Out & ...

in

Dublin

Did you know ...
... that in Dublin you can:

Windsurf in the heart of the city?
Join the Junior United Nations?
Learn acrobatics?
Get lost in four different mazes?
Find a tree that's gobbling a chair?
Tap into a vast database that's kept under a
mountain in Utah?
Take a ride on a steam train?
Say hey to a ray?
Join a marching band?
Build a raft?
Visit two and a half islands?
Meet two dodos?
Learn to play traditional Irish music?
Be a Viking slave?
Meet your own TD?
Eat Middle Eastern food in the shade of a mosque?
Sit in the stocks?
Whizz up a chimney?
Send your face to Hollywood?
Cook your own barbecue?
Learn to be a museum curator?
Feel what it's like to be inside the Book of Kells?
Say Bon Voyage to a wild seal?
See Mediterranean-type lavender fields?

Out & About
in
Dublin

Mary Finn

WOLFHOUND PRESS
Celebrating 25 Years

Published in 2000 by
WOLFHOUND PRESS
68 Mountjoy Square
Dublin 1
Tel: (353-1) 874 0354
Fax: (353-1) 872 0207

British Library Cataloguing in Publication Data
A catalogue record for this book is available from the British Library

ISBN 0-86327-767-5

Text Illustration: Aileen Caffrey
Illustration of Ha'penny Bridge (p. 163): Ann Fallon
Maps: Sarah Cunningham
Cover design: Terry Foley
Cover photos courtesy of: Surf Dock, The National Sea Life Centre, S. Cashman, Terry Foley
Typesetting by Wolfhound Press
Printed in the UK by Cox & Wyman Ltd., Reading, Berks.

Contents

Symbols used in this book:

Chapter 1

Wheelchair access

Chapter 10

Museum or heritage site

Houses and/or gardens

Activity site

In memory of my parents,
Daniel and Agnes Finn,
who took us places.

acknowledgements

I owe many debts of gratitude, to family, friends, and especially to Daniel, for putting up with my madwoman-in-the-attic impression during the research and writing (and possibly permanently). Their kindness and forbearance helped tremendously, as always.

I would also like to thank everyone who helped me, wittingly and unwittingly, in their professional way. I can state, hand on heart, that Dublin Corporation and Dúchas/OPW have the most courteous and helpful staff that a city and country could ask for. They also do us excellent service.

Starting points

So Dublin, like the rest of the western world, is having a 2000th birthday. Mind you, Dublin is a special case. This is its second Millennium in twelve years. We like to party.

Since *The Adventure Guide to Dublin* first appeared, much has happened. Lots of new and exciting places to visit. Some of them didn't properly exist when I was writing about them but there were hardworking enthusiasts to tell me what to expect. They wanted their places or their work included for the Big Birthday. And no, I don't just mean the Millennium monument on O'Connell Street, the LUAS, the soccer stadium. Or the Millennium Liffey Boardwalk or the new walkers' Liffey bridge. You'll more than likely find all these in their places one of these days without any need for directions.

The Adventure Guide to Dublin was originally devised as a guidebook to Dublin for children. But as long as it remained in print I found that all types of people used it, Dubliners, visitors, children, families, teachers and common or garden adults like myself. Which pleases me because it's the kind of book I would use myself. I would not wish to categorise *Out & About in Dublin* any more than its predecessor, except to say that it also has a bias for putting independent-minded young people in touch with interesting places and things to do. And Dublin, bless its millennium heart, is still blessed by all the history and geography fairies. You don't have to go to the Antarctic to have an uncharted adventure or to Rome to have historical encounters. You can act and sing and dance your heart out in Dublin too.

People travel more now, so in *Out & About in Dublin* there is a much larger section on excursions outside the city and county. Dubliners use their city more (I think) so there is a chapter on all the ways you can travel around Dublin in the hands of experts.

Two things must be said before the Party begins. Our city traffic drives people mad. Children like to be able to get around on their own but, for many, cycling to school or to town is not safe. *The Adventure Guide to Dublin* included lots of advice for cyclists because cycling remains the best way to get around a city. Sadly I've had to change that emphasis. So here's my advice this time. Get properly mad! Shout at politicians and planners. Tell them you want safe paths and more cycle-ways.

The second thing is that we now meet more and more visitors on Dublin's streets. Not all of them are rich, and some of them are very frightened. Whatever their reasons are for coming to Dublin, we should welcome them. *Out & About* includes a page of contacts for aid organisations. Young people can do brave and wonderful things abroad; but remember, the line is — you don't have to travel to have amazing encounters.

Please get in touch with me through the publisher to tell me about all the treasures that I have, no doubt, left out. May Dublin, Dubliners and guests (and this book, naturally) prosper in the twenty-first century. Enjoy!

dos and don'ts

You think Marco Polo didn't have a list of Dos and Don'ts? Of course he did — all survivors do. And since some of the outings in this book involve exploration and scrambling around I've drawn up a very basic survival list. All the accidents hinted at in this list have happened and do happen to people. Don't let them happen to you. And yes, there *are* more Don'ts than Dos, but consider that all the other pages in this book contain a gigantic number of Dos.

Going

1. **DO** tell at least one adult exactly where you are going, especially on outdoor trips. Say *how* you are travelling. It's no use leaving a trail of crumbs.
2. **DON'T** go on any long expedition on your own. Even a museum though safe as a house is more fun in company.

Out and about

3. **DO** bring something satisfying to eat — sweet things lose their appeal on a long trip.
4. **DO** bring a puncture repair kit (if you cycle!) Buses don't take kindly to sick bicycles and it's *ALWAYS* a long walk home.
5. **DO** remember, if you bring a small brother or sister, they can't walk as fast or as long as you can, and they get bored easily. Boy, do they get bored. Make sure you have a bit of extra money to distract them.
6. **NEVER** cross a railway line. You just don't know the timetables and the DART is both fast and quiet-moving.

7. **DON'T** swim in canals, rivers or reservoirs — they contain weed — or on deserted beaches. Swim parallel to the shore, near to other groups of people.

8. **DON'T** go into wrecked or just-built houses, they are dangerous.

9. **DON'T** eat mushrooms or berries even if you're a dab hand in biology.

10. **DON'T**, if you end up somewhere exotic like a dump — and this is very specific — get into a derelict fridge, wardrobe or anything with a door that can jam shut. People may not hear you.

Coming Home

11. **DON'T** hitch-hike unless there are at least twenty of you thumbing the same car. When out on a day trip, it's good advice for you to carry a phonecard (or better still a mobile phone), or at very least keep 50p as a reserve for emergency phone calls.

12. **NEVER** assume that just because it's the end of the day and someone has disappeared, that he/she has gone home. If they don't turn up check with their parents.

Chapter 1

DO NOT FEED
THE ANIMALS
— .. —
PRE-STUFFED

Museums Plus

Come on, out with it. Museums are for school projects and cranky family Sundays — right? Have I got news for you! In the first edition of this book this chapter was the longest. For this millennium edition it has had to be divided into three sections like Julius Caesar's Gaul. The first part is called simply **Museums**; the next section is called **Castles,**

Grand Houses and Extraordinary Buildings; the final section is called **The Creepy! The Experience!**

The secret about enjoying museums is to know a little about what to expect, and that is what this chapter is about. It offers you a list of things to look out for, the kind of list I wish I'd had starting out myself, if you follow me. I hope you do. Dublin museums (and other such places) are crammed full of treasures, ranging from famous paintings to ferocious weapons, from emperors' silken robes to enormous doll's houses. They tell stories about the past from the Jurassic period up to yesterday, about science and animals, about work and war, about geniuses and ordinary people. Some museums, of course, are better than others. However, since this book was first published, not only are there new and exciting places to go, many museums and galleries have also taken giant steps to make themselves more interesting and accessible. You will find special activities, treasure hunt leaflets, computer guides in the great free (remember that magic word FREE) national museums and galleries. Many other places have installed audio-visual aids to tell their stories. Some that I have included here contain material that might be considered to be of adult interest only; the houses of great Irish writers for example, or the workings of a brewery. A good guide can even make a crisp bag interesting, however, and there are many good guides around, especially for organised trips. And of course, sometimes even the smallest visitor can find something that no one else will. This chapter aims at least to let you know what's out there to be explored. Some places will work for you, some probably won't yet but may another time.

Have a look at the long list of places to go. The division goes like this: **Museums** (and galleries or libraries) are either officially called 'museum' or 'gallery' or else they contain collections of art and artefacts to be admired. (Sorry, manta ray, I know you're actually a lean, mean eating-machine, not an artefact.) **Castles, Grand Houses and Extraordinary Buildings** are so-called by me because people like to visit such places on account of their architecture and the evidence of the lifestyles that they once accommodated. Some have splendid gardens and plenty of A&A (but rarely manta rays) inside — just like the museums. **Creepy** places have a definite whiff of the goosebumps off them, while **The Experience** offers an all-in time-trip. The general plan of this chapter is that amenities with city-centre addresses are listed first, followed by northside, then southside locations. Have fun! Just remember that, in Museumworld, Monday very often means CLOSED, so remember to check the times listed before setting out. Always arrive *at least* one hour before closing time to avoid disappointment.

If you're visiting Dublin as a tourist (or are a very busy native) there are savings to be made on site visits. Dublin Tourism offer a SuperSaver ticket for the sites they manage (ask at HQ in Andrew Street) and Dúchas, the government service which manages a large number of heritage sites throughout the country, sell a bargain Heritage card which allows you visit any and all of their sites as many times as you wish during the year. 1999 price: £15 for an adult; £6 for a child; family £36. Excellent value. Dúchas fee-paying sites are indicated in this book by an asterisk*. You can buy the heritage cards at the larger sites, or from HQ at 51 St Stephen's Green.

Museums

Natural History Museum

Merrion Street, Dublin 2 (beside the Dáil)
Ground floor only

Tel: 677 7444

Open: Tuesday–Saturday: 10.00 a.m.–5.00 p.m.; Sunday: 2.00 p.m.–5.00 p.m. Admission free.

If you belong to a species whose hackles rise at the thought of visiting a museum, this one might convert you. Shaped like a Victorian helter-skelter, it's a fascinating place; a museum that should itself be in a museum. It was built and stuffed with specimens at a time when people thought nothing of bagging animals and birds and having *them* stuffed. In those days even people like Charles Darwin did this — taxidermists must have been as busy as taxi-drivers are these days.

As far up as you can go (not the very top gallery) you are surrounded by exotic leeches and tapeworms. From here you can look down on the suspended skeletons of whales and giant elks. If these don't take your fancy you can also view a dodo's remains or a roc's egg or a tarantula eating a hummingbird. The birds and bats are super realistic while the baby gannet looks like he's going to throw a tantrum. There's (almost) a 'flight of the condor', and the Greenland falcons are truly noble. The fur seal and the walrus are ENORMOUS.

Best of all, stay down to earth with the Irish animals exhibition on the ground floor. It's the ideal place for learning how to recognise native birds and discovering how animals look in their own habitats. Don't miss the beautiful snowy owl, the osprey — who is more punk than anything walking the streets — and for an idea of what might be swimming below you in Dublin Bay, have a look at the sunfish.

Books and leaflets are available in the Kildare Street National Museum, though in summer a shop operates here. Why not petition for all the galleries of this unique building to be opened up for the twenty-first century? Meanwhile if you have a query about any Irish fauna you can telephone the Keeper of this Museum at the above number.

The National Museum (1)

Kildare Street, Dublin 2 (beside the Dáil)
Tel: 677 7444.

Ground
floor only

Open: Tuesday–Saturday: 10.00 a.m.–5.00 p.m.; Sunday: 2.00 p.m.–
5.00 p.m. Permanent collection with occasional visiting exhibitions.
Group visits should be arranged beforehand. Activity sheets available.
Admission free but adults charged for guided tours (2.15 p.m.,
3.00 p.m., 4.00 p.m.)

The National Museum houses all the Celtic treasures you have ever heard of, from the Tara Brooch to the Ardagh Chalice and back again, and anything of historical value you find with your ferret or metal detector should be turned in to them too (if you find anything like the Derrynaflan Hoard you will be very lucky). Gold, silver, pewter, amber and yew-wood were the Celts' favourite materials and their taste passed down into early Christian art. Look out for the way artists and craftspeople worked tiny spirally animals into everything. Look out also for Ireland's oldest wheel and a nasty neck chain for prisoners. These are all part of the **Treasury** exhibition, and to concentrate your mind and eyes, you can watch an excellent audio-visual show before roaming.

The main floor exhibition is called **Ór** — (Gold) which, if you close your peripheral vision and forget that this is a museum, might make you think you had walked into Tiffany's jewellery stores in New York. These gold ornaments, beaten thin, twisted or scrolled, are shining bright and perfectly to twentieth-century taste. Many of them are over 4,000 years old, and come from Ireland's great gold rush during the Bronze Age. Think again of panning a river!

There are prehistoric remains on show too, including a flint axe dated at 400,000 BC (but nobody's making claims for who owned it). The huge hewn-out Lurgan longboat is spectacular, like a war canoe from the South Pacific. Upstairs is the **Viking Dublin** exhibition — the oldest remnants of city-life in Dublin. Here you'll find everything from vicious swords to homely pots and pans, gaming boards, dice, jewellery, toys, shoes and graffiti, which were dug up mainly in the Christ Church/Wood Quay area of the city. For centuries, layers of waterlogged matter had kept them preserved like pickles. There is also a full skeleton of a very tall warrior dug up in Islandbridge; it measures 5 feet 10 inches — much taller than the native Irish of its time. Other exhibitions include the **Egyptian** room, done up like a tomb, crammed with mummies (including a long thin cat), a fantastic model boat, amulets, hieroglyphics and, cutest of all, a reliquary for a pet gecko. Downstairs there's a video wall in the 1916 room, and many mementoes, including James Connolly's blood-stained vest. There's a good museum shop in the lobby, and you can post a specially franked letter or card, in several languages, in the oldest postbox in Ireland.

The National Museum (2) at Collins Barracks
Benburb Street, Dublin 7 (near Phoenix Park)
Tel: 677 7444
Open: Tuesday–Saturday: 10.00 a.m.–5.00 p.m.; Sunday: 2.00 p.m.–
5.00 p.m. Activity sheets available. Admission free. Adults charged for
guided tours. Shop and restaurant.

Collins Barracks was first of all the Royal Barracks, built in 1701, which makes it a senior building by any standards. Once it had the biggest barrack square in Europe; today as you enter you can see the paces marked out in huge figures for the soldiers to square-bash. In front of the Museum is 'Croppies Acre' where many of the 1798 revolutionaries were buried after execution, and it was in this Royal Barracks that Theobald Wolfe Tone cut his throat rather than be executed. The barracks was re-christened for Michael Collins and went out of military business in 1993.

We should be glad because it's a fabulous museum. So many of the treasures of the National Museum were hidden away because there was no space in Kildare Street (above) to show them. Here the clever museum people not only show them off — and give us computers to figure out what is which, and when, and why — they also show off the day-to-day business of running a museum.

There are three floors each of which has two wings and there are plans for further expansion. Floor one offers Curators' Choices — from a 2,000-year-old Japanese bell, which dongs as you approach, to the tiniest pair of grown-up ankle boots imaginable. There's also a display of beautiful Irish silver, from Georgian big dinner party stuff to super-modern teapots. Out of storage is a two-floor display of wonders that had previously been under wraps, including a giant teapot that would take not just a dormouse but a Dalmatian, salvage from the *Lusitania,* and a Japanese emperor's palanquin. Further up is a range of Irish furniture from open-up settle beds to the delicate parlour pale woods of cabinetmaker James Hicks and also a collection of scientific instruments — dig the giant camera and the exquisite orrery, or model of the planetary universe. Every artefact is beautifully lit and displayed against period illustrations. You won't miss the barracks' original pendulum clock which hangs down a shaft like a lift. There is a shop which has books, cool T-shirts and the cheapest and prettiest museum cards *anywhere.*

Collins Barracks runs a regular programme of workshops with schools and, on certain Saturdays, with families also. Ring for information, or check the website or Event Guides.

National Gallery of Ireland

Merrion Square West, Dublin 2 (other side of Dáil)
Tel: 661 5133

Wheelchairs
available

Open: Monday–Saturday: 10.00 a.m.–5.30 p.m.; Thursday: 10.00 a.m.–8.30 p.m.; Sunday: 2.00 p.m.–5.00 p.m. Activity sheets available.
Admission free.

The National Gallery is the most popular place on the Dublin visitor map and it's getting bigger and better all the time. A new wing stretching all the way to Clare Street is scheduled to open in late 2000, and will contain new exhibition rooms, a multimedia centre and a winter garden, as well as a larger shop and restaurant. It's also FREE — even hanging your wet coat is free — and many foreign visitors can't believe their luck. The Gallery is a place to conquer in parts rather than all at once. If you like pictures that tell a story and are full of characters and adventures, visit the Irish, Flemish and Dutch rooms — Breughel, Vermeer and Steen are great story-painters. The showpiece painting by Caravaggio has an exciting Cinderella story behind its recent discovery, and there are faces that you might recognise by Hals, Goya, Rembrandt, Van Dyck and El Greco. Renaissance master Fra Angelico has a bloodthirsty miracle on show in gloriously fresh colours, while each January there's a display of stunning watercolours by Turner, which can't be seen at any other time. The twentieth-century Irish painter Jack Yeats has a new section to himself where you can compare his magical pulsating pictures with those painted by others in his family — even by his brother, the famous poet W.B. Yeats.

The best introduction to the paintings is to attend some of the free lectures or guided tours. The porter's desk has an up-to-date news list of events called the *Gallery News*. Among these are:

Public tours on Saturdays at 3.00 p.m., Sundays at 2.15 p.m., 3.00 p.m. and 4.00 p.m.

Family activity programmes (including music and literature) on Saturdays at 3.00 p.m. Come early as numbers are limited.

Annual holiday painting activities for young people during Christmas and summer.

Drawing studies: a two-term course for people of all abilities. Fee-paying.

Multimedia presentation with activity sheet: Touch and feel all the valuables you like!

I-Spy hunts for different age levels.

Lectures and projects for school students — these are free.

Night-time lectures for anyone who enjoys art history (fee-paying).

The Picture Clinic. Got a picture in your attic? (Remember the Caravaggio.) The Curators have an advice session on the first Thursday of each month, 10.00 a.m. to 12.00 noon — just bring your painting for this free service.

Some **special exhibitions** may have an entrance fee but many are free.

The Gallery bookshop is dangerously good, with books for every taste and age, posters and prints, calendars, postcards and videos. There is a **library** but places have to be reserved by appointment. The Gallery also hosts **concerts** in the enormous Shaw Room (and why is it called that? See page 33). Last, but definitely not least, the **Restaurant** is excellent.

Hugh Lane Municipal Gallery of Modern Art
Entrance: Parnell Square North, Dublin 1
Tel: 874 1903
Open: Tuesday, Wednesday, Thursday: 9.30 a.m.–6.00 p.m., Friday, Saturday: 9.30 a.m.–5.00 p.m.; Sunday: 11.00 a.m.–5.00 p.m. Summer time late opening on Thursday until 8.00 p.m. Guided tours by prior arrangement. Art materials for children on request. Admission free.

This gallery welcomes everyone with open arms. It was built as a townhouse for Lord Charlemont — his suburban house was in Marino complete with rhyming Casino (see page 66). The art collection dates from just over one hundred years ago right up to the present. Some of the most famous paintings are the French Impressionist works which were left to be shared between this Gallery and the National Gallery in London by Sir Hugh Lane, who was drowned when the *Lusitania* was torpedoed in 1915. There are plenty of interesting sculptures here too. The coloured Big Bird is a hit, as is the anti-Bullfight installation; and if you go into the stained-glass gallery you will fall in love forever with the colour blue, thanks to artist Harry Clarke. Another colourful place is the Roderic O'Conor room; O'Conor was an Irish artist who went to France and worked with the very famous Paul Gauguin.

A new acquisition is the actual studio of Irish-born painter Francis Bacon, another exhibit which was left to the Gallery by will. If you get inspired by his brushes, palettes and paints and the interesting shapes and colours around, some art materials are available at the desk. The Gallery also runs an Art Club for three different age groups on Saturday mornings — call in or telephone for more details. There's a special video on the paintings in the gallery which has its own book, available from the gallery shop. In addition, almost every Sunday at noon, there are free concerts, which are advertised in the weekend papers.

The Irish Museum of Modern Art (IMMA)
Royal Hospital, Kilmainham, Dublin 8
Tel: 612 9900
Entrance: follow the signs from St John's Road, beside Heuston Station.
Open: Tuesday–Saturday: 10.00 a.m.–5.30 p.m.; Sunday: 12.00 noon–
5.30 p.m. Admission free but special exhibitions have a charge.
Buses: 21, 51, 78, 79.

This is an art gallery but it's also a very historic building (see below). The old soldiers who retired here would be amazed to walk the long bright corridors and peer into their former bedrooms to see what the late twentieth-century contents are. Works of Irish and world artists are on view here, together with many prestigious visiting exhibitions — from Andy Warhol to the Chinese terracotta army. Even the Irish works don't stay on permanent view; the collection rotates so that there's always something new to admire and exchange opinion on. IMMA has a committed community and education programme for its catchment area, so quite often there is themed work by young people on view. You might also catch the regular Explorer trolley which tours the museum like an ice-cream van with art materials and various artefacts. With certain exhibitions there are also activity sheets and more information on these can be obtained at the desk. Although many of the books in the bookshop are fabulously expensive, there are great postcards and small gift ideas. There is a restaurant in the courtyard.

There are many small galleries in Dublin with changing exhibitions. Keen art students should check event guides. One to remember is the **RHA Gallagher Gallery** at 15 Ely Place (Tel: 661 2558) which has regular large-scale exhibitions. Government Buildings (see page 224) has a large collection by modern Irish artists. Outdoor sculpture events take place in summer in several gardens such as Malahide Demesne and Fern Hill (see Chapter 2). See also the Sculpture Walk.

National Photographic Archive

Meeting House Square, Temple Bar, Dublin 2
Tel: 603 0200
Entrance: under the archway entrance, off East Essex Street.
Open: Monday–Friday: 10.00 a.m.–5.00 p.m.

This new space is another branch of the National Library which owns over 250,000 photographs. There is an exhibition area that makes the most of an interesting layout centred around two bridges. On display are samples from the many collections dating back to Victorian daguerreotypes, tintypes and stereo photographs, right up to modern postcard prints and stunning aerial views. There are samples of early glass negatives and private photo-albums here, all of which tell stories about Irish life. But if you are searching for something in particular, there's a reading room, with catalogues of the collections, plus several publications. Help is available and photocopies and prints can be ordered here. There is also a selection of sepia postcards on sale, along with Library publications.

The Gallery of Photography

Meeting House Square, Temple Bar, Dublin 2
Tel: 671 4654/670 9293
Entrance: across the Square from the National Photographic Archive
Open: Monday–Saturday: 11.00 a.m.–6.00 p.m.

The Gallery runs exhibitions by particular photographers, Irish and foreign, and functions as a gallery rather than an archive. Some very famous images can be on view here and there's a shop with books, posters and prints. Sharing space with the National Archive is the DIT School of Photography, the Irish Film Institute Library and an entrance to the Irish Film Centre. The Square itself is used in summer for free open-air movies (see page 344) so altogether it's a place for eyes to have some serious fun.

Heraldic Museum and Genealogical Office

2 Kildare Street, Dublin 2
Tel: 603 0200
Entrance: at the Nassau Street end; the handsome redbrick building.
Open: Monday–Friday: 10.00 a.m.–12.45 p.m.; 2.00 p.m.–4.30 p.m.
Admission free.

If you ever wanted to design a personal family crest/motto/seal or whatnot the Heraldic Museum is the place to fill your mind with dragons rampant and severed arms or *fleurs-de-lys*. It's just one room with a mixed selection of exhibits: seals, heraldic stamps, family banners, an armoured helm and a herald's tabard like the White Rabbit's from *Alice in Wonderland*. Not for all tastes, but if you like design and knights-at-arms you should drop in. For details of ancestry tracing see National Library above.

Dublin Civic Museum

South William Street, Dublin 2
Tel: 679 4260
Open: Tuesday–Saturday 10.00 a.m.–6.00 p.m.; Sunday: 11.00 a.m.–
2.00 p.m. Admission free. Guided tours for groups by prior arrangement.

This is a little magpie of a museum. It's lodged in a small eighteenth-century house, which despite its comfortable doll's house neatness, has always been associated with the public, first for artists' exhibitions, then as the City Assembly House. During the War of Independence the Supreme Court used to meet here in secret.

The Corporation owns so many different items of city life that it's hard to say what's on show here at any one time. Exhibitions change all the time, but they range from, for example, Dublin and World War 1, the Emergency, Canal Life in Dublin, Radio, plus the lives of different famous Dubliners. There are old shop signs, street furniture, and a monstrous thing, the stone head of Admiral Nelson, which he lost when his O'Connell Street Pillar was blown up in 1966.

What the Civic Museum is best at is being a resource centre. The Old Dublin Society meets and holds lectures here (visitors welcome) on Wednesday evenings at 8.00 p.m. from October to April. Research work can be done by arrangement in the little library room. The City Archives (covering everything from medieval sheriffs to Victorian rat-catchers to the current Lord Mayor's 'D No. 1' registration plates) are in transit during 1999/2000. Some are housed here; some are stored in City Hall (see page 62), but they will soon all be housed at the Corporation's transformed Gilbert Library in Pearse Street. The Irish Theatre Archive is also maintained by the City. For more information telephone or write to the City Archivist, or Civic Museum Curator.

Findlater's Museum
Harcourt Street, Dublin 2
Tel: 475 1699
Open: Monday: 9.30 a.m.–5.30 p.m.; Saturday: 10.30 a.m.–5.30 p.m.
Admission free.

Findlater's cavernous vaults under the old railway stretch on for ever and give the impression that a Roman emperor *did* made it to Ireland despite what everyone thinks. The air is perfect for storing vintage wines and the smell of it is everywhere. Parents might get very mellow....

As well as their wine business, Findlater's used to run a chain of grocery stores throughout Dublin. They were the Superquinn of their day, which kicked off in 1823, when Mr Findlater, a Scot, arrived to make his fortune. Down in the vaults' entrance there's a shop front with lots of items from the old stores; inside there are posters, bills, shop furniture and photographs, and, some days, you'll find wine-tasters on the premises spitting good wine into barrels, like bad babies. You can certainly demand a cool drink upstairs in the Odeon, the converted station bar, when you're through underground.

Trinity College and Book of Kells
College Green, Dublin 2
Tel: 677 2941
Other entrances on Nassau Street and South Leinster Street.

College campus open to visitors seven days a week. Guided tours during the summer — ask at porter's desk.
Long Room (Library): entry through bookshop, signposted. Monday– Friday: 9.30 a.m.–4.45 p.m.; Saturday: 9.30 a.m.–12.45 p.m. Admission fee. (Dublin Experience: see below.)

Trinity College is a private institution but is very beautiful inside and no one is barred from entering unless they are troublesome, or unless the Trinity Ball is on and they don't have tickets. Queen Elizabeth I founded the College in 1592 on the site of a monastery. Her aim was 'to "civilise" the Irish and cure them of Popery'. And, originally founded by a woman, it was the first university in these islands to award women degrees, in 1904.

Four hundred years ago Dublin people were allowed graze their pigs and cows on Hoggen Green, a space just in front of Trinity and the Bank of Ireland. There were executions here also — that's when plays and tournaments weren't being staged. So Trinity was built beside a kind of Elizabethan Funderland site and at once made the area upwardly mobile.

It's a residential university and some students are lucky enough to live in the eighteenth-century quadrangles and have their rooms cleaned for them — a very ancient college custom.

Buildings to look out for are: the matching **Chapel** and **Exam Hall** buildings and the **Dining Hall** which is on your left, set back a bit and looking like a miniature Trinity College itself. Eating here is called 'dining in Commons' with High Tables and Low Tables — High Table diners wear gowns. Ahead is The **Rubrics,** the tall redbrick block, and it's the oldest dwellingplace left in Dublin — 1700 being its construction date. **No. 25** The Rubrics is said to have its own ghost — an unpopular master, who was shot by an unknown student, walks out at dusk every day (they say).

The **Museum Building** beside the 'new' (1967) Library contains lecture rooms and some giant elk skeletons. It's a beautiful building, a bit like a Venetian palace, designed by Victorian architects Deane and Woodward. Inside it changes to Turkish, worked in multi-coloured marbles. Almost all the materials are Irish and there's a display showing where they come from. Stare carefully at the window design. You'll be able to recognise the work of these designers all over the city from the windows alone. (Try Dame Street and Kildare Street for starters.)

The **Long Room** is where the busloads of tourists head for — it's got the 800 AD **Book of Kells** on display, with different illuminated (illustrated) pages being turned every day. It's reckoned that 185 calves/cows died to produce the vellum on which anonymous monks transcribed the Gospels. The illustrations are not just beautiful, they are a kind of code in which the word of God is concealed as if in a puzzle. The countless animals and fantastic beasts which are depicted are also magnificent. The colours are very rich and it's thought that the rich blue was made from lapis lazuli which was mined in farthest Afghanistan. A full reproduction of the Book of Kells will cost you over 12,000 Euros. The real thing is priceless, but you can buy postcards and other mementoes in the shop.

Trinity also has some more modern best-sellers like first editions of Dante and Shakespeare. The Trinity Library receives a first edition of every book published in these islands — even *this* one should be there. Even if you think the Book of Kells is a taboo sight for true Dubs have a look at the library. It's all gleaming lines of shelves, ladders, and books that act as a background for the beautiful carved spiral staircases. Readers used to study at the top of the long ladders, perched like owls or bats in the gloom. While you are there, be sure to look out for Brian Boru's harp (or at any rate someone's ancient harp).

A lot of building has been happening in Trinity over recent years. There is the **Samuel Beckett Theatre** hidden away on the Pearse Street side of the campus. It has the appearance of a Shakespearean theatre and belongs to the Drama Department. On the South Leinster Street side are gleaming new genetics and dentistry buildings. Thankfully there's still a great deal of green space and you can pick up brochures on the wildlife of Trinity in the bookshop.

The modern Arts Block (housing the entry from Nassau Street) is home to the **Douglas Hyde Gallery** which regularly features good art and photographic exhibitions. This is also the site for the **Dublin Experience** and there's a cheap coffee shop. If you go out this way, take a look at the grille on your left. Down below is said to be St Patrick's Well — the former name of Nassau Street was St Patrick's Well Lane.

National Library of Ireland

Kildare Street, Dublin 2
Tel: 603 0200
Entrance: on the left of the Dáil.
Open: Monday: 10.00 a.m.–9.00 p.m.; Tuesday–Wednesday: 2.00 p.m.–9.00 p.m.; Thursday–Friday: 10.00 a.m.–5.00 p.m.; Saturday: 10.00 a.m.–1.00 p.m.

Though the Library was originally declared 'free to respectable persons' you will need a reader's ticket to enter the domed Reading Room, and unless you're a student doing valid research it's not likely you'll get one. Here newspapers are on microfilm and a treasury of Irish literature, history, manuscripts, maps is also stored. Although the catalogues are computerised now and not in great ledgers as they once were, the system is the same: you take a desk seat, note its number, write down what you need and the books are brought to you, the scholar. It's a wonderful place on a winter's evening with the green glowing reading lamps and the great dome like an encouraging brain. However, if you're interested in genealogical research, there are day tickets available for the genealogical room (proof of identity needed) and detailed start-you-off leaflets and a computer database to help you begin your search. If you do get through the security gates you must visit the glorious Victorian toilets. Anyone can walk into the shop and the National Library has a collection of facsimile documents for sale on various subjects — they are superb.

Marsh's Library

St Patrick's Close, Dublin 8 (beside St Patrick's Cathedral)
Tel: 454 3511
Open: Monday, Wednesday, Thursday, Friday: 10.00 a.m.–12.45 p.m. and 2.00 p.m.–5.00 p.m.; Saturday: 10.30 a.m.–12.45 p.m. Admission: children free, small fee for adults.

Archbishop Narcissus Marsh built this library in the Close in 1701 which makes it the oldest public library in the country. You can't borrow from the Archbishop's store of books but you can see what the perfect scholar's library was supposed to look like. It's like a pocket edition of the great library in Trinity College. If all the dark wood panelling and ghost stories were not enough to make a student work he could ask to be locked into one of the special wooden cages at the end of the room.

The alleged resident ghost is supposed to be that of old Narcissus himself, who, it is claimed, searches through the books at night for a letter that his niece wrote him before she eloped. And if that isn't sad enough, there is an account in the library of '... the accidental death of an elephant by burning in the city of Dublin in 1689'.

Chester Beatty Library

Dublin Castle, Dublin 2
Tel: 407 0750
Entrance: beside Dubh Linn garden.
Open: Tuesday–Friday: 10.00 a.m.–1.00 p.m., 2.00 p.m.–5.00 p.m.;
Saturday: 2.00 p.m.–5.00 p.m. Admission free.

After a long history of living in Embassyland, Ballsbridge, the Chester Beatty Library re-opens in spacious new/old quarters in Dublin Castle in early 2000. The good news is that the facilities will be superb; the bad news is that this guidebook can't describe them yet. However, the contents can be outlined as they will be much as they are in the Chester Beatty's current location.

The Library is really a museum and art gallery rolled into one. Its benefactor, Sir Alfred Chester Beatty, was a collector of oriental treasures which he left to the Irish nation. So this is actually the kind of place where Indiana Jones might have made his discoveries before setting out. Famous biblical scholars come here to examine incredibly ancient fragments of 'The Word'. If the Book of Kells doesn't appeal to you, you may not want to look at oriental manuscripts either. But if you like books, bindings, brightly coloured and golden illustrations, calligraphy and general whiffs of the Orient, you will be very happy walking around here. If you wake at night wondering what real papyrus and hieroglyphs look like, you'll find those here as well. There are two permanent exhibitions, one based on the world's great religions, the other on arts patronage. These cover a variety of subjects from Chinese emperors and their dragon robes to Reformation courts in Europe.

In the Library's new location there will be stacks of modern technology for exploring the museum's artefacts and stories, as well as an audio-visual theatre and lecture room. Schools will be able to book guided tours and there will also be two libraries, one for research and one for general readers. Many beautiful images and books will be on sale in the shop and there will be a restaurant. The roof garden *may* be open for close inspection of the fine peacock weathervane: we're told this lively model is called Harry and he also features on the interior mosaic.

Dublin Writers' Museum

18/19 Parnell Square North, Dublin 1
Tel: 872 2077
Entrance: beside Findlater's Church, opposite Garden of Remembrance.
Open: Monday–Saturday: 10.00 a.m.–5.00 p.m.; Sundays and Bank
Holidays: 11.00 a.m.–5.00 p.m. June, July, August: open until 6.00 p.m.
Monday–Friday. Schools and groups by arrangement. Admission fee.
Free access to bookshop and restaurant.

The Writers' Museum is a unique amenity — and not just because this magnificent house contains another miniature house that you can find....

The exhibition rooms celebrate a roll-call of great Irish writers, gathering first editions of their books, their writing implements, portraits, letters and other clues to their characters — such as the flying goggles of Oliver Gogarty or the animal-embroidered waistcoat of James Joyce. Upstairs the house itself comes into its own. It is a Georgian townhouse, completed in 1769, but embellished also by its later owners. Thus the magnificent Gallery of Writers which looks like a wonderful place for a party (and is) also boasts a ceiling and friezed walls unlike any other house in the country. Downstairs again, you can go through the annexe, past the Zen garden, and upstairs into the exhibition room that houses Tara's Palace.

This doll's palace was built by Irish craftspeople to replace another treasure, Titania's Palace, which was sold, of all places, to Legoland in Denmark. The floors, pictures, fittings and furnishings on display are tiny and intricate; some of the ivory pieces were made by French Napoleonic prisoners of war. Next door is a Hall of Fame of Irish children's writers, complete with Magic Pool.

Downstairs again are the restaurant and bookshop. There's a good young people's selection — check that they have this book!

James Joyce Centre
35 North Great George's Street, Dublin 1
Tel: 878 8547
Entrance: through its beautiful Georgian door with fanlight lantern.
Open: Monday–Saturday: 9.30 a.m.–5.00 p.m.; Sunday: 12.30 p.m.–
5.00 p.m. Admission fee. Tea-room.

Probably you should read some of James Joyce's work, unquestionably Dublin's greatest writer, to get the best from this house. Whatever — here are some things to tick off. First, Joyce never lived here. But you can see his school, Belvedere College, at the top of the street, and he certainly made his Jesuit teachers famous in his *Portrait of the Artist as a Young Man*. This is a typical north-city Georgian house, once classy, but which became a tenement building, home to many families. Joyce wrote much about places like this — he left Ireland but never stopped writing about it. His book *Ulysses* is all set on the one day, 16 June 1904. This date is now celebrated every year as Bloomsday, after the book's hero, Leopold Bloom, who is really a Dublin version of Homer's hero Odysseus/Ulysses.

The library is situated in the upstairs part of the house and shows some of the many translations of *Ulysses* — the most famous novel in English of this century. There is a short video about Joyce and the house itself is to be admired as a fine piece of restoration work — its stucco ceilings were by a master *stuccodore* — an artist in plaster. There are many photographs and paintings in the James Joyce Centre, but it's definitely best if you are interested in writers and writing. Singers Sinead O'Connor and Shane McGowan once lived on this street as did a lot of Irish patriots — you are on holy ground. (See page 71 for the actual Joyce Museum. Even though that's called 'museum', I've included it in the 'extraordinary buildings' section, because it's inside a Martello tower.)

Ten Names for Dublin made up by Joyce in Finnegans Wake	
Dubbyling	Londub
Hurdlebury Finn	Eblana Magna
Dublovnik	Babbalong
Tumbin on the Leafy	Old Brawn
The Heart of MidLeinster	Dungbin

The Shaw Birthplace
33 Synge Street, off the South Circular Road
Tel: 475 0854
Entrance via basement.

Open: May–October. Monday–Saturday: 10.00 a.m.–5.00 p.m. Sundays and Holidays: 11.00 a.m.–5.00 p.m. Closed for lunch: 1.00 p.m.– 2.00 p.m. Admission fee.

There are several reasons why you might come to the birthplace of George Bernard Shaw: (a) if you have discovered his plays; (b) if someone else has; or (c) because this house has the power to make Victorian stories come alive. Everyone gets an audio guide, and this one is more like an atmospheric radio programme than a tour commentary. Shaw, aka GBS, did not have a happy childhood — there are no toys and few books but lots of heavy velvet, brass beds, lace curtains and po-faced photographs. Nevertheless, he grew up a brilliant and kindly man; a sort of skinny Santa Claus figure, who gave money away everywhere, and especially to Dublin's National Gallery which can afford to buy more paintings because of the Shaw Bequest.

Watch out for the round plaques which can be seen on many houses in the city. They show where many other famous writers, artists and historical figures used to live.

National Wax Museum
Granby Row, past Parnell Square West
Tel: 872 6340
Open: Monday–Saturday: 10.00 a.m.–5.30 p.m.; Sunday: 12.00 noon–
5.30 p.m. Schools by arrangement. Admission fee.

A Swiss woman called Marie Tussaud started the waxworks craze during the Reign of Terror of the French Revolution. She was made of stern stuff, Madame Tussaud, because she worked on famous heads straight from the guillotine. She is in the lobby of this museum waiting to greet you, along with some other friendly figures.

The Museum is divided into sections. There's the Children's World of Fairytale and Fantasy which has all the best-known characters (including some fantastic bits of Giant), a hall of goblins, crazy mirrors and, best for some, secret Tunnels that lead somewhere if you dare ... There is a pageant of Irish historical and cultural figures that is added to all the time. The museum also features international figures (Hitler is dodgy on several counts), a hall of Megastars, and, with a separate entrance, a Chamber of Horrors which is hallmarked with gruesomeness. The tunnel here is *not* for claustrophobics, toughies will love it though.

All the wax figures are made on the premises by a resident sculptor. Live Irish personalities have a face mask made; others are worked on from photographs and other records. A head can take up to three months' work. Interested art students could enquire about seeing the workroom. Before this Museum opened in 1983, there hadn't been a waxworks in Dublin since 1916, when the last one burned (very steadily) to the ground.

The Story of Banking

Bank of Ireland Arts Centre, Foster Place
Tel: 671 1488
Open: Tuesday–Friday: 10.00 a.m.–4.00 p.m. At weekends, large
groups by appointment only. Admission fee.

You get to print your own money here, which is what an amazing number of people were doing right up to the nineteenth century — legally. One of them was David La Touche, who was the genius behind the making of the Bank of Ireland, and he tells his banking adventures in a time-trip film. Before that there's a history of the bank building in its first and glorious days as the Irish Parliament (see page 59), including an eavesdropping on some of the heated debates. There is also a visit into an eighteenth-century cash office including a look at the original bank ledgers and bank notes. A push-along armoured cart and a bank soldier on the stairs are some of the other exhibits here, along with the historical layout and, of course, your own bit of counterfeiting.

This exhibition is quite separate from the tour of the House of Lords (see page 60) which is free and is also situated in the Bank building.

GAA Museum

Croke Park, Dublin 1
Tel: 855 8176
Entrance: under the Cusack Stand, via Clonliffe Road.
Open: May–September, every day: 9.30 a.m.–5.00 p.m.; October–April,
Tuesday–Sunday: 10.00 a.m.–5.00 p.m.; Sunday Match Days: 12.00 noon
–3.00 p.m. only. Admission fee. Buses: 3, 11, 16.

The most state-of-the-art, media-stuffed museum in this book, if not the country, is the GAA Museum — it takes at least a match-long period to work through. History is downstairs, interactive pucking, kicking and testing your own athletic reflexes are upstairs. As you enter under the majestic Cusack Stand you get a ticket-cum-map to help plot your way around. You can follow the chronological story of the Games revival from 1886, or wander around dipping into different stories. The links with the nation's history are powerfully told in film and display. There's a clever comparative exhibit of the state of sports in different countries at the same time — the modern Olympic Games, soccer, baseball and the GAA had a lot in common. The story of the foreign games ban is here; so is the story of transport to Croke Park — the 'Special' buses. Kits from everywhere, ancient hurleys, little Setanta, serious camogie, trophies and the smart structure of the GAA's structure today are all on offer. Upstairs you can get dug right in, and afterwards there's a supercharged look at the most recent and exciting finals in the mini-theatre. A kit and souvenir shop together with a coffee bar make certain that you won't get out before extra time.

National Transport Museum

Howth Castle grounds, Howth, County Dublin

Not between exhibits

Tel: 832 0427; Queries: 848 0831
Entrance: to the right, just before the Castle.
Open: June–August, weekdays: 10.00 am–5.00 p.m. All year:
Saturdays, Sundays and Bank Holidays: 2.00 p.m.–5.00 p.m. Saturdays,
Sundays and bank holidays, 26 December–1 January: 2.00 p.m.–5.00 p.m.
Admission fee. Bus: 31; DART.

You get an old tram ticket on entry here. If you loved Richard Scarry books as a small child, or just generally like having large recognisable chunks of the past to stroke, the Transport Museum is a wonderful place. Here, in a gigantic shed belonging to this old Gothic castle, are housed ancient tractors, mineral water trucks, gorgeous old double-decker buses, fire-trucks, and the pride of the collection — several Belfast and Dublin trams, including the Hill of Howth tram, which racketed faithfully up to Howth Summit until the 1950s. Film companies vie for the hiring of many of the vehicles here. All the workers are voluntary, and are delighted to talk about their beloved charges, and their plans for them.

The castle isn't open to the public. Don't take it personally — it wasn't open to pirate queen Granuaile, either. Consequently, she kidnapped the eldest child of the family in a huff. But it is permitted to walk past the grizzly towers and barbican and up towards the Deerpark Hotel and golf club. During May and June there's a riot of purple rhododendrons to admire.

Irish Jewish Museum

**Ground
floor only**

*3/4 Walworth Road, off Victoria Street,
Portobello, Dublin 8*
Tel: 453 1797 (outside opening hours: 475 8388/676 0737)
**Open: May–September, Sundays, Tuesdays, Thursdays: 11.00 a.m.–
3.30 p.m. October–April, Sundays: 10.30 a.m.–2.30 p.m. Closed on
Jewish holidays. Admission by donation. Groups and schools can visit
by arrangement. Buses: 14, 15, 16, 19.**

This museum is located within two ordinary houses which
were thrown together, and you'll only spot it by its longer
windows and the Hebrew plaque outside. Inside it
incorporates a small local synagogue which is no longer in
use. Part of the Orthodox rules ordained that one had to
walk to the synagogue, not drive, so there were several
small synagogues around the South Circular Road area of
Dublin, which was the principal Jewish district in the city.
The exhibition traces the history of the Jewish Community
in Ireland from 1079 (five arrived and were sent away)
through all the different migrations that occurred, usually
after persecutions in Europe. History students can check out
the wretched anti-Semitic spoutings of some prominent Irish
public servants, preserved in twentieth-century newspaper
accounts which are also available for inspection.

There is a reconstruction of a 1920s Dublin Jewish
kitchen, laid out for Chanukkah, with all the kosher foods
represented. There's also information on Jewish writers
and artists, as well as Dublin-based Jewish schools and
youth organisations. The most famous twentieth-century
novel in English has as its hero a Dublin Jew, Leopold
Bloom, in James Joyce's *Ulysses* (its other hero is Dublin
itself). He is here too. This museum is full of stories and the
synagogue has a powerful atmosphere.

> On Richmond Road in Drumcondra there is a small
> Jewish cemetery where you will find the year 5618
> carved.

National Print Museum

Beggar's Bush former barracks, Ballsbridge, Dublin 4
Tel: 660 3770

Main
level only

Open: May–September, Monday–Friday: 10.00 a.m.–12.30 p.m.; 2.30
p.m.–5.00 p.m, weekends and holidays: 12.00 noon–5.00 p.m. October–
April, Tuesday, Thursday, weekends: 2.00 p.m.–5.00 p.m.
Admission fee. Buses: 7A, 8, 45.

From outside, the former garrison chapel looks neat and
perfect; inside, the printing presses and jumble of metal
slugs, inks and crammed drawers give the Print Museum
the appearance of an old revolutionary press with
handbills you could be hanged for producing. Except
there's no noise. A huge and truly fabulous 1894 banner of
the Bookbinders' Consolidated Union hangs from the
rafters — printing here covers everything from wax tablet
to vellum and from a book like this one to the feint-ruled
copybooks that were marked out like fields. Find out what
it means to be really 'typecast', when 'hot off the presses'
actually meant what it said, and check out some glorious
front pages of Irish newspapers in history. Take a bow Mr
Gutenberg, this was a wonderful craft you invented. The
funny thing is that the first batch of computers up in the
gallery look even more ancient than the wonderful
Monotype machines. There's a short video introduction to
hot-metal printing and afterwards you might even get to
print something yourself.

There's also a pleasant café.

*Waterways Visitor Centre**

Grand Canal Basin, Ringsend, Dublin 4
Tel: 677 7510

Main
level only

Entrance: just off Ringsend end of Pearse Street.

Open: June–September, daily: 9.30 a.m.–6.30 p.m. October–May,
Wednesday–Sunday: 12.30 p.m.–5.00 p.m.
Admission fee. Bus: 3.

They call this centre the 'box in the docks'. When you
cross the bridge you seem to be floating in the deep canal
water and it's a pleasant sensation. This is the world of

Ireland's — and Dublin's — inland waterways, the canals and navigable rivers. Downstairs are working models of canal locks and flood-systems, and some of the most ancient river boats. You can test your surveying knowledge by computer and track the history of the two great canals. Upstairs check out an antique diving suit used in the Shannon, and watch the waterways video that will make you want to rush up to the roof (you can) and scan the great view all around for a canalworthy boat to charge the locks. Better still, turn to Chapter 5 and plan your day out along one of the canals.

The Classical Museum

UCD, Belfield, Dublin 4
Tel: 706 8166
Entrance: in the Classics Department, Arts Block, Room K216.
Open: in term time, Tuesday and Friday: 10.00 a.m.–1.00 p.m.;
Thursday: 1.00 p.m.–5.00 p.m. Groups by prior arrangement. For any
visitor, telephoning beforehand is advised. Admission free.

How do we know so much about what Greek gods and heroes got up to? From Homer and other writers, of course, but also from the many storytelling vases and sculptures that have survived. In the glass cases of UCD's small Classical Museum you can see Zeus, Herakles, Apollo, Dionysus and company just as the Ancient Greeks did. This is a collection of thousands-of-years-old originals first 'acquired' by Grand Tourists, the way Lord Elgin 'acquired' a large amount of the Parthenon for the British Museum. As well as the wonderful vessel shapes of *amphora, kylix, krater, alabastron* and suchlike, with their black and red figures, there are much earlier sacred items from Minoan Crete and from Cyprus. Roman coins in superb condition, right down to different imperial noses and warts are here, as well as funeral sculpture and some Egyptian ware. It's not for everyone, but classical studies students love seeing the real thing and there are special activity sheets for schools. Questions are welcome. You could begin by asking why one of the vase painters is known as the 'Dublin' painter....

The Pearse Museum/St Enda's
Grange Road, Rathfarnham
Tel: 493 4208

Open: Daily: 10.00 a.m. Closes at 4.00 p.m. November–January; at
5.00 p.m. in spring and autumn; at 5.30 p.m. from May–August. Closed
for lunch all year: 1.00 p.m.–2.00 p.m. Group tours by prior
arrangement. Admission free. Bus: 16.

The Hermitage is a famous museum in St Petersburg — it is also a third name for this museum. A fourth is the Fields of Odin; its first owner, Thomas Conolly called the estate by this name. St Enda's was the school founded by Patrick Pearse for Irish Catholic boys. Pearse called other schools of the day 'murder machines' — and he may well have had a point. Belonging to his school was a bit like being in the ancient Fianna, if the uniform is anything to judge by. But he was a talented and idealistic teacher who brought music, drama and art into his young students' lives. You can see the dormitory, study and some of Pearse's letters, family photographs and writings which are now on display. His final letter to his mother, written on the eve of his execution, is both brave and heartbreaking.

The grounds of St Enda's are wonderful to explore and you can pick up the nature/river trail in the courtyard nature study centre. Robert Emmet and his girlfriend Sarah Curran used to meet here in secret — try finding the structure that's named Emmet's Folly. Closer to the house the gardens are very pretty and give a happy air to this small stately home.

The **Nature Awareness Centre** is open to schools, by arrangement, from Wednesday to Sunday, and there are open activities on Saturdays from 11.30 a.m.–1.00 p.m. There is also a Junior Bat Club and competitions and special exhibitions at Hallowe'en and Easter. Summer camps also run right through the summer. For details telephone St Enda's. All in all a very pleasant, busy and interesting place to visit.

The National Maritime Museum of Ireland

The Mariners' Church, Haigh Terrace, Dún Laoghaire   Certain
Tel: 280 0969   *areas only*

Open: May–September, daily, except Mondays: 1.00 p.m.–5.00 p.m.
April and October, Sundays only: 1.00 p.m.–5.00 p.m. Schools and
groups outside these times by arrangement. Admission fee.
Buses: 7A, 8; DART.

The Museum is in a converted mariners' church which is down a narrow street. To get to it just turn left off George's Street after the Dún Laoghaire Shopping Centre.

There are two things that you can't miss — the giant lens from the Baily Lighthouse and the longboat. The lens is beautiful, rotating like the eye of a god with two million candle-watts reflecting in its mirrors. The longboat is possibly the oldest surviving ship's boat in the world. It came ashore in Bantry Bay with the French invasion fleet in 1796 and is painted in its original French revolutionary tricolours. There are dozens of ships' models — both steam and full-rigged sailing vessels, logs, compasses, 'sin bins', a scale model of an oil rig, charts, telescopes and even a nail from the mutinous *Bounty*.

National Sealife Centre

Bray, County Wicklow
Tel: 286 6939
Entrance: halfway down the Esplanade. Open: 10.00 a.m.–5.00 p.m.;
Easter–September every day. Rest of year: weekends only, or for
guided tours by arrangement. Admission fee. Bus: 45; DART.

This is not 'national' in the sense of National Museum; it's a multinational aquarium enterprise. But the fish here are truly paid-up nationals — they are, with very few exceptions, from Irish coastal or fresh waters. This makes them dark creatures rather than dramatically coloured and shaped ones. The guides have lots of information and if you take time to study the different tanks you'll find amazing things going on. For instance it was thought that sea horses were lost from Irish waters, but two were found and bred from and they are here in their shy non-macho (the males give birth) beauty. There's a convent-pool of cuckoo wrasse, all born pink and female, then one changes to blue and becomes a male. The catfish and their cartoon lips glare out from their dim pool and in another pool the scary horseshoe crabs clamber over each other while the contents of a fishmonger's slab swan around above them. There's a mock-up river with all those river fish who get thrown back by fishermen, but who has ever seen the *sterlet*? It is here and it's a spacey character. Best of all — better than the shark show — are the rays in the Bay of Rays. They're curious as cats and like to check out human smells and voices so they stick their noses out, treading water — cute as aliens. There's a gift shop crammed with sea-life goodies, cheap and expensive, an Explorers Club (free admission with adults), and parties can be arranged here too. An admission ticket lasts all day, with multiple entries, if you want to swim or boat and look for the real thing.

The Steam Museum

Straffan, County Kildare
Tel: 627 3155/628 8412
Entrance: Dublin/Naas by-pass, turn right for Straffan village. Take
right turn at the Straffan Inn; the Museum is about half a mile on the
right in the grounds of Lodge Park House.
Open: April, May, September on Sundays and Bank Holidays: 2.30 p.m.–
5.30 p.m.; June–August: every day except Monday: 2.00 p.m.–6.00 p.m.
Admission fee (except for proven technical students!) School groups
and guides by prior arrangement.

Here be dragons — steam dragons, heroes of the Industrial Revolution which changed our world for ever. Now these old industrial engines and the perfect working models of locomotives and Victorian plumbing systems are dinosaurs, but they can still puff their hearts out though many are creeping up on 200 years of age. The Museum is located in a beautifully restored Gothic-style church. The Power Hall contains five fantastic engines, taken from brewery, distillery, factory and ship, and on a working day, the combined power presents an awesome sight. The Engineers Hall has the dwarves — models created for a purpose (but there must have been pleasure too) by the great Men of Steam. Included is Richard Trevithick's (the First M of S) third model of 1797 — the oldest of its kind in the world. The train locomotives are quite perfect, each one unique and distinct as no modern vehicle is. There's a portrait gallery of steam persons and a souvenir shop of steam artefacts. More everyday steam happenings occur in the tea-room. Lodge Park's walled garden is also open to visitors in June, July and August, Tuesday–Friday afternoons. (For more about steam activities see pages 42 and 305.)

Other museum-type exhibitions to note are:

The Garda Museum
The Record Tower, Dublin Castle. Tel: 671 9966. In summer this is included in Castle Tour Number 2, but you can knock at the door (under the blue light) or telephone for an appointment. The shape is wonderful, of course, and way up, past all the DMP helmets and trouser presses, toy constables and written reports, you may even find a 'dead body' across the stairwell.

The Freemasons' Hall
Molesworth Street. Tel: 679 5465.
Open during June, July and August, or by arrangement for groups. Of great interest for historical and artistic research. This Victorian building contains Masonic jewels, pennants and regalia and there's a reconstruction of an eighteenth-century lodge meeting, as well as the different meeting rooms of today.

Fire Brigade Museum
Training Centre, Malahide Road. Tel: 833 8313.
In construction, but a computer-friendly research area on fire-fighting history plus many artefacts is planned for this training HQ. By appointment only.

The Plunkett Education Museum
Church of Ireland Training College, Rathmines
Road. Tel: 497 0033.
Open to groups only and strictly by arrangement.
School groups would enjoy this nineteenth-century
classroom reconstruction and exhibition of school-
ing. Staff are limited so plan ahead.

The Lambert Puppet Theatre/Museum
Clifton Lane, Monkstown. Tel: 280 0974.
If you attend one of the regular puppet shows you
can see the unique collection of puppets and
marionettes from all over the world.

Mercy International Centre
Baggot Street. Tel: 661 8061.
Guided tours at 10.30 a.m. and 2.30 p.m. every day.
Admission fee.
A Dubliner, the Venerable Catherine McAuley (of £5
note fame), born in 1778, founded the world's
largest religious order of nuns— the Sisters of Mercy.
This Centre traces their work in Ireland and
worldwide, along with the story of Catherine herself.
Her tomb is in the peaceful water garden. Watch for
the delicate artwork of Sister Clare Augustine — she
modelled her style on the ancient Irish monastic
illuminators. There's a shop with a variety of goodies
and admission includes tea and scones.

Maynooth College
Maynooth, County Kildare. Tel: 708 3576.
Open: all year. Visitor Centre May–September.
Monday–Friday: 11.00 a.m.–5.00 p.m. Weekends:
2.00 p.m.–6.00 p.m.
For history, architecture and garden enthusiasts.
The Visitor Centre shows a short video of the 200-
year history of this diocesan university. It was set up
before Catholic Emancipation, so it's no surprise to
find the wax death mask of Daniel O'Connell here. A
modern water garden is an interesting feature of the
extensive grounds which also include the biggest
choir chapel in the world, and many mementoes of
the visit of Pope John Paul II in 1979.

Castles, Grand Houses and Extraordinary Buildings

Here is how this part of the chapter works. Listed first is anything that calls itself a castle, or was once a castle. Next come cathedrals and other religious buildings. After that come civic buildings and city houses which are open to the public, followed by excursions to grand houses with big parks. Finally, there is a list of unique buildings which don't fit into any of the previous categories.

Dublin Castle*
Castle Street, off Dame Street, Dublin 2
Tel: 677 7580

Except tower and Undercroft

Open: Monday–Friday: 10.00 a.m.–5.00 p.m.; Saturday and Sunday: 2.00 p.m.–5.00 p.m. In summer there is a separate tour of the Record Tower and Chapel. The Chester Beatty Library is now based in the Castle area (see page 30) and there is also a theatre, The Crypt. Admission free to Castle yard, Chapel Royal and Dubh Linn garden. Admission fee to State Apartments, including Undercroft.

As you enter the gates you will notice there's no moat, no drawbridge and no portcullis, although there are sentry-boxes. The former *were* there when the Castle was built in

1204 by King John. However, the Castle was rebuilt in the sixteenth and seventeenth centuries so that the English Viceroys could live and work here in style. (The style is the bit you pay to see.) Unfortunately, they had to do some unplanned rebuilding when there was a fire which spread to the Gunpowder Tower and blew the whole place up, something no rebels ever managed to do.

The Castle has a medieval plan of two courtyards — in the lower one, over in the right corner, is one of the original towers. This is the famous **Record** or **Black Tower** from which Red Hugh O'Donnell escaped not once but twice, in the freezing winters of the 1590s. You can climb the Tower on the summertime tour (or, indeed, if you call in on the Garda Museum — see page 43) but don't miss the little **Chapel Royal** beside it, accessible at any time of the year. It is a tiny romantic Gothic-style church crying out to be peopled with knights and damsels, though it was really built in 1807 by Francis Johnston — much later than the era it conjures up. His design, apart from being medieval-looking, was very crafty; although all the work looks as though it's solid masonry, it is in fact crafted from wood and plaster, painted to look like stone. Touch it and see. You can see why if you go round the back of the chapel, along by the multi-coloured blocks, and look into the pretty **Dubh Linn garden**, with its Celtic swirls and mosaic sculptures. Underneath this, it's claimed, is the original 'dark pool — dubh linn' which was formed by the River Poddle. The Normans diverted it to make their moat and still today the Poddle flows underneath the castle — you will see it if you do the tour. A solid stone chapel would sink — and they did — which is why this pretty chapel is also crafty.

The Castle was always the seat of English power. There's a famous joke about the figure of Justice over the main entrance: (a) she has her back turned on the city, (b) she's not wearing her customary blindfold, and (c) when her scales filled up with water they tilted. During the Great War of 1914–18 the Castle was used as a military hospital and an attempt was made to capture it during the 1916 Rising. Now it's maintained by the State for the inauguration of a President, for entertaining foreign heads of state and for European Community functions. The **State Apartments** are on view when there is no State business going on there. The tour includes the Throne Room, the even more regal St Patrick's Hall, the elegant Apollo Room and the Gothic-style Supper Room. In one of the smaller rooms there's a very beautiful and intricate table made by a prisoner for Queen Victoria — she snubbed it. The Apartments are in the style of a Grand House, not Castle-like; they are beautifully maintained eighteenth-century rooms with stuccoed ceilings and gorgeous chandeliers where balls and receptions took place during the 'Castle' season — from Christmas to Easter.

Across from the Apartments entrance, in the trim little building with its octagonal Clock Tower, is one of the Castle's great crime scenes. It was from here that the Irish Crown Jewels were stolen in 1907, while under a heavy guard — just like a Pink Panther film. They have never been found, so away you go, Sherlock.

The tour of the Apartments ends with the meaty medieval bit, in the **Undercroft**. Many feet under the yard level you do the time warp and see the original city wall with clumsy arches where the moat flowed, the postern steps for deliveries and a pool of the actual Poddle, looking as if pale big-eyed creatures might stir in it. Heads used to roll in here.

Ashtown Castle and Phoenix Park Visitors Centre*
Phoenix Park, Dublin 7
Tel: 677 0095

Ground floor only (FREE)

Entrance signposted from the Phoenix Monument.
Open: Every day, June–September: 10.00 a.m.–6.00 p.m.;
March/October: 9.30 a.m.–5.00 p.m.; April/May: 9.30 a.m.–5.30 p.m.;
winter months: 9.30 a.m.–4.30 p.m. Admission fee.

The park is its glorious self — it doesn't need words or pictures to be enjoyed. The centre is also a very pleasant place, if only to enjoy good tea and cakes. In addition, it has also got the bonus of a long-hidden construction, Ashtown Castle, which can be explored along with its miniature maze. When the deer park was laid out for the monarch, the castle passed to a keeper who had to prevent the 'spoil and embezzlement of the vert or venison'. He also got to keep some for himself. The castle was later attached to a more regular house and plastered over — it was only discovered when this house, belonging to the papal ambassador, was knocked down in the 1980s. The Centre offers a video and displays of the history of the Phoenix Park; you can find out where the burial ground lies that is even older than Newgrange (which itself is older than the Pyramids!), learn about the murders, the motor races, the millions who've gathered on religious occasions here — and more. The animal exhibit is a little strange with its utterly non-Phoenix Park mammoth and elephant bird news, but you can always be guaranteed a real deer outside.

Farmleigh House
Phoenix Park

Farmleigh is an enormous house on the Castleknock side of the Park. Once owned by the Guinness family, it has recently been bought by the Government. It is planned to have it as a Grand House for entertaining visiting heads of state, but it is also planned that Farmleigh will have hours of public access.

Swords Castle
Main Street, Swords
Tel: 872 7777 (weekdays for information)
Tower Open: Monday, Wednesday, Thursday: 10.00 a.m.–4.00 p.m.;
Friday: 10.00 a.m.–3.00 p.m. Buses: 33, 41, 43.

Swords is well-named, for the eventual plan for the Castle reconstruction includes actual medieval-style tournament events. In the meantime it's planned to open up different parts of the castle as they are worked on by FÁS. Swords

Castle looks both medieval and castle-like. It belonged, not to a sheriff or a knight, but to the Archbishop of Dublin who maintained a large household here and took the townspeople inside his thick defending walls when there were marauders about. When the battlement walk is fully restored the sheer size of the place will be evident; it comprises a gatehouse, the archbishop's apartments, a banqueting hall, rooms for retainers, a chapel and farm buildings, plus the great yard which must have been packed with horses and tradesmen at their work. What you can enter now is the Constable's Tower, a little keep of its own facing the Ward River and park, and part of the battlement walk.

Ardgillan Castle and Demesne
Skerries
Tel: 849 2212

Almost all areas

Castle open: April–September, Tuesday–Sunday: 11.00 a.m.–6.00 p.m.; October–March, Wednesday–Sunday: 11.00 a.m.–4.30 p.m.; January, Sundays only: 2.00 p.m.–4.00 p.m. Admission free to park and gardens. Fee for castle tour. Bus: 33. Train from Connolly Station. Signposted from the main Dublin–Skerries road.

Ardgillan didn't always look like a Victorian castle — it started life as an early Georgian country house in 1738 and just grew from there in the continual ownership of the same family, the Taylours. They were blessed with the most glorious sea views from their house as well as a train that stopped like a bus at the bottom of their lawns. The old hall is now a display room for various curiosities such as a miniature cannon and two sad-looking stuffed bears from North America, one of which appears to have a dental problem. The butler's pantry and the kitchen have many clever tricks — check out the cheap roasting spit. However, pride of place must go to the library. It contains the classic mystery-story cliché — the door hidden behind false bookshelves. Only there are *two* doors, and the clue to opening them is contained in the title of one of the false books. There's also a display of valuable early Irish maps, the Down Survey (because they were written down) of 1655. The coffee shop serves good cakes.

> For what to see in the superb *free* gardens see page 92.

Malahide Castle and Demesne
Malahide Road, just before Malahide village
Tel: 846 2516/846 2228
(Separate entries for Fry Model Railway Exhibition and Castle Gardens in Chapter 2)

Demesne open during park hours (See Parks — Chapter 2). Castle open: Monday–Friday: 10.00 a.m.–5.00 p.m. (all year); November–March, Saturdays, Sundays and Bank Holidays: 2.00 p.m.–5.00 p.m.; April–October, Saturday: 10.00 a.m.–5.00 p.m.; Sunday and Holidays: 11.00 a.m.–6.00 p.m. Admission fee. Bus: 42. Train from Connolly Station.

Talbot Street is the city bus terminus for the Malahide bus, and the Talbot family were the owners of Malahide Castle from 1185 until the 1970s. Now the 268 acres belong to Dublin County Council and you can visit without an RSVP all year round. There's great rolling parkland, some of which has been turned into tennis courts and playing fields, but most of it can still be raced and tumbled upon. Behind the car park closest to the Castle is a fine adventure playground hewn of wood.

You can do a tour of the Castle inside. From outside it's a mixture of styles, mainly Loch Ness movie, and it has a very small door for its size. Inside, the rooms have been turned into a walk-around museum of Irish interiors and furniture — from a medieval banqueting hall to a Victorian nursery. Portraits of faces from history books hang everywhere. Upstairs there's a gentleman's, a lady's and a child's bedroom, just like the Three Bears. Try spotting the different period styles in the castle by watching details like window shapes, room sizes, ceilings and colours. In the Great Hall there's an entrance known as Puck's Door after the resident ghost. Puck turns up when changes occur that he doesn't like. He may have done that when one of his secret treasures, original manuscripts of the famous Scottish writer and scandalmonger, James Boswell, were disturbed here in 1928.

Drimnagh Castle
Long Mile Road, Crumlin
Tel: 450 2530

Ground
level only

Entrance: through the grounds of the Christian Brothers School.
Open: April–October, Wednesday, Saturday, Sunday: 12.00 p.m.–5.00
p.m. October–March, Sundays only: 12.00 noon–5.00 p.m. Other times
for schools and groups by arrangement. It is advisable to telephone as
the castle is regularly hired for functions. Admission fee. Buses: 56A
(or 50, 55 to Crumlin village only).

This is a very likeable Norman castle that is not much larger than an average modern semi-detached house. However, in its time, it probably slept thirty or more people, as well as horses, hounds, cats and other less welcome four-footed creatures. The moat sports ducks rather than fearsome pike but there's an ancillary burglar-alarm in the shape of a 'murder-hole' leading into the undercroft, or medieval store and kitchens. Upstairs the Great Hall (living-room-cum-bedroom to us) has been lovingly restored in tiles and oak by craftspeople, who (fittingly) have had carvings of their faces worked into the roof-space, like any medieval workers worth their salt. Outside there's a seventeenth-century knot garden and some exotic fowl.

Rathfarnham Castle*
Rathfarnham
Tel: 493 9462
Entrance: signposted from Rathfarnham village by-pass.
Open: May and October: 10.00 a.m.–5.00 p.m. every day; June–
September: 10.00 a.m.–6.00 p.m. every day. Easter weekend:
10.00 a.m.–5.00 p.m. Admission fee. Buses: 16, 17, 75.

The first version of the castle goes back to the reign of Queen Elizabeth I. Her not-so-loyal subjects in Wicklow had a habit of attacking this great house so when it was done over in the eighteenth century by another generation of the founding Loftus family they retained the fortifications and the dizzy-shaped rooms that grew out of them. Sir Henry Loftus invited the best architects and decorators of the day to take their paint and plaster to the walls and ceilings. Some of the work was so good that the original gold leaf paint still gleams on one of the ceilings — one with Greek gods, naturally. However, the house still has miles to go before it sleeps — a lot of restoration work has yet to be done. This aspect makes the tour more interesting in a way, as the guides point to all the detective work and clues that the OPW restorers are working with. Plenty to see — beautiful spacious rooms with a classical theme, strange smells (chemicals and death-watch beetle corpses), a wall with a ghost, a one-way front door and all kinds of stories from eighteenth-century life. There is also a model of early Rathfarnham, a nice coffee shop and parkland (only a tiny proportion left of what the Wicklow raiders would have stomped through) and also a small lake complete with its own doggy ghost story. Would-be architects/ historians, this is your life.

Goat Castle/Dalkey Heritage Centre

Ground floor only

Main Street, Dalkey
Tel: 285 8366
Entrance: the larger castle on Castle Street.
Open: April–October, daily: 9 a.m.–5.00 p.m.; weekends: 11 a.m.–5.00 p.m.; November–March, weekends: 11 a.m.–5 p.m. Admission fee.
Bus: 8; DART.

At one time, there were seven castles on this street; now there are two. This one is called Goat Castle. Dalkey was the important port of Dublin during medieval times because it had deeper water than the Liffey and the castles were important defence and storage systems. It's thought that the Black Death arrived in Ireland via Dalkey port in 1348. There was also a lot of tax dodging going on around the town. Upstairs you'll find the *bartizan* or boiling-oil hole that put invaders off their stride if they were stupid enough not to know about it. Downstairs there's a display of works by famous Dalkey residents — from George Bernard Shaw to Maeve Binchy, and life through the different ages of Dalkey. Upstairs there are some beautifully made models of the stone quarries together with the famous Dalkey train that ran on air, and the tramways.

Religious Buildings

St Patrick's Cathedral

Patrick Street, Dublin 8
Tel: 475 4817
Entrance: at main doorway on St Patrick's Close.
Open: Monday–Friday: 9.00 a.m.–6.00 p.m.; Saturday: 9.00 a.m.–
5.00 p.m. (4.00 p.m. in winter); Sunday: 10.00 a.m.–11.00 a.m.; 12.45
p.m.–3.00 p.m. Admission fee.

St Patrick's Park is a green oasis; this whole site was, at one time, a riverside location (still is, only *seven* feet underground) courtesy of the Poddle river, which used flow alongside and flood the early cathedral buildings. Long before that, the real St Patrick is said to have baptised fifth-century Dubliners on this very spot. Inside the cathedral there's an ancient stone cross that was found 'six feet down and 91 feet due north of the north-west angle of the tower' — where St Patrick's Well is said to be. The clock on the bell tower is one of three that Queen Elizabeth I allowed the city so that Dublin people could tell the time. Outside you see the chess bishop-like Liberty Bell sculpture by Vivienne Roche. This cathedral was begun in 1191, in a 'liberty' area —outside the bossy paws of Dublin city. It is now the most Dublin of all Dublin churches and was saved from falling into ruin during the last century by a very rich Guinness magnate — the brewery lords also

built the housing and school buildings around the park.
Inside it's all soaring stony Gothic — but the gargoyles you
see on the columns are Victorian not medieval. Not to
miss are the monstrous tomb of Richard Boyle, who
stuffed all his family in as wooden statues around him, the
free-standing door with a hole in it (it tells you why, and
also how the hole-maker invented the idea of 'chancing
your arm'), the grave of the man who devised a recipe for
roast child (it *was* a satire) aka *Gulliver's Travels* author
Jonathan Swift, who was Dean of St Patrick's from 1714.
Near him lies the woman who loved him, Stella. The war
memorials are fantastically sad; the bright flags are those of
Irish regiments and of the Knights of St Patrick. Don't miss
the organ console with its dramatic organ stop commands
'well to great; hautboy; bombard' — it may very well be
your only chance to examine an example of the longest-
working 'synthesiser' keyboard in musical history. Be sure
to admire the beautifully crafted needlepoint kneelers —
each one is different and they all celebrate different
aspects of Ireland, from surfing to birds to the Burren. You
can hear Evensong Monday to Friday at 5.35 p.m. or at
3.15 p.m. on Sundays; the choirboys go to school across
the road.

Christ Church Cathedral

Except
to Crypt

Lord Edward Street, Dublin 8
Tel: 677 8099
Entrance: either via Dublinia or main entrance facing High Street.
Open: daily: 10.00 a.m.–5.00 p.m., 5.30 p.m. in summer. Admission
fee.

The first birthdate of Christ Church is 1038 when it was
developed by the Dublin Viking king, Sitric Silkenbeard. It
was built high up on the great hill of the city — but we
don't know what it looked like. What we see today dates
from the treacherous days of the twelfth century — the
Normans had just invaded and wanted to build a fine
stone cathedral. You'll find yourself stepping down in time
to enter if you come in the main entrance (Dublinia

visitors enter over the stone bridge). However, the oldest
part of the cathedral is the crypt, entered from the right-
hand side of the nave. It's vast — looking and smelling
more like Roman vaults than anything else. During the
seventeenth century taverns and shops carried on business
down here and had to be evicted. It's the biggest cathedral
crypt in these islands and can be said to have its own
mummies — a poor cat and rat that got stuck in an organ
pipe. There's an on-going Crypt Stone Identification
Project and the crypt itself will be closed for renovation
between September 1999 and May 2000. Upstairs in the
cathedral it's best to follow the map you get with your
ticket (there is an excellent I-Spy Young Person's Guide) to
discover the alleged tomb of Norman knight Strongbow,
husband of Aoife, plus the mysterious half tomb alongside.
The tomb was used as a cashpoint by medieval landlords.
You can pick out the two architectural styles, rounded
Romanesque and pointed Gothic in the window shapes.
Check out the 'Foxy Friars' and stone faces, the repository
with the heart of Archbishop Laurence O'Toole and read
the story of the Boy Pretender King, Lambert Simnel, who
had his Andy Warhol famous 15 minutes when he was
crowned as Edward VI here in 1487, during the English
Wars of the Roses. He spent the rest of his life as a kitchen
boy. There's a special Peace chapel and prayers for world
peace are offered every day at 12.00 noon. Outside in the
grounds you can see the remains of a chapter house. The
Cathedral website is superb (see page 348); you can find
out many things including bell-ringing practice times and
the story of their movable belfry.

St Audoen's Church*
Cornmarket, near Christ Church
Tel: 661 3111/453 5984
Apart from the cathedrals, St Audoen's is the only working
medieval church in Dublin. Its unusual name recalls the
busy Norman saint Ouen/Audoen who built a monastery
near Brie (of cheese fame), and travelled widely. His

Dublin church is now divided into four parts, two with roofs, two without; there is also a tower which contains beautifully-sounding fifteenth-century bells. The exhibition is through the roofed area facing the street, and leads into the actual Church of Ireland that is parallel to the city walls. St Audoen's was a Guild church, the Lord Mayor's church and Dublin Corporation's church — you'll see the city's three blazing castles in the glass of the east window. So it was a very important part of city life. But before its foundation in 1190 there was most likely an older church here and evidence is the Lucky Stone in the porch. Give a rub to this eighth-century graveslab which is now safe back where it belongs. There's a story that it used to walk and terrify people; it certainly defied all attempts to steal it. You'll see the Portlester tomb where the fifteenth-century Earl of Portlester and his wife lie in stately stone; and inside the church the wall-based memorial to two families, the Sparkes and the Duffs, who are fixed like a seventeenth-century stone version of the Simpsons. After a visit, it's essential that you walk down the passageway to St Audoen's Arch, the only medieval city gateway still standing.

St Mary's Abbey Chapter House*
Tel: 872 1490
Entrance: Meeting House Lane, off Mary's Abbey, Capel Street.
Open: mid-June–mid-September, Wednesdays and Sundays:
10.00 a.m.–5.00 p.m. Admission fee.

It's a case of that cave smell again as you descend eight centuries into this Cistercian abbey's chapter house or monks' common room. St Mary's was a huge business enterprise as well as an important religious house and the maps and drawings will show just how much land it took up on the north side of the Liffey. The monks also had their own harbour at Dalkey and 30,000 other acres, so they had plenty to talk about in their special sign language — some of it illustrated in the display. By reason they were based in the Pale; they belonged to the

English brand of the church, very different from the feisty Irish branch. Above you is some very plain but very clever architecture, with ribs like umbrella spokes holding up the roof. The Chapter House is most famous, not for its monks' neat manuscripts or herb gardens, but for the smashing down on a table of the sword of state by Silken Thomas, the Geraldine knight who could take no more interference from the Crown. This happened in 1534; he lost his head, and the King of England (who, being Henry VIII, was fond of a head or two) shortly afterwards did his best to wipe out all the monasteries of Ireland, including this one. So this little room is a tough cookie to have survived.

St Doulagh's Church

Very limited

(No telephone)
Entrance: on the Malahide Road, near Kinsealy.
Open: May–September, Sunday: 3.00 p.m.–5.00 p.m. Admission by donation. Bus: 42.

If God made Wendy churches this is one. Everything is pint-sized in this thirteenth-century church which is nearly perfectly preserved. Perhaps the monk who wrote the Irish poem 'Pangur Bán' about his white cat, lived here because the building has a sense of humour about it. From the road you see the myriad tiny windows set at angles where nothing except a toe has any business to be. Inside miniature crooked staircases lead round and up into the tiny, boxy rooms, one on top of the other. There are stone seats and cubbyholes and the hairy watercress grows in all the windows.

St Doulagh was an anchorite. That is a monk who chose to be walled up in a cell for the rest of his life and fed by his trusted fellows through a cubbyhole. There's also a leper window here so that the unfortunates could attend Mass without meeting squeaky-clean people. Outside in the grounds is the holy well and baptistery; so old that St Patrick is said to have happened along to oversee the work.

Lusk Heritage Centre*

Lusk
Tel: 843 7683
Entrance: walkway in the centre of Lusk village.
Open: mid-June–mid-September, Fridays only: 10.00 a.m.–5.00 p.m.
Admission fee. Bus: 33.

Unfortunately, no entry to the round tower here, but clinging on to it is the square medieval belfry and its several floors and thoroughly medieval staircase which you are free to explore. There are displays from tombs in the Fingal monastic area, but pride of place goes to the Elizabethan married couple in effigy on their tomb. These were Barnewalls (same family as in Drimnagh Castle), lying peacefully on their stone pillows with their stone dogs. It's very like a castle keep — apart from the twentieth-century perspex that has been added to the windows.

Sacred Heart Oratory

Library Road, Dún Laoghaire
Tel: 205 4700 for details
Opening hours not allocated at time of printing.

When you come round the dramatic red protective shell that has been built around this tiny oratory, you'll find swirls of all kinds. In the tiles, in the floor mosaic, and in the specially planted Celtic peace garden that surrounds it. But when you enter the oratory, which is smaller than most living-rooms, you'll see the reason for the spiralwork. This is like walking *into* the Book of Kells. Every inch of the surface, walls and ceiling is covered in the triskels and fantastic wriggling animals that we associate with Celtic illumination. There are snakes, birds of paradise, cats, and a zooful of imaginary gymnastic creatures.

The oratory was built in 1919 in the Dominican convent as a thanksgiving for the end of the First World War. Sister Concepta Lynch was the artist and she worked entirely with ordinary domestic paints, plus touches of gold. She was a born and bred artist: her father Thomas Lynch ran one of Dublin's most established Celtic Revival

illumination businesses. Sister Concepta made stencils of
her ideas so that work could be faster; these are now in
the National Gallery. The stained-glass windows were
made by the Harry Clarke studio, and have a strong
medieval charm. As a war memorial, the oratory seems to
say 'make art, not war'. Sister Concepta died, mercifully,
just before the Second World War.

Historic Houses and Buildings in or near Dublin City

Bank of Ireland
College Green, Dublin 2
Tel: 677 6801
**Entrance: College Green portico, ask for admission to the House of
Lords which is open unless meetings are taking place.**
**Open: Normal banking hours, Monday–Friday: 10.00 a.m.–4.00 p.m.;
Thursday: open till 5.00 p.m. On Tuesdays only, there is a guided tour
of the original House of Lords by Dublin historian Eamonn Mac
Thomáis. Tours are at 10.30 a.m., 11.30 a.m. and 1.45 p.m. Admission
is free.**

An accident of history turned this vast building into a bank
— it was designed to house the very proud Irish
parliament that was largely responsible for the growth and
importance of Dublin in the eighteenth century. Though
there were mud streets outside it, the people of Dublin
took a great interest in the doings of parliament, coming
into the Commons galleries to watch, or sometimes to riot.
Banned books were burned at the gates.

The architect, Edward Lovett Pearce, designed this
building — the most splendid parliament house in Europe
at the time — when he was only 29. His 1729 design did
not include the curved walls — they were added later by
James Gandon and they are actually fakes. Not that they
would fall down if you kick them but there's no enclosure
behind them. This part of the building is like a giant

thermos, with an inner wall and an outer wall. Inside all is
much smaller than it seems from without. The old House
of Commons chamber is gone; it was octagon-shaped, with
a dome and galleries for onlookers. The Bank's Cash Office
is worth a look — it was originally the Court of Requests.
Best of all, you can ask the porters to show you the old
House of Lords. It's a beautiful temple-like chamber — no
traffic noise can be heard in here — and contains an
original Dublin chandelier and chiming grandfather clock
that have outlived all the great speeches and the
corruption of the Act of Union in 1800. You will be sat
down and told which bishop's or duke's place you have
taken — almost 200 lords and bishops were crowded in
here, with places for the King and the Earls of Dublin and
Belfast. On the walls are enormous tapestries celebrating
Williamite victories, posh versions of what can be seen on
walls in east Belfast, except here King Billy's horse is *not*
white (visit the Battle of the Boyne site, page 242). If it's
winter, warm your hands in the entrance hall on the way
out at what must be the biggest coal fire in Ireland.

Number Twenty-nine — Georgian Townhouse
29 Lower Fitzwilliam Street, Dublin 2
Tel: 702 6165
Open: Tuesday–Saturday: 10.00 a.m.–5.00 p.m.; Sunday: 2.00 p.m.–
5.00 p.m. Large groups by arrangement. Admission fee (children free).

Eighteenth-century children had it tough; the rich ones
were banished to the nursery at the top of the house while
the more numerous poor ones hauled coals and water,
brooms and linen to the top of the house and back down
five storeys to the basement — that is, if they were lucky
enough to have a job. You can enter briefly into their lives,
and those of the adults around them, in this beautifully
restored Georgian townhouse, maintained by the ESB, the
friendly guides being some of their retired staff. The house
was built in the 1790s by an eighteenth-century property
developer and it cost its first owner £320. The audio-visual
show at the beginning of the tour introduces this lady and

her family life; then a guide shows visitors through the tall narrow bathroomless house — two rooms on each of the five storeys. The furnishings are completely in period. Watch especially for the everyday details of heating, lighting and toiletries — whale-oil lamps, petticoat mirrors, cricket cages and ruff-irons aren't found in the average house today. The most lively rooms are the kitchen and, of course, the nursery, which has a selection of playhouse-sized doll's houses, as well as a two-hundred-year-old baby-walker.

Newman House
85/86 St Stephen's Green, Dublin 2
Tel: 706 7422
Entrance: through number 86. Open: June–September, Tuesday–
Friday: 12.00 noon–5.00 p.m.; Saturday: 2.00 p.m.–5.00 p.m.; Sunday:
11.00 a.m.–2.00 p.m.; also open for groups by arrangement. Admission
fee.

Enter under number 86's delightful dozy (*couchant*) lion. A former owner of this house, the rather scandalous Mr Buck Whaley, jumped successfully from the lion onto a carriage for a bet. The tour begins in the smaller house which was built to the design of the busy Richard Cassells — he also made Leinster House (now the Dáil) and Russborough House — in 1738. This makes Newman House the oldest townhouse on view in this book. When the original owners moved in, there was nothing between the back garden and the mountains except countryside and highwaymen. Off the hall is the Apollo Room where the god Apollo and his nine muses with their tongue-twister names are worked in large-scale plaster work, surrounded by little cherubs or *putti*. The Swiss Family Lafranchini did the plaster marvels here and also upstairs in the great salon where the plump angelic legs actually dangle in the air. Both the small and large houses are joined because they became home to the Catholic University (grandparent of UCD) during the last century. Cardinal Newman was the Rector — hence the name — and another famous teacher here was the poet Gerard Manley Hopkins, whose study is on also view. The Catholic management did a decoration make-over on number 85, dressing all the nudes in plaster clothes, all of which have now been removed except for Juno's grungy shift. James Joyce was a student here, walking up the stairs with its plaster musical instruments, snake-like birds and baboon heads made by Robert West. Newman House — you'll have guessed — is famed for its plaster work; and yes, you *can* get into the dreamy gardens behind the wall — see Iveagh Gardens (page 94).

City Hall

Lord Edward Street, Dublin 2 (facing Parliament Street)
Tel: 672 2222

After 2.00 p.m.

Open: Daily: 9.15 a.m.–12.45 p.m., 2.15 p.m.–4.45 p.m. Admission free.

The City Hall was originally the Royal Exchange, built in 1769, which thirty years later acted as a torture chamber for the nearby Castle during the 1798 Rebellion. Now it's the most historic home of Dublin Corporation and the councillors still meet here (see page 226), although the Corporation's main business happens in the Civic Offices on Wood Quay making these gleaming riverside boxes the most useful buildings in the city, although they have a dark history (see page 158).

Inside the entrance hall you step into a rotunda which makes this the nearest building in Dublin to Rome's wonderful round temple, the Pantheon. Take a look up into the dome and count the elaborate half-columns which couldn't make up their mind which style to be Ionic, or Corinthian, and decided to be both. The statues (check out the 18-feet-high Daniel O'Connell) and frescoes turn the Hall into a civic temple altogether much more sedate than when traders were rushing around and coining money here. You can pick up a pamphlet about Dublin's coat of arms which depicts three blazing castles — in heraldry fire usually means zeal, not incendiary devices. When you come out of the City Hall take a look down Parliament Street, subtract the buses, bike couriers and MPVs, and the vista is much the same as it was for the rich Georgians who did business both here and in the handsome Newcomen Bank to your left. All that the poor got was the Bank's free drinking fountain, now nicely lit up in blue at night.

City Hall has a splendid new display area for the city treasures. Due to open to the public in 2000, the exhibition includes the gigantic **City Sword** and **Mace**, which are so big that only a tournament knight could have carried them. The Corporation also owns a very awesome article — the Ancient and Original **Charter of the City of Dublin**, dated 1171, with the signature of Henry II and all the Norman nobles.

The **Chain Book** of Dublin is also a prize possession. It was a kind of medieval Golden Pages that used to be chained to the Tholsel (Danish word for Guildhall) which was opposite Christ Church Cathedral. It's written for the most part in middle English, middle French and Latin but there are early Dublin 'Corpo' gems like the ruling that millers who diddled their customers would be hanged from their own mill beams, or the inventory of all the hideous types of chains and tortures in Newgate prison. There's also a list of brewers — all women.

Tailors' Hall
Back Lane, Dublin 8
Tel: 454 4794
Entrance: opposite Mother Redcap's Tavern.
Open: weekday office hours.

This building is the working office of An Taisce, the conservation organisation, but it started life as the party house of Dublin's tailors. The sheepskin-wearing St John the Baptist was their patron saint, perhaps because he was a man who definitely needed a tailor. You can see the master guildsmen's names inscribed here, going back to an incredible 1464. Interested people are allowed look at the hall which will very soon have its 300th birthday. It was finished in 1707, which makes it a Queen Anne building (what's yours — a De Valera? a Clinton?) You go through a handsome stone gate into a peaceful paved area, which is worth a visit even if you don't go inside the building. The hall itself has meeting-house-style windows, and a gallery for minstrels as all kinds of parties were held here. They still are, but no Wolfe Tones these days — he used to hold United Irishmen meetings here.

The Custom House Visitor Centre
Custom House Quay, Dublin 1
Tel: 878 7660
Open: mid-March–October, Monday–Friday: 10.00 a.m.–5.00 p.m.;
Weekends: 2.00 p.m.–5.00 p.m.; November–mid-March, Wednesday–
Friday: 1.00 p.m.–5.00 p.m.; Sunday: 2.00 p.m.–5.00 p.m. Admission
fee.

The Custom House is really an outside job, and best seen with its river godheads from across the Liffey (see page 168), but your tour allows you into the dab-hand and tricky shaped interiors that clever Mr James Gandon provided for the tax collectors of the eighteenth century. You can see in the beautiful stone where the notorious fire of 1921 burnt so fiercely — it reached over 1,800 degrees Fahrenheit. The display here is architectural and historical. All the powers that be who worked in the Custom House left a story — from the people who oversaw Famine workhouses (there's a giant soup pot, big enough for a cannibal's wedding feast) — to the poteen catchers.

Royal Hospital, Kilmainham
Tel: 612 9900
Follow the signs from St John's Road, alongside Heuston railway
station.
Guided tours by prior arrangement only. Buses: 7, 90.

The Royal Hospital, now home to the Gallery of Modern Art, cries out to be looked at for itself. The building is the nearest thing Dublin has to a Great Parisian Building. The Duke of Ormond, who also had the great idea of the Phoenix Park, saw the new home for King Louis XIV's old and wounded soldiers, *Les Invalides,* and decided that King

Charles's soldiers should be just as well served. So, this beautiful, classical, square hospital was built and finished in 1684. The soldiers lived in little rooms, two to a bed, and wore a blue uniform. For exercise, there were the anything but secret gardens, and for a long walk, a trip down to Bully's Acre, the oldest known graveyard in the city. The soldiers had little rooms in the upper storeys. The architect, Sir William Robinson, saved his genius for the Dining Hall, the Chapel and the Master's rooms, now all beautifully restored. Oak trees from Scandinavia provided the panelling, and sheer genius (or extravagance) provided the Chapel's ceiling. If you want to know what 'baroque' means don't look in a dictionary, come here instead. The building cost £23,000 three hundred years ago and it cost £20,000,000 to restore it. After your visit to IMMA have a snack in the restaurant and try to figure out how the clock facing the quadrangle works. The formal gardens are also open to the public.

Some other notable city buildings you can enter (or peek into) are:

The Four Courts (see page 227): — noted for its elegant great drum. It was built by James Gandon of Custom House fame. It was spectacularly blown up in the Civil War in 1921 with many state archives lost.

St Catherine's Church, Thomas Street — open on Saturdays and Sundays, this stern church, saved from decay by the evangelical church which now owns it, does not tell many stories. However, it is notorious for being the backdrop to Robert Emmet's execution in 1803.

Powerscourt Townhouse — now mainly a shopping centre so, no problem gaining access. The smart original 1774 entrance is on South William Street and was built of stone from the Powerscourt estate in Enniskerry.

The GPO — in O'Connell Street. Stamps, Cú Chulainn, Greek columns and the bloody site of the Republic's birth.

King's Inns — come to find the tree devouring a park bench in the open park belonging to King's Inns. Peek in past the caryatid figures at the doors of Mr Gandon's legal palace. Upstairs is a huge Dining Hall where barristers are supposed to learn nice manners. Walk out the archway into Henrietta Street which was once the grandest street in Dublin.

The Rotunda Hospital Chapel — every baby born in this first (1748) maternity hospital in Europe must have its match in the riot of cherubs on the ceiling in the beautiful baroque Chapel. Ask for entry at the desk between 8.30 a.m. and 4.00 p.m.

Grand Houses outside Dublin City Centre

The Casino*
Marino, Dublin 3
Tel: 833 1618
Entrance: signposted (and visible) from the Malahide Road.
Open: June–September, daily: 9.30 a.m.–6.30 p.m.; May and October: 10.00 a.m.–5.00 p.m. November and February–April, Sundays and Wednesdays only: 12.00 noon–4.00 p.m. Admission fee.
Buses: 20, 27, 42.

Don't come expecting fruit machines. Casino really means 'little house' and that is what the first Earl of Charlemont commissioned his genius friend and architect Sir William Chambers to make, in 1762. What it does have in common with the other kind of casino is trickery. This 'little house' has three storeys, a secret window, Grecian urns for chimney pots, and, of course, a secret tunnel. The excellent guides will tell you about the pineapples that once grew here (the plaster work shows spades and rakes as well as fancy Greek gods), about the spiteful spoiling of the view, why green paint was more expensive than yellow and about the four friendly stone lions with Tipperary smiles. The original 'good goods in small parcels' and beautiful restoration work would make anyone want to be an architect.

Newbridge House
Donabate
Tel: 843 6534
Entrance: right-turn for Donabate from the Dublin/Belfast road, after Swords — signposted.
Open: April to September, Tuesday–Friday: 10.00 a.m.–5.00 p.m. (closed 1.00 p.m.–2.00 p.m.); Saturdays: 10.00 a.m.–5.00 p.m.; Sundays and Bank Holidays: 2.00 p.m.–6.00 p.m.; October–March, Saturdays, Sundays and Bank Holidays: 2.00 p.m.–5.00 p.m. Admission fee. Reductions for families and groups. Bus: 33B; train from Connolly Station to Donabate.

Newbridge House, its traditional farm and its parkland (see Parks chapter, page 91) are over 250 years old, and a national treasure. The family who gave Newbridge to the public, the Cobbes, kept a flat in the huge house that was begun by their great (multiply by '*n*' times) relative, Archbishop Charles Cobbe. There are plenty of admirable eighteenth-century rooms, including a dramatic Red Drawing Room. There are also two other fine rooms which are particularly of note; one is the private museum of curiosities, the equivalent of a holiday video or after-dinner chat. Here you can see giant scarab beetles, moths of revolting appearance, python skins, a hookah, wheat from a Roman camp, an egg laid by an ostrich in Dundalk (?) and great stuff from the bottom of the ocean, dredged up by the science ship *Challenger*. The kitchen is the other great room in this house — it really is like something out of a storybook.

You can take a separate tour of Newbridge Traditional Farm (see page 91).

Marlay House
Marlay Park, Rathfarnham
Tel: 493 4059 (information only)
Entrance: path from car park off Grange Road.

Not yet open at time of printing, Marlay House promises to
be a credit to its restoration team of master craftspeople
and apprentices. Three of its sides have mountain views;
they also have beautiful bow windows giving great light
and elegance to many of the rooms. One is a small
ballroom which must have hosted some of the best
suburban parties in Dublin. Back in Henry VIII's time, this
land was called the Grange of the March — that is why
you approach it via Grange Road — and there was a
house called the Grange here. Marlay House itself was
begun by the Taylor family (Taylor's Lane) and finished by
the La Touche family of Bank of Ireland fame. The
courtyard has been colonised for years by artists,
craftspeople and a coffee shop; the walled gardens are
being restored in eighteenth-century style. Another Marlay
project for restoration is the fairy-ale house known to
everyone who travels through the woods to the adventure
playground.

Castletown House*
Celbridge, County Kildare
Tel: 628 8252
Entrance: from Celbridge Main Street.
Open: April/May, Sundays and Bank Holidays: 1.00 p.m.–6.00 p.m.;
June–September weekdays: 10.00 a.m.–6.00 p.m.; weekends:
1.00 p.m.–6.00 p.m.; October weekdays: 10.00 a.m.–5.00 p.m.; Sundays
and Holidays: 1.00 p.m.–5.00 p.m.; November, Sundays only:
1.00 p.m.–5.00 p.m. Admission fee. Buses: 67, 76A.

Castletown House is enormous but once it belonged to an
average sized family, the Conollys. William Conolly was
Speaker of the Irish House of Commons; he rose from
obscurity to become the richest man of his time in Ireland.
His perfect house was built to show off his wealth and was
begun in 1722. Several architects were involved: one, an

Italian, Galilei (yes, like Galileo) designed the main block, another was Edward Pearce of Bank of Ireland (Irish Parliament) fame who added the colonnaded wings of the house. Palladian is the name for this style of architecture modelled on sixteenth-century *palazzo* townhouses.

You will see plenty once you step inside the enormous hall. There is a cracked mirror in the dining-room, said to have happened when the devil was discovered at the dinner table tucking in. (The devil seems to have liked this part of Dublin, and the Conollys in particular, as he turned up in the Hellfire Club in the Dublin mountains, also built by Speaker Conolly.) There's also a Print Room, which is an early and genteel forerunner of the habit of adorning rooms with posters and stickers and which was favoured by the ladies who applied their favourite works to the walls. Visitors to the Conolly household were entertained in a number of drawing-rooms, but the favourite was the Long Gallery, an enormous and beautiful mirrored room that the family used much as Norman barons used their Great Halls. The elegant staircase is *cantilevered,* that is, held up on its inside only. From the first floor there's a fine view of the Conolly Folly, two miles away. It is 140 feet high and was paved with good intentions — to give famine relief in 1739.

There is no coffee shop at the moment. A full restoration of the stable yards is planned. On a fine day, you could take a picnic down by the banks of the Liffey which sweeps past Castletown.

Russborough House
Blessington, County Wicklow
Tel: 045-865 239
Entrance: to the right past Blessington on the Donard road.
Open: April, May, September, October, Sundays and Bank Holidays:
10.30 a.m.–5.30 p.m.; every day in June, July and August: 10.30 a.m.–
5.30 p.m. Admission fee. Bus: 65 to Donard.

Russborough was built in 1741 for a rich brewer called Joseph Leeson (Leeson Street is named for him). He spared no expense, hiring the best of Italian plaster-workers for the interiors, after using the design of possibly the busiest and most expensive architect in Ireland, Richard Cassels. Russborough's winged and Palladian frontage is the longest in Ireland — at 700 feet it is longer than some streets are. Everything in the house is polished and perfect, and, like nowhere else, there's an air of utter luxury in the rooms you are guided through. Every piece of porcelain and every strand of carpet looks like it was intended to be here from the day it was made. The collection of Old Masters only adds to this impression — it was built up by the uncle of the house's owner, Sir Alfred Beit. Unfortunately, there have been some notorious art robberies from Russborough and, in 1987, Sir Alfred donated the most valuable pictures of his collection to the State, at the National Gallery.

There is a shop and a fine restaurant. The house faces the lake, all greys and greens. Behind the quaint indoor riding school is an excellent development for stately homes in Ireland — a **maze**. Planted with fast-growing beech, the maze is open in summer to puzzle visitors and torture toddlers. Be there with your ball of string! (For more mazes see pages 111, 253, 333.)

Other Kinds of Buildings

Skerries Mills Centre
Skerries
Tel: 849 5208.
Open: April–October: 10.30 a.m.–6.00 p.m.; October–March: 10.30 a.m.–4.30 p.m.; closed 20 December–1 January. Admission fee.
Bus: 33; train from Connolly Station.

Up on a height to catch the winds, the two windmills add an exotic touch to pretty Skerries, but they were built with a job to do, to grind grain for the Jenkins bakery. One has four sails, the other five, and they can be reefed just like yacht sails, depending on wind conditions. When days were calm the watermill worked even harder on the same business. Beautifully restored by FÁS apprentices over several years, the stone-built mills are now in business again, grinding away as a working trades museum. While windmill power is an easy mechanism to understand, the watermill is more subtle and more hardworking. As you go through the different floors and spaces of the great mill, you will see each cog and gear and pulley literally earning its bread. The water powered everything, from millstones to sack hauling. Bad chaff got separated from good wheat in a winnowing machine. Grain was loaded into hoppers and dramatically released. On the non-moving side of the mill, a furnace dried the grain through a perforated tile floor. With the ladders and staircases and smell of grain (and bread baking for the restaurant below) it's easy to think back to all the fairy stories of millers, millers' sons and magical sacks of grain, not forgetting determined armies of mice and cats. Buy bread straight from the ovens! Craft shops make up the complex and the land around forms a great green island in the heart of Skerries.

The Joyce Museum

Sandycove
Tel: 280 9265
Entrance: the Martello Tower, down by the Forty-foot swimming place.
Open: April–September, Monday–Saturday: 10.00 a.m.–5.00 p.m.
(closed 1.00 p.m.–2.00 p.m.); Sundays and Bank Holidays 2.00 p.m.–
6.00 p.m.; out of season by appointment only (tel: 280 6984).
Admission fee. Bus: 8; DART.

The Joyce Museum is in a Martello tower on the sea front in Sandycove where the writer James Joyce lived in 1904. Inside there are letters and manuscripts, some of his very stylish clothes, his guitar and his death mask. Even if you are not particularly interested in Joyce's personal effects, it's a chance to get inside a Martello tower and see what it was like to live in one. These stone Rolos were built as watchtowers in case Napoleon decided to drop in — some have since been converted into private homes. You can see the round rooms inside this one. One room is restored to match the description in the first chapter of *Ulysses*. As in the book, you can also climb right up onto the battlements of the tower — James Joyce's favoured place for shaving.

Round Towers

Clondalkin, Lusk and Swords
Tel: 647 3000 (Dúchas)
Entrances: see individual towers.
Admission free.

Dublin has three very well-preserved round towers, one of which can be entered. The towers are at Clondalkin, Lusk and Swords, and they aren't hard to find!

Probably everyone in Ireland knows that round towers were built by monastic communities to protect themselves and their valuables from Viking raids during the ninth century and onwards. That is why the doors are set so far up — when all the monks, plus manuscripts and cats, were inside, up came the ladder. But the doorway is a piece of cake — wait until you open the door and see what lengths they went to escape the fury of the Norsemen. Naturally, they couldn't use a staircase inside in case the outside door failed and the enemy got within — so they had more ladders connecting the various floors which could also be pulled up. The Vikings' answer to all this was (sometimes) to throw in a lighted match and that was that.

You can go up the tower at Clondalkin but this guide can't give it the personal seal of approval since she would rather have faced a thousand Vikings instead. It's perfectly safe if you aren't afraid of heights, but you do need a torch.

Clondalkin Round Tower

Key from Mr J. O'Connor, 2 Millview, Clondalkin. Bus: 51.
You should check this availability first with OPW/Dúchas at 661 3111, weekdays.

Dates from 776 and was plundered by the 'Horned Ones' in 832. It's still almost perfect.

Lusk Round Tower

The tower is attached to Lusk Heritage Centre (see above) so you can get close. Bus: 33.

Swords Round Tower

No access. Buses: 33, 41.

Brian Boru's body spent the night here after the battle of Clontarf, on its way to Armagh.

The Creepy! The Experience!

Kilmainham Gaol*

Partial access only

Tel: 453 5984
Entrance: Inchicore Road.
Open: April–September, daily: 9.30 a.m.–6.00 p.m.; October–March, weekdays: 9.30 a.m.–5.00 p.m.; closed Saturdays; Sunday: 10.00 a.m.–6.00 p.m. Guided tours.

The dank chill of Kilmainham's enormous historic walls will have entered into your soul by the time you have edged along its narrow passages, trodden on its wire cage netting and walked over the Fenian dead under the flagstones in the prisoners' yards. Ireland's political and social history from the 1790s to the Civil War in 1922 breathes here through every stone, and sounds to every footfall and clang. And if the atmosphere itself wasn't enough, the excellent expanded museum section, in galleries that echo prison structure, has the artefacts to prove it. There is an introductory audio-visual display in what used to be the prison chapel and then a guide leads visitors through the cell corridors and the execution yards, filling in the heartless background to prison life. Although the Gaol became particularly notorious after the leaders of the 1916 Rising were executed in the stonecutters' yard, debtors, transportees and famine victims also had their tragic tales told here (an 8-year-old child was sentenced to 5 months' hard labour in 1839 for stealing a cloak). The three-tiered exhibition centre includes, naturally, a history of the 1916 Rising and Civil War, but also an introduction to penal history. Learn about the Panopticon or 'all-seeing eye' of Jeremy Bentham, see the hateful treadmill, locks and shackles, and worst of all, the physiology of the gallows. An Irishman made hanging more 'merciful' by inventing the Long Drop — there's even a mathematical formula for it.

There are fascinating document kits available here for both primary and secondary school students. The gun-running boat *Asgard* is in final 'dry dock' in one of the yards.

See page 88 for information on the free tour of Glasnevin Cemetery. Many ex-inmates of Kilmainham Gaol are buried in the Republican Plot there, and others are interred in nearby Arbour Hill Cemetery.

Another city gaol was the **Black Dog Debtors' Prison**, beside Green Street Court/Halston Street. Restored, but not for public access, its peculiar horseshoe shape can be seen; life was dark and dreary for the poor debtors whose cells looked in on each other.

St Michan's, Church Street

Access to church only

Tel: 872 4154
Entrance: the church on the left, just up from the north quays after the Four Courts.
Open daily except Sunday. November–March, weekdays: 12.30 p.m.– 3.30 p.m.; March–October: 10.00 a.m.–5.00 p.m. Closed: 1.00 p.m.– 2.00 p.m.; Saturday: 10.00 a.m.–1.00 p.m. Admission fee. Bus: 134 from Middle Abbey Street.

Pronounced 'Mickan' (not 'Mike-an') this church's original birthday was 1095; but that isn't why it's is filed under 'creepy'. No, this square stone church is Dublin's answer to the tombs of the pharaohs. Down in the vaults here, in open coffins, are three exceptionally well-preserved mummies, brown and leathery-like bog bodies. The guide leads you into the chill but dry depths, locking and unlocking trapdoors, all the time telling you science, myths and histories about the mummies and about the other burials here (who equally must be mummies, only they are privately buried). Here you find the unfortunate but famous 'Crusader', also a mystery woman and a man beside her who may have been executed. Two people who really *were* executed, and buried here, are the Sheares Brothers of the 1798 Rebellion; there's a full gory history of what happened to them. The guide does the underground part of the building only and visitors are free to walk around the graveyard and the church interior themselves. Inside you can see the Penitent's Pew, where sinners confessed in public, and there's also a magnificent organ on view. A small village-type shop sells snacks and souvenirs.

In Whitefriars Carmelite Church, off Aungier Street, at the top right-hand altar, is a casket that's claimed to have the remains of **St Valentine**, the patron saint of lovers. Or at the very least, his heart. At the right back of the church is a very old and very beautiful wooden statue called Our Lady of Dublin. It is thought to have belonged to the monks of St Mary's before it went wandering southside.

For details of Dublin's Ghostbus and some spooky walking tours see page 211. For the Hellfire Club climb see page 102.

Dublinia

Partial access only

St Michael's Hill, Dublin 8
(opposite Christ Church Cathedral)
Tel: 679 4611
Open: April–September, daily: 10.00 a.m.–5.00 p.m.; October–March, Monday –Saturday: 11.00 a.m.–4.00 p.m.; Sundays and Bank Holidays: 10.00 a.m.–4.30 p.m. Admission fee.

Here, perched on the highest hill in old Dublin city, you can enter the hurly-burly of medieval Dublin in Christ

Church Cathedral's twin, the Chapter House. The colourful pennants and the convincing stocks for photo opportunities will give you a flavour of what's inside. Inside you get an audio guide to walk you through the collection of merchants, knights-at-arms, plague-ridden victims, Normans, fighting Irish and other characters. The explanations are *not* short on details. Upstairs there's a super model of medieval Dublin, a quayside scene, and lots of artefacts dug up just down the road at Wood Quay. Best fun is the interactive Medieval Fair. Learn about spices and alchemy, try on chain mail and helmets, have a sniff of a pie from nearby Cook Street. There are medieval-type clothes and shoes for fitting, entertainments like a reprobate's dancing bear, an all-too-vicious dog and lots more. Snacks in the coffee bar will build you up for the climb up St Michael's Tower, which offers telescopes to spy on Celtic Tigerish Dublin. On the way out is the rather splendid Great Hall, then you continue into Christ Church Cathedral as part of your admission goodies. There's a gift shop on this level too. Dublinia is also where Irish Young Archaeologists meet. Ask for details.

Dublin Viking Adventure

Essex Street West, Temple Bar, Dublin 2
Tel: 679 6040
Entrance: continue from main Temple Bar thoroughfare across Parliament Street.
Open: All year round, Tuesday–Saturday: 10.00 a.m.–4.30 p.m.
Admission fee.

At the entrance to this adventure, there's a sculpture showing the sea and star chart of the Viking route to Ireland. It's by Grace Weir, and is worth looking at in detail.

The adventure inside is launched in darkness with howling winds and sea spray and a hairy sea captain, but don't worry, you won't have to row the boat, it moves nicely on its own. You 'land' at the Viking settlement of Dyflin sometime during the period coming up to the end of the first millennium. A hearty bunch of citizens are at hand to question you and welcome you — that's if they don't try to sell you as slaves. Cesspits, fleas, hard work, no detail is spared in this encounter. Afterwards you pass through a mock-up of the great Wood Quay dig, that despite well-organised protests in the 1970s, failed to stop the Civic Offices being built on the best Viking site ever discovered in Ireland. There's a compact museum showing some of the artefacts like the proto-chess game Hrefatafl (visit the National Museum for more), and also a very nifty exhibition of how archaeologists do their work, including the mysteries of carbon-dating. A mini-archaeology workshop displays tools, delicate cleaning instruments and permitted chemicals.

Upstairs you exit through the Viking banqueting hall. There are night-time feasts here with traditional entertainment but be warned, they are not cheap. (Phone 490 6077 for details.)

The Dublin Experience
Trinity College, Dublin 2
Entrance: Arts Block, Nassau Street.
Open: end of May–end of September: 10.00 a.m.–5.00 p.m. Admission fee.

For visitors, this is a good starting point for a general flavour of the city and its history — especially on a wet day when the real thing is more difficult. A dramatic audio-visual presentation develops the story of Dublin and Dubliners from the days when the Liffey was like a seashore, through battles, sieges, blood and glory, streets broad and narrow. Or you could stick to this book and write your own script.

Ceol — Irish Traditional Music Centre
Smithfield, Dublin 8
Tel: 817 3820
Open: Monday–Saturday: 9.30 a.m.–6.00 p.m.; Sunday and Bank Holidays: 10.30 a.m.–6.00 p.m.

Fancy playing the bones? Knowing the ins and outs of accordion playing? Synchronising your feet to the rhythm

of a Riverdance rave? The brand-new interactive Ceol is
the place to experience Irish music, ancient and new, with
twenty-first-century technology. Through Chief O'Neill's
Hotel — he was an Irish-born Chicago Police Chief who
collected Irish tunes — you enter the first level of Ceol
(there are twelve altogether). Here, via touch screens,
friendly robots and magic floors, you can test different
instruments, from flutes to fiddle to feadóg, hear the story
behind the music, learn the different song traditions, try
out dance steps, learn the Who's Who of great Irish music,
and enjoy their company via a superb 180-degree film.
The special children's room features tricks of touch and
light to help visitors create their own music. The Centre
has two satellite-wired concert rooms where live sessions
can be either recorded or broadcast. School groups can
check out their exam music syllabus and have fun at the
same time. Ceol has its own shop and is linked to a
complex of open space, shops and eating places in
Smithfield via Duck Lane, the old street that has been
reopened.

The Chimney
Smithfield, Dublin 8
Tel: 817 3830
Scheduled to open in 2000.)
Opening hours similar to Ceol. Admission fee.

Its birthday is printed on the side — 1895; its height is 60
metres (175 feet), and it has the most magical views of
Dublin city ever. This is because of its height — extinct
Nelson Pillar was only 134 feet — and also because of its
riverside location near the ancient ford. Chimney expert
Santa himself must be very happy with this Millennium
present that Dublin has made for itself. You travel up in an
exciting glass lift to the two-deck observation platform and
can spend as long as you like training falcon eyes over the
360-degree city vista. There are two other former distillery
chimneys behind, standing like medieval Italian towers.
Size definitely matters in cases like this.

The Guinness Hopstore and Visitors Centre

Crane Street, Dublin 8
Tel: 453 8364
Entrance: signposted off James's Street.
Open: Monday–Saturday: 9.30 a.m.–5.00 p.m.; Sunday and Bank
Holidays: 10.30 a.m.–4.30 p.m.

The Hopstore (hops, malt, barley, yeast and water are what Guinness is made of) is an art gallery and a museum and today it's an enormous, stunning building. What it was like crammed with hops is anybody's guess. You will hear that this is the site where the Emperor of Morocco's son was kidnapped, but once Arthur Guinness set his heart on brewing dark porter that was it for non-Guinness stories. He fought with the Dublin City fathers for his own water supply to come to him through hollow elm trunk pipes — then he built up his huge empire of gallons. You can walk through the old brewery equipment, and sit through an entertaining audio-visual show, before going downstairs to look at the transport models and into the big bar where adults get a free sample fresh from the brewery and others a soft drink. Upstairs, the galleries usually carry exhibitions well worth visiting.

The Dublin Brewing Company

141-146 North King Street, Smithfield, Dublin 8
Tel: 872 8622
Open: Monday–Friday: 10.00 a.m.–5.00 p.m. Tours by arrangement
only. Admission fee.

Best to check tour availability by phone first because this is a David operation, with a small staff, standing up to the Goliath Guinness just across the river. The young brewers here claim they are restoring to Dublin the glory days of small breweries when over thirty companies produced oceans of ale and stout. Here four different beers are manufactured in gleaming kettles and vats; the admission price includes a lecture, tour, and four free samples for adults in the bar, while children are admitted free, with a free soft drink. The long building used to be a soap factory and it's still very clean, with an astonishingly different smell of fresh roasted ingredients. A bigger visitor centre is planned and meanwhile the place can be hired for parties.

The Old Jameson Distillery
Bow Street, Smithfield, Dublin 8
Tel: 807 2355
Entrance: back of the new Smithfield complex.
Open: daily, 9.30 a.m.–5.30 p.m. Admission fee.

Elementary chemistry here — what is *distilling* then? It's pure alcohol boiled off a malted fermented mixture and cooled down in shiny fat copper stills, that look like a giantess's wedding gifts. Irish whiskey gets distilled three times — that's one thing you will never forget after this tour which is definitely designed for tourists. All the Irish whiskey makers are now united (and French owned) but this really was the great Dublin distillery of John Jameson and the guided tour takes you through all the steps of whiskey making and its history, and blasts you with smells, from alcoholic porridge to 'gold' in the glass. They have even stuffed the distillery's Great Mousing Cat. What they don't tell you, surprisingly, is that the distillery was seized as a base by the rebels during Rebellion week in 1916 and the company tried unsuccessfully to claim £2,138 in compensation. There's a free drink in the bar and it can be a soft one, but whiskey drinkers are the real winners here and there's even a tasting session for volunteers.

The Hot Press Irish Music Hall of Fame
57 Middle Abbey Street, Dublin 1
Tel: 878 3345
Open: daily, 10.00 a.m.–6.00 p.m.

Be a rock star for a day — well, an hour or so anyway — in this centre-city palace of sounds that also incorporates HQ, a live performance venue. Your tour includes a journey along the irresistible rise of Irish music, from folk to the glitter ball showband era, grunge and garage, the great empire of U2, Celtic rock and teeny boy and girl stars.

Multimedia, soundtracks, touch screens and visuals, along with the stars' personal effects, are all accessible on the interactive tour. There's a pub session experience, a peep-hole on a garage band, even a Backstage 'visit', and more. You can, of course, also do the Rock & Stroll Trail which begins from here, depending on seasonal availability (telephone first) and takes in several miles of sites in the city.

Oscar Wilde House
1 Merrion Square
Tel: 662 0281
Open: Monday, Wednesday and Thursday: 10.00 a.m.–12.00 noon.
Admission fee.

The Wilde family lived in this elegant corner house for 23 years, until 1878. Now Oscar's statue looks across from the Square. The American College who occupy the house offer guided tours — another opportunity to see a townhouse. The Salon is where Oscar's dramatic mother, Speranza, also a writer, used to hold her famous literary evenings. Watch for the stained-glass window showing 'The Happy Prince'.

Chapter 2

Parks, gardens and farms

Parks, Gardens and Farms

This chapter heads for the great outdoors — the outdoors that were made especially for city slickers — parks. Dublin is lucky in the number of parks it has, and I haven't covered even half of them here. Let's face it, some parks are as ugly as sin, but they can still be favourites because you are used to them. Here I am taking a look at some of Dublin's oldest parks, plus some special gardens and open farms which are a short drive from the city at most. So if your local park is not here, don't be insulted. Public parks follow seasonal opening times depending on daylight hours; opening times for private parks are given below.

Northside parks first!

Phoenix Park

(see separate entries on Áras an Uachtaráin, page 223, and the
Phoenix Park Visitors Centre, page 47.)
Buses: 10, 14, 38, 39.

The easiest way to 'the Park' is to walk, bus or cycle up the
quays to Parkgate Street with the Wellington Monument
(Duke not boot) as your Pole Star.

The park is huge (1,752 acres, enclosed) and walking
from one end to the other is no laughing matter, but it's
worth getting to know the various corners, and also where
it gets its name from. There's a lovely statue of a phoenix
bird in the centre park but he is really there under false
pretences. If anything he should be an albatross because
the name 'phoenix' comes from the Irish 'fionn uisce',
clear water, referring to a spring still to be seen in the
grounds of the Zoo.

Phoenix Park was turned into a Park in 1662 by James,
Duke of Ormond. He wanted to have a royal deer-park,
within easy reach of the city presumably in case the king,
Charles II, ever turned up on the doorstep looking for
some *craic*, but from the start, the deer-park was taken
over by Dubliners.

The main road through the park to Castleknock takes
you past the sports grounds and also the turning for the
Zoo. (More about that later.) This main road is lined with
old Dublin gas-lamps which have been restored to working
order.

As you go upwards towards the Castleknock Gate, look
out for all manner of strange sportsmen, especially on
Sundays. **Horse-riding** is commonplace, but **walking
races** are good to look at and real pony **polo** is played in
its own grounds on the right, on three afternoons a week:
Wednesday, Saturday and Sunday, May to September. It's
free to watch and a very skilled, old-style, sport it is. You
might also see, or at least hear, the buzz of **model
aeroplanes** flying above. You will certainly hear the buzz
of full-throttle Formula X engines here during the annual

motor races, which are free and a great spectacle, with a circuit of closed roads. During the 1920s there were even Grand Prix races here and even today Formula 1 drivers have been spotted in the Park. (Once a red squirrel held up a race — I saw it happen, honestly!)

More ordinary sports are played in the Phoenix Park also. On your left, as you go from the Parkgate Street entrance, you pass a huge area called the Fifteen Acres (multiply that by thirteen to get its actual size). As this area is so wide open, it was the perfect place for a million plus people to gather, in September 1979, to hear Pope John Paul II say Mass. It was a colossal spectacle.

The deer should not be missed. They are usually found in the spinneys near the Castleknock Gate. These deer are the dappled, fallow variety and the young ones are quite tame, but watch your dog if you have one with you. Although the deer aren't native, they have been here since Charles II's time and so they deserve a bit of respect. The Office of Public Works keeps their number secret but you could try counting them. (The other Irish deer, the native red deer, are becoming very rare throughout the country.) Despite their cheekiness, red squirrels are also less common than they used to be, so if you do see any make or class of squirrel, it's more likely to be a grey one.

At the Knockmaroon Gate in the extreme south-west of the Park is an **Information Centre** which can supply details of the park's wildlife and walks. Just beside it is an easily followed Nature Trail which heads down deep into the Furry Glen. Good for a family afternoon.

On the main road through to Castleknock you will also see two white houses — **Áras an Uachtaráin** on your right (see page 223) and the American Ambassador's residence on your left. At the Phoenix monument you take the signposted turn for the **Visitors Centre** and **Ashtown Castle** (see page 47). Near the Castleknock Gate, on your left in a hollow, is the **Ordnance Survey**.

The OS is responsible not just for plotting every needle in every haystack in every field in every townland in every barony in every county in every province in Ireland, but also, in the early days of the OS, intrepid nineteenth-century gentlemen collected songs and folklore, put tops on some round towers and dug castles out of manure heaps, all in the name of the OS. In fact, in the process they also built up a large part of Irish history that would otherwise have been lost forever. If you are an interested and fairly advanced geography student, you may be able to make an appointment here — otherwise, it is strictly private.

Poised at the top of the Hollow is the excellent Phoenix Park Tea-rooms, restored from Edwardian days which now serves cakes, snacks, and, in summer, strawberries and cream.

Now for the return journey. If you come back by the rear of Áras an Uachtaráin — which was formerly the home of the Viceroys to Ireland, and where the President now lives — you are doing what last century's Dubliners often did, hoping to get a gawk at the Lord Lieutenant and his entourage. Coming back round towards the Park Gate, you find the People's Park where bands used to play and nannies used to try to keep their charges from rolling down the Hollow. Today the same nannies could make their task much easier by going into the great little adventure playground just inside the gates of the Park. Across the way, large Dublin Metropolitan Policemen used to march smartly up and down in the barracks yard — it's now the Dublin headquarters of the Garda Síochána.

Ashtown Castle (see page 47), in the Phoenix Park, is now also open to the public, and you are able to go right into this medieval keep, built most likely by Norman Crusaders. Later it became the home of the British Under Secretary, whoever that should be, one of whose perks was as much venison as he could eat, from the herd.

The Zoological Gardens
Phoenix Park
Tel: 677 1425
Open: Monday–Saturday: 9.30 a.m.–6.00 p.m.; Sunday: 10.30 a.m.–
6.00 p.m. Admission fee. Buses: 10, 14.

If someone in the family takes out family membership for a year, everyone gets in free as often as you like to go; you can also have special lunches, and you get copies of the Zoo's newsletter. Admission to Fota Wildlife Park in Cork is also included in this membership.

Feelings run high about the keeping of large wild animals in captivity and there is controversy about city zoos all over the world. You may prefer to visit a free-range park like Fota in Cork. However, Dublin Zoo is by no means the Victorian garden park enclosure it once was. (Actually, it was founded in 1830 and its only inhabitant on the day was a solitary wild boar.) It has a successful breeding programme and works with zoos and wildlife societies world-wide. It has been completely re-designed and new space — a gift from the President — will soon be included for the African large animals. As you come in the new entrance gates you can choose right or left. Left is for the themed enclosures — the lions, apes, monkeys-with-offshore-islands, the pack of seriously wolfish wolves, a Tundra Trail and the Fringes of the Arctic which includes polar bears, sea lions and Arctic foxes. Every few feet, it seems, there's a slice of climbing equipment for small people to try out monkey-stuff. The other side of the lake leads to the darkened Bat House, Reptile House, the glorious lemurs and the new City Farm which is the place for hands-on petting and cuddling of donkeys, sheep, goats, calves, rabbits and guinea pigs. (They even have cats who have their own sitting-room!) Search the Zoo for other special show-offs like the lemurs and meerkats — and all through the day there's a chance to meet particular keepers who'll answer questions.

Other services available: the Zoo runs summer week and day camps. The Education Officer works with schools and other groups. Visitor Services can organise personal visits with animals (you must write in). You can also become a member of the Zoo and get reductions on family visits. There are several eating places, and the entrance shop has a huge range of soft-toy animals.

Lastly, did you know that the MGM lion, who snarls at the beginning of MGM movies, was a Dublin Zoo lion?

National Botanic Gardens
Glasnevin
Tel: 837 4388
Admission free. Buses: 13, 19, 19A.

The Botanic Gardens are on somewhat the same lines as the Zoo, except that it's free and the inhabitants don't move. If the dreaded triffids ever hit Ireland, this will be their headquarters. The gardens are national property so they belong to *you*. They became 'botanical' when the Royal Dublin Society acquired them in 1795.

The summer is the best time for visiting. The plan inside the gate will tell you where everything is, even Thomas Moore's 'Last Rose of Summer'. The herb garden is a delicate and delicious, nose-educating spot, and nearby is the poisonous garden. There are also bog, Burren, vegetable and glorious herbaceous gardens, plus thousands of tall specimen trees. For sheer, unbearable jungle heat, see how Tarzan-ish you can be in the Palm House which is complete with banana trees. You will also find the now extinct-in-the-wild primitive cycad tree there. The Palm House is tall enough for the huge Amazonian creepers and the building is a lovely piece of Victorian glass construction. Currently, it is awaiting restoration like its companion iron and glass-work house — Richard Turner's famous Curvilinear Range.

If you visit during the summer ask for directions to the giant Amazon water lily which, not surprisingly, is housed indoors. Dublin was the first place to grow this jungle monster in the 1850s and people came to see it as they would a panda.

The River Tolka forms one of the Garden's boundaries and it also forms a water lily pond in the gardens. If you sit here very quietly on a warm May afternoon, you are likely to see the most enormous dragonflies, like model helicopters, blue and whirring. There are red squirrels here too — a good spot is around the walnut tree near the glasshouses. You will also see lots of young gardeners — the Department runs a degree course in horticulture here, supplying all the parks' gardeners and many private nursery gardeners. You can ask for advice yourself — if you have a project or a digging bug, it's a good place to go. The interesting-looking Herbarium plus library is a place for serious research (by arrangement), and a Visitor Centre is to house exhibitions, lectures and tea-rooms.

Nearby is **Glasnevin Cemetery** (the main entrance is on Finglas Road), a very large and a very famous one, and the most traditional Dublin cemetery. Over one million people have been buried here since it opened its multidenominational gates in 1831. Absolutely the best way to visit here is to do the free tour (Wednesday, Friday at 2.30 p.m. from main gate). If you don't manage that here are some musts to spot. The memorial round tower (not that you could miss this one) was built in 1869 as a monument to Daniel O'Connell. He is buried here and so is Charles Stewart Parnell who had the biggest funeral of any Irishman; he asked to be buried in a mound made up of the unmarked graves of cholera victims. The Republican Plot contains so many famous historical names that it's quite astonishing, but one who is not there is Michael Collins (who had the second-biggest funeral of any Irishman). He is buried separately and his grave always has flowers on it, as do many of the historical plots. The guides are superb — as well as the people-talk they point out the designs of gravestones. In the last century stonemasons rediscovered Celtic art and all its twirly animals and letters. You can even pick up a leaflet on the trees of the cemetery. Flowers are available from street-sellers outside the gates at weekends — they aren't allowed inside. Nowadays, the caretakers have an easier job; in Victorian times they were kept up half the night on the watch for body-snatchers who took rings and other valuables and then sold the bodies to medical students.

St Anne's Park
Raheny
Buses: 30, 44A.

It's called St Anne's because there was a holy well of that name near the sea road part of the park. Dublin girls used to have a prayer for the busy saint: 'Dear St Anne, send me a man, as fast as you can.'

The park used to belong to the Guinness family, and when the Corporation first took it over just before the Second World War, the area was used for growing wartime vegetable rations. Now it's the biggest public park after the Phoenix Park, stretching from Raheny to Clontarf. You will find forty football pitches and eighteen hard tennis courts as well as the huge and glorious rose garden which can be located by smell.

Apart from the flower gardens, it's not a formally laid-out park so there's a lot of room to move around, roller skate, fly kites and model planes, do cartwheels or just go for a ramble and explore. Sometimes there are free open-air concerts. Just remember — dogs like flower beds for different reasons than human beings, and rose gardeners can be thorny people.

However, you can join in the Choose Your Rose Competition which is held every year on a Sunday in July. If you prove to be a good judge of roses you could win a prize.

Malahide Castle Demesne and Talbot Botanic Gardens

Tel: 846 2516

Open: May–September: 2.00 p.m.–5.00 p.m. Guided tour on Wednesdays at 2.00 p.m. Admission fee adults; children under 12 free. Bus 42 from Talbot Street; train to Malahide from Connolly Station.

You might never get to see the actual gardens because the huge park is so well worth exploring. Even when it's full of Sunday families there are hidden corners, playing fields, tennis courts and acres of velvety grass with not one forbidden inch marked out. Very small children go into ecstasies at the sight of all this grass. Then they find the adventure playground up close to the castle.... Perfect for a social kind of picnic, but make sure to clean up because the park is so well kept and so welcoming. It's also free.

The gardens are behind the Castle — you go through a small lodge to reach them. Once inside the gardens two things that must be seen are the giant thistles, about eight feet tall and straight from a science fiction story, and the oak tree. The latter is an amazing thing with branches taller than itself and looks as petrified as its Latin name *(quercus petraea)* suggests. However, the tree is not actually petrified — it's just a sessile oak, grown ancient and hoary. In other parts of the gardens the shrubbery, which has numerous narrow grass paths through it, makes a good hiding area. However, it is certainly not a good idea to venture beyond the paths — they're not there for no reason. Another big plus for small persons is the grassy slope that would once have been the castle's moat — nowadays superb rolling can be practised here.

In the rest of Malahide Castle grounds you could search for Yourell's Well or the Lime Kiln, using the free leaflet to assist you. The leaflets are available from the Castle admission desk.

Fry Model Railway Exhibition
Malahide Castle
Tel: 846 3779
Entrance: beside Castle.
**Open: April–October, Monday–Saturday: 10.00 a.m.–5.00 p.m.;
Sunday: 11.00 a.m.–6.00 p.m.; November–March, Monday–Friday:
10.00 a.m.–5.00 p.m.; Saturday–Sunday: 2.00 p.m.–5.00 p.m.; closed:
1.00 p.m.–2.15 all year. Admission fee. Bus 42: from Talbot Street;
train to Malahide from Connolly Station.**

The Fry collection is the Crown Jewel of Irish model
railway layouts. It was built up by an engineer, Cyril Fry,
during the 1920s and 1930s and it's now beautifully
housed and maintained in part of the Malahide Castle
outbuildings. There are all kinds of full-scale railway
mementoes on display in the waiting-room, but save your
admiration for the tiny and perfect railway systems inside.
You will find the DART going to Howth where the Howth
Tramway snakes up the Hill, the famous West Clare
Railway and other narrow gauge lines, Belfast and Cork
railway stations, as well as miniature replicas of familiar
bits of Dublin like the Poolbeg power station and more.
Anyone who is interested in crafts will love the tiny
throwaway details.

Newbridge Demesne and Traditional Farm
Donabate
Tel: 843 6534
**Entrance: right-turn for Donabate from the Dublin/Belfast road, after
Swords; signposted.**
**Open: April–September, Tuesday–Friday: 10.00 a.m.–5.00 p.m., closed:
1.00 p.m.–2.00 p.m.; Saturdays: 10.00 a.m.–5.00 p.m.; Sundays and
Bank Holidays: 2.00 p.m.–6.00 p.m.; October–March, Saturdays,
Sundays and Bank Holidays: 2.00 p.m.–5.00 p.m. Admission charge for
farm, park free. Reductions for families and groups. Bus: 33B; train to
Donabate from Connolly Station.**

You can take a separate tour of Newbridge Traditional
Farm, through the beautiful cobbled courtyard. With your
ticket comes a leaflet explaining the layout. Round the

yard are the dairy, forge, tack room, carpenters' workshop, and, incredibly, the Lord Chancellor's Coach, golden and beautifully sprung (check for pumpkin seeds!), together with some other magnificent horse-drawn vehicles. From the courtyard you go through to the farmyard, via the hatcheries where you can check for eggs cracking. Remember — this is a Big House farm that bore no similarity to the average sized farm of the time, but this farmyard somehow looks like farmyards from every folk and fairy tale. There's a small but noisy collection of birds and beasts — gigantic hens and cocks with feathery breeches; a sow, human-friendly sheep, goats and miniature ponies. There is also a killing shed — not now in use. You pass by the duck pond and the vinery to the paddocks where there's a small herd of traditional cattle. Head back through the walled orchard and garden to the courtyard where you can call in at the coffee bar for some refreshment.

Wandering through the park itself is free, and it's unbeatable for an outdoor party — you could take the train for a treat. A river runs right through the park and you will also discover a castle inside the gate, meadows, woodland, a secret pond (be careful) and acres of space to hang out.

Ardgillan Demesne and Castle
Skerries
Tel: 849 2212
Entrance: signposted from the main Dublin–Skerries Road.
Open: April–September, Tuesday–Sunday: 11.00 a.m.–6.00 p.m.;
October–March, Wednesday–Sunday: 11.00 a.m.–4.30 p.m.; January,
Sundays only: 2.00 p.m.–4.00 p.m. Admission free to park and gardens.
Fee for castle tour. Bus: 33; train to Skerries from Connolly Station.

'High Wood' is the Irish meaning of Ardgillan; it's accurate but it *should* have included a reference to the sea. This is a glorious location with the castle overlooking a great green sweep down to the sea and the islands off Skerries village, with the railway threading in between. There are plenty of forest trails among real trees, picnic areas, and access via a haunted railway footbridge (the Lady's Stairs) to an interesting beach — not recommended at full tide. But the glory of Ardgillan is its gardens. These are serious Victorian walled gardens — herb, rose, vegetable, fruit and an 'Irish' garden — bursting with health and wafting scents everywhere. There is a tunnel from the gardens to the house which runs underneath the beautiful glasshouse with its tropical plants. In fact, there's a whole network of underground pathways used for storing fuel for the hundred or more fireplaces, and another tunnel which leads to the old icehouse in the forest. Here, meat and dairy produce was stored and kept cool using ice which had been broken from ponds and rivers.

(For Castle entry see page 49.)

St Stephen's Green
Open until sundown, whenever it is, all year round.
Buses: you can walk from anywhere in the City Centre! Routes from O'Connell Street, Westmoreland Street.

Dubliners call this park simply Stephen's Green. In one form or another, the Green (as it is known) has been around for a long time. When Dublin was a walled city, the Green was a common grazing ground where citizens could 'walk and take the open aire'. But, as ever, the Corporation needed more money so, in 1663, they offered the Green to the well-off burghers and bigwigs to stake their claims. They could build houses or not, as they wished, around the Green and if they did, the house had to have two storeys and a basement. There was a wall around the Green itself with a ditch, and every householder had to plant six healthy sycamore trees near this ditch. Whether this was to keep the citizens out or in is not certain. There were several gruesome executions here; reports exist telling of the boiling alive of a female cook who had poisoned several people. That was as recently as 1773. In 1798, the year of the Great Irish Rebellion, there was one shopkeeper who obviously did not mind the commotion, because he built an amazing tower and toyshop on Stephen's Green. He gave his store a great name, the Pantheon Phusitechnikon. It was near the Shelbourne Hotel, and you can find a drawing of it in the National Gallery. At any rate the Green grew up fast and was eventually claimed by Dubliners, just as the Phoenix Park was.

Nowadays the Green is famous for its pond with its ducks and geese, for sunbathing, for statues and for free lunch-time music in the summer. The pond is fed with water from the Grand Canal at Portobello and it's a very strange sight to see it being cleared annually. One half at a time gets drained and looks like a mud swamp while bewildered ducks try to figure out what's happening. Mallard and greylag geese are the common water-birds here and you may be lucky enough to see all the traffic stop while the famous ducks who hatch their eggs on Leinster House lawn bring their offspring up to take the waters in the Green. Early June is usually the best time to see this.

There are ten statues in the Green — see if you can find them all — including a modern memorial to W.B. Yeats (with holes in it) by Henry Moore. (There is another Moore sculpture in the Front Square of Trinity.) There's also an adventure playground.

Iveagh Gardens
Entrance: behind the National Concert Hall on Earlsfort Terrace, or Clonmel Street, off Harcourt Street. Admission free.

Iveagh Gardens are like a giant Secret Garden — while the world and his wife are lounging around Stephen's Green just across the road, only a select few are in the know about these magical grounds. They were once part of the Guinness estate and designed to be green and formal — flowers are few and far between. They have since become grown over, but that is part of their charm; let's hope the restoration work is not too tidy-minded. You can wander down paths through trees, meet classical sculptures and feel that the Emperor Hadrian is just around the corner. Fountains, steps, a sunken area, a grotto, and a rose garden with real smells make up an old-fashioned idyllic place that is easy to pretend belongs to you. Great for picnics — then off to join the *hoi polloi* in the Green.

Merrion Square

Admission free. Buses: 7, 7A, 8, 45 and, if there are no buses, you can walk. Route from O'Connell Bridge: Westmoreland Street, College Green, Nassau Street, Clare Street.

Merrion Square has been transformed from a private residents' square into a park. (Fitzwilliam Square nearby still has the former status — only the residents of the square have keys and the privilege of disporting themselves inside the railings. See page 60 for entry to an original square-house.) The Catholic Church owned the green square and had plans for building a cathedral on it. That would have made three and a half cathedrals in Dublin. But in 1974 the Square was handed over to Dublin Corporation — lock, stock and barrel.

Merrion Square is now yours — and you can survey the three sides of Georgian houses as if you owned one of them. The gardens are beautifully landscaped, there's a small playground and interesting sculptures lurking in all parts of the square.* Lots of open-air events happen here during the summer, and it's a perfect place for a city picnic.

*See Georgian Walks with Statues in Chapter 4 — I-spy Walks (page 162).

Herbert Park
Donnybrook/Ballsbridge
Buses: 7A, 8, 10, 45, 46A.

A perfect park. On the Ballsbridge side you can watch bowling (very sedate) or play tennis (very cheap).

The Donnybrook side of the park has everything else that you would expect to find in a park — pond, swings, an Edwardian drinking-fountain, bandstands, Brothers Grimm-type shelters, playing fields, hidden levels and corners, and the Park extends right over to the river Dodder.

Herbert Park had its summer of glory when King Edward VII opened the Great Exhibition here. It looked like a cross between the Arabian Nights and a willow-pattern tea set; there were sunny pavilions everywhere and the pond had boats and a water-chute, with little bridges crossing over the bottlenecks. Because this was Imperial Britain there was even a Somali village and inhabitants packed into the grounds for Dubliners to stare at. When a Trinity student kidnapped a Somali baby the visitors terrified the Donnybrook residents by threatening war.

Irishtown Wildlife Park
Sandymount
Open: access all year. Bus: 3.

This park is somewhat Dutch in that it's built entirely on landfill dumped on former seabed. Walk out towards the power station chimneys, take the right turn by the water and follow any of the trails. It's a wild place that has industry on one side and sea on the other. Dogs absolutely adore it. Although it's still a relatively young park, many kinds of wild flowers and herbs have colonised it already and you can hear even larks in season. It's the kind of park that has its own evolution going on and is interesting for that, as well as for delivering healthy ozone to humans and animals alike.

Ranelagh Gardens
Ranelagh Village
Bus: 11, 13, 48A.

A strange little park, with many peculiarities. One is the number of gates — although it's just a small walk-around area it seems to have as many entrances as the Phoenix Park. Another is the strange carvings on the stones of the old railway bridge entrance; who knows what they mean?

Then there is its glorious history. Ranelagh Pleasure Gardens was Dublin's most exciting event venue in the late eighteenth century, a kind of Point-cum-Funderland of its day. That was why the first Irish air enthusiast took off from here in January 1785. Richard Crosbie had rather meanly sent an unfortunate cat up in an earlier balloon ascent. He took off himself to the cheers of a huge crowd and came down safely and gloriously in Clontarf. The gardens later became the property of a convent before being passed on to Dublin Corporation; they aren't very well known any more.

UCD Grounds
Belfield
Buses: 10, 11, 46A.

The university grounds are officially private but at weekends the university is unofficially glad to welcome people like you and me. There are many sports pitches and a most luxurious sports complex which is open to non-students in summer for a fee.

The grounds are pleasantly laid out complete with little spinneys and shrubberies, and even a little 'temple' for investigation. More unusual is the great fire-pond in the heart of the university buildings. Every weekend, modellers bring radio-controlled boats here and have races, wars, embarkations and even ice-breaking or so it's rumoured. Sundays at noon you can also find miniature Formula One racing in the car park near the campus church.

Killiney Hill/Dalkey Hill
Bus: 59 from outside Dún Laoghaire railway station to Killiney (ask to be let off near gate to Killiney Hill); DART.

Killiney and Dalkey Hills are big rambling places with parklands, woods, huge rocks, bracken and gorse undergrowth and, of course, some of the best views in Dublin. You can go for a leisurely walk (about four miles) around the summits of the two hills gazing at the view. Or else you can plunge into the undergrowth and hide and then creep up and ambush people. Be sure to wear thick clothing if you're going to do the latter. If it's a windy Sunday, you can watch people hang-gliding off the top of Killiney Hill in the afternoon, and you can also see people rock-climbing in the old quarries on the side of Dalkey Hill in any weather (see Chapter 11 — Joining In — page 314).

The obelisk at the top of Killiney Hill has a plaque which reads: 'Last year being hard with the poor, the walks around these hills, and this was erected by John Mapas, June, 1742.' John Mapas also built Killiney Castle which looks more like a French chateau from the hill. He did a good job on the paths — there is one right around Killiney Hill and another right around Dalkey Hill, and the two join to make a figure of eight. There are a couple of paths leading down to the Vico Road and the owners of Killiney Castle used to walk over to catch the train into Dublin.

In case you are wondering, the Wishing Stone on the top of Killiney Hill was built in 1852, why, nobody knows but if you walk around each level from base to top and stand facing Dalkey Island and make a wish, it's bound to come true!

Marlay Park
Grange Road, Rathfarnham
(see separate entry for Marlay House, Chapter 1)
Bus: 16c.

This is a huge open park with acres of mown grass and some woodland. It's perfect for Frisbees, gymnastic displays, or kites. The courtyard of old Marlay House has been turned into a craft centre and you can drop into the workshops just to have a look, or to buy, or try the coffee shop.

Marlay also has Dublin's largest public adventure playground, a BMX track, and, in summer, a model railway which gives under-tens a real Orient Express-type ride. The playground is quite a walk, about half a mile from the entrance, diagonally and to your right across the large field — but it's really worth it. Similar in appearance to a Red Indian camp — everything is made of wood, built to take assault: a wobble bridge, a fortress with slide-down pole, a tower with rope for swinging, tunnels, and lots of milder but similar stuff for small kids. Across from the playground (no dogs) is the BMX course — you are required to have safety gear. On your way over you pass the miniature railway. In summer, on Saturday afternoons from 3.00 p.m. to 5.00 p.m., the railwaymen run their model steam trains on real coal and it's entirely free. There is always a queue but it moves quickly. (For more steam see the Steam Museum, page 42.)

If you have walked round all the parks listed in this chapter and still haven't had enough, Marlay Park has just the thing for you. There's a twenty-mile walk through forest and heather, all the way to Enniskerry and Roundwood. It is called the Wicklow Way and is the first stage of a planned footpath the whole way around Ireland. You can get a copy of the route and instructions for the walk from Dublin Tourism in Suffolk Street. Alternatively take OS Map sheet 16 of Kildare and Wicklow and study the route on show in the car park in Marlay. The route is signposted all the way so you can't really go too far wrong. Bring warm clothing, stout shoes, food and drink.

The experts say you average only 2 miles per hour in hilly terrain, so the walk to Enniskerry will probably take the whole day. You could break the walk here and catch the bus (44) back to town or stay in the youth hostel at Knockree near Enniskerry and carry on to Roundwood the next day.

Memorial Park
Inchicore/Islandbridge
Buses: 21, 65, 79.

This park's proper name is the Irish National War Memorial Park and it was laid out in 1938 in remembrance of the 49,000 Irishmen who died in the First World War. Happily, they are now also commemorated in the part of the world where they died, in Belgium, where another special garden-memorial was opened in 1998. The architect of the Memorial Park in Dublin was the very famous Sir Edwin Lutyens, who created dream buildings not only in Ireland, but all over the world. He used a hollow, surrounded by avenues of trees, and designed living wreath-gardens of beautiful roses and lilies, along with huge fountains and towers. The towers themselves contain book rooms with all the dead soldiers' names and these can be consulted by appointment. Ahead is a lovely stretch of the Liffey where all the boat clubs practise. It's a quiet park, very different and well worth rambling in and exploring.

Powerscourt House, Gardens and Waterfall
Enniskerry, County Wicklow
Tel: 204 6000/286 7676
Entrance: by gate just outside Enniskerry village.
Open: House and gardens (daily): 9.30 a.m.–5.30 p.m.; Waterfall (summer): 9.30 a.m.–7.00 p.m., (winter): 10.30 a.m.–dusk. Admission fee. Buses: 44 (from Dublin), 85 (from Bray DART).

You can enjoy one of the most beautiful estates in Ireland, free, if you just wish to visit the restaurant and shops in the house, or the garden centre. There are usually horses and donkeys to meet and exceedingly handsome tall beech trees along the way. If you have seen the beautiful scenes of England from the Laurence Olivier film, *Henry V*, the trees might look familiar — the film was made here during the Second World War. There's also an excellent mini-adventure playground laid out beside an avenue of dark evergreens.

If you've never been, it would be a shame not to pay at least once into the gardens proper. These are dream gardens, the kind that needed as many servants to mind them as the house itself had. Statues of gods and monsters were copied and brought back from Italy. So were Italian steps and watery ideas. However, the view is pure Wicklow, and there are other secrets in the garden too, a Japanese garden with bridges, a grotto, woods, a tower with cannon, a pet-cemetery — look out for the faithful Jersey cow's tombstone — and good slopes for toddler-rolling.

The winged Palladian house, the interior of which was burnt in 1974, has been partially restored, and there is a plan to rebuild and redecorate the beautiful galleried ballroom. You can pay to see the archive film and exhibition. A snack or a meal on the terrace offers the most stunning meal location in this book. The shops are expensive but good.

You can also visit the Waterfall a couple of miles away. This tallest cascade in Ireland is best seen after some rain but do *not* try climbing it — people have been killed here. (George IV just missed being washed away.) There's fine nature trail by the river. All in all an excellent place for a picnic, but do note, it's a separate cost from the house.

Killruddery House and Gardens

Bray, County Wicklow
Tel: 286 2777
Entrance: signposted from Bray/Greystones roundabout.
Open: Gardens, April–September 1.00 p.m.–5.00 p.m.; house, May,
June, September: 1.00 p.m.–5.00 p.m.
Admission fee/s. Bus: 84 to Greystones.

The house is still occupied by the original Brabazon family and the tour is brief. You might spot more of it in films — it has featured extensively, from Australian children's series to *My Left Foot*. Killruddery is one of the Great Irish House venues for classical concerts in summer. Best to come here for the gardens which were laid out a long time ago, possibly in the seventeenth century. Trees, water and statues provide the most distinguishing features but flowers do not get a look in. But if it's formal, it's also fun. There are all kinds of places to explore, like the double beech hedge with its concealed path, dozens of cheeky statues to find, an overgrown outdoor 'theatre', fish-stealing herons by the long canals and several ponds. Picnics are permitted.

Fern Hill Gardens

Tel: 295 6000.

Entrance: Enniskerry Road — just up from Lamb's Cross.
Open: March–September, Tuesday–Saturday: 11.00 a.m.–5.00 p.m.;
Sunday 2.00 p.m.–6.00 p.m. Admission fee. Bus: 44.

Fern Hill Gardens belong to the Walker family who are said to be garden geniuses. They have made this a beautiful place with everything from great redwoods to a laurel maze, from a huge rockery to an old-fashioned vegetable garden and from a stream with secret picnic places to wild ground and a lookout rock. It's a wonderful location at most times of the year and if you are entranced with gardening there's a very good nursery which sells unusual plants. You could build a very good herb garden with stock from Fern Hill and have fresh herbs right outside your kitchen window.

Massey Woods

Killakee

Entrance: over the wall, opposite Killakee House Restaurant, on the
Killakee Road, Rathfarnham.

Despite the 'over the wall' bit these woods are open to the public, and they are included here, from all the different woods that clothe the Dublin mountains, (a) because they are close to the city and, (b) because they comprise real mixed woodland, not just Christmas tree woods. There's a little river running through the rocky valley which can be followed by path or by water (pools, falls and glades and all) for picnics. Throughout Massey Woods you can try to identify the different kind of trees — great beeches, oaks and others.

On the other side of the road is the ascent up Montpelier Hill to the Hellfire Club. It's an easy climb with a super view. The club is a very smelly ruin now, but in its eighteenth-century heyday it was the haunt of rich young layabouts, including the famous Conollys of Castletown House. The story goes that one dark and stormy night a group of these fellows were playing cards all out, and somebody noticed, as one does, that the winning player had a cloven hoof. It could have been a sign that the use of prehistoric monuments to make the house was not a good idea.

Mount Usher Gardens
Ashford, County Wicklow
Tel: 0404-40116
Entrance: on the main Dublin–Wexford road.
Open: March–October: 10.30 a.m.–6.00 p.m. Admission fee. Buses: Bus Éireann routes to Wicklow, Arklow, and Wexford.

Early summer Mount Usher is positively Tahitian looking, with its rhododendron and azalea blossoms luxuriating themselves by the riverside. The Vartry River is crossed here by little suspension bridges which bounce as you walk over them. There are many kinds of trees, including lots of tall eucalyptus, and even though there can be hundreds of people here on a fine weekend, it's a very tranquil and dreamy place. Mount Usher also has shops and its own café. Alternatively, afternoon tea can be taken in the nearby Hunter's Hotel, which also has a pleasant garden.

Model World
Newtownmountkennedy, County Wicklow
Tel: 281 0877
Entrance: signposted from the Dublin–Wexford road.
Open: April–September, Saturday–Sunday: 10.30 a.m.–5.00 p.m. Admission fee.

Six acres of mini-mountains, tiny lakes and slender working canals, Model World traces all the habitations of Irish people over 7,000 years. Miniature Stone Age tents start the trail off, leading to ráths, wattle houses, magical stone circles, Norman castles, medieval villages, rural cottages and Georgian townhouses. There's a Famine workhouse too, as well as dwelling-places along the canals and railways. Everything is made to the same scale — 1:22.5. You get a map and there is a gift shop and coffee shop.

National Garden Exhibition Centre
Kilquade, County Wicklow
Tel: 281 9890
Entrance: signposted from main Dublin–Wexford road.
Open: Monday–Saturday: 10.00 a.m.–6.00 p.m.; Sunday: 1.00 p.m.–
6.00 p.m. Admission fee (under 16s free).

This is one of the many places that garden-mad people come to get ideas, and that is exactly what it was planned for. Sixteen different mini-gardens have been designed by experts and lead into each other like scented classrooms. All the watery ones are big hits, as is the dragonfly pond with its lone giant carp. Small (and free) visitors can blackmail away in the café while parents spend money in the gardening shop. Glenroe farm and the beach are both very near the Garden Centre and either makes a suitable choice for possible afters.

Celbridge Abbey Grounds
Celbridge, County Kildare
Tel: 627 5508
Entrance: turn left entering Celbridge village.
Open all year: weekdays: 10.00 a.m.–6.00 p.m.; Sunday: 12.00 noon –
6.00 p.m.
Admission fee. Bus: 67.

These grounds which are located beside the handsome (and deep) Liffey and its fast-flowing mill race are packed with charms and surprises. The most famous person to live in the Abbey was Esther Vanhomrigh who was Jonathan Swift's ladyfriend, Vanessa. So, not surprisingly, one of the trails leads to her bower, past a collection of life-size Swiftian figures. Under a spreading plane tree there's an irresistible 'zoo' of garden sculptures, from a baboon to a feeding robin. You can cross and uncross the mill race by various bridges, including a narrow and venerable stone one. In one corner there's a cute playground, and on occasion a model railway is on view there. The grounds also have several beautiful old yew trees and there is no shortage of places where you can have a picnic amongst them. Schools can do the ecology trail and there are regular local entertainments. The Abbey itself is owned by the St John of God Brothers who work with people with special needs, so all of the money that you spend when you visit is put to very good use. The restaurant is in the old Gate House and it is excellent. There is also a garden centre.

Devil's Glen
Ashford, County Wicklow
Entrance: driving towards Wicklow, turn right at the Ashford House Hotel; the wood is signposted a couple of miles further on.
Open: access all year.

The forested glen along the Vartry River has only one devilish problem — mud when conditions are wet. Otherwise, this is a beautiful place to walk and explore. On very frosty days icicles hang in the sheltered rockfall area and dippers are often spotted in the river. The wood is also a sculpture park — large objects all, hewn and formed from different types of wood.

Japanese Gardens, St Fiachra's Garden and Irish National Stud
Tully, County Kildare
Tel: 045-521617/045-522963
Entrance: at Kildare town follow the signposts.
Open: daily mid-February–mid-November: 9.30 a.m.–6.00 p.m.
Admission fee.

Your admission fee is for all places so this can be a glorious trip in late spring (for the blossom), summer and early autumn (for the maples). The horses are glorious to see all the time. The Stud is all about the after-history of the famous four horses who were the beginning of thoroughbred horse stock. Kildare's lush grass grows on mineral-rich soil which gives horses lots of calcium for their bones and that is why there are so many stud farms in this particular county. This stud was begun in 1900 by a Scottish colonel who believed in astrology for horses. He had their horoscopes cast at birth and built his stable blocks aligned to certain planetary paths. It worked! (Or maybe his horse-trading abilities did.) You can walk the paddocks and see millionaires' stallions at grass. However, the real hit is the selection of miniature Falabella horses and their foals. The adults of these mini-equines are smaller than many breeds of large domestic dog. There's a horse museum, which houses brave Arkle's skeleton, old tackle, videos of famous races, and, in a loose box, you can watch footage of a prize foal being born. Alongside the stud is a Celtic monastic garden which is dedicated to St Fiachra, the patron saint of gardeners — and also of taxi-drivers. The garden features an underground passage, crystal garden and even a 'spider' from the Skelligs in Kerry.

The Japanese gardens have something for everyone — not surprising because Tassa Eida, the gardener who plotted them, was tracing the Life of Man from Oblivion to Eternity, through the design of the layout. You can scuttle into caves, climb miniature mountains, tramp paths of adventure and cross torrents via significant stepping-stones. When your race is done, there's a very handsome pagoda-like restaurant (lego included!) and a bonsai and garden centre if you fancy making your own Japanese garden.

> You can read more about this Japanese garden in the haunting children's story, *Japanese Whispers* by Romie Lambkin, published by Wolfhound Press.

Farms

Airfield Trust — Gardens and Farm
Upper Kilmacud Road, Dundrum
Tel: 298 4301
Gardens and tea-room open during the summer: Tuesday: 10.00 a.m.–
1.00 p.m.; Thursday: 2.00 p.m.–5.00 p.m.; Saturday: 2.00 p.m.–
5.00 p.m. (These hours are scheduled to be extended.) Farm open
during school year only and by prior arrangement only. No dogs
allowed.

If you enter Airfield from the busy suburban road, walk up the yew-treed drive, turn round and open your eyes, a gasp is guaranteed. Here in the heart of Dundrum, you suddenly find that you are standing right in the middle of forty acres of gardens and mixed farm; the noise and commotion of the city has shrunk away to nothing and hens, sheep, pigs and cattle are as loud as their country cousins, completely unaware that they actually live in Dublin 14.

Airfield was owned by two legendary sisters, Naomi and Letitia Overend. They ran the farm, drove an antique Rolls Royce (sometimes with a calf trailer attached) and did some enormously useful charitable work. In their will they left Airfield to a private trust who are developing the farm and outhouses into an educational resource. When it's up and running, local schools will be able to arrange a visit to Airfield, seeing how the farm is run, doing related projects and artwork in the craft area. All queries must be directed to the Airfield Education Officer and all school visits must be by prior arrangement.

Meanwhile the gardens are open to the public, initially at no fee. A car park is being built and until it is completed, there is pedestrian entry only. Visitors can stroll through the grounds, the charming walled garden, the kitchen garden area and the Victorian greenhouse while enjoying both the farm, and the splendid views of the mountains. At various times throughout the year, plants, eggs and other farm produce, are available for purchase.

Larchill Arcadian Gardens and Farm
Kilcock, County Kildare
Tel: 628 4580
Entrance: signposted from Kilcock town square (leave N4 at Maynooth or Kilcock).
Open: May–September, every day: 12.00 noon–6.00 p.m. Tours by arrangement. Admission fee.

Not to be confused with the Boy Scouts Dublin camping area, this Larchill was once a theme park for eighteenth-century folk who rolled up in carriages to explore this famous ornate farm. Its original Dublin owners had a lake dug, where they built two islands (shades of the Famous Five), one with a temple and one with a 'Gibraltar' fort. All through the estate there were follies, and there's a fancy fox earth complete with exits which was built by the master of the Meath hunt who was convinced he would be reincarnated as a fox. You will also find fairy trees, boat houses, and nearer the long farmhouse, a farmyard with Gothic houses for pigs and poultry, and a walled garden where the south wall was once heated to grow peaches.

Nowadays this area includes not only forest walks and a picnic area, but also lots of exotic breeds of cattle (including red Highland cattle with curly horns), sheep in all colours, ridiculously friendly donkeys and Babe-smart piglets, plus hens with pants on — well, so they seem. School tours get the full treatment here and families can wander throughout the farm with a printed pamphlet to guide them. There is a gift shop and tea-rooms. This is also the centre for learning rural crafts like wall building (see page 335).

Newgrange Farm
Slane, County Meath
Tel: 041-24119
Entrance: turn right at the crossroads in Slane Village and follow the signposts. The farm is famously situated beside the Newgrange Megalithic Tomb (see page 238) but there is no entry to Old Newgrange on this side.
Open: Easter Saturday–early September (daily): 10.00 a.m.–5.00 p.m. Admission fee.

This is a very handsome farm which is located in the oldest part of Old Meath, and comes complete with traditional stone stable yard and loose boxes where the cuddly farm young are kept (most of which are petable). After the film *Babe* everyone loves the piglets, but you will also find rabbits, lambs, goats and ponies here. Out the back you will find poultry of all feathers, great barns complete with livestock (and their prize rosettes), a wool storyboard and the pungent aroma of both hay and food. Depending on the date that you choose to visit, there might also be demonstrations of rural crafts or even the Newgrange Farm Stakes Sheep Race. Tractor-and-trailer rides around the farm are available and are a huge hit. There is also a toy tractor play area for the tinies to practise their driving skills and manoeuvres. The excellent restaurant is well worth investigating or, alternatively, you can also eat at the indoor and outdoor picnic areas.

Straffan Butterfly Farm
Straffan, County Kildare
Tel: 627 1109
Entrance: Dublin/Naas by-pass; turn right for Straffan, left at
T- junction in village, farm is signposted.
Open: May until the August Bank Holiday weekend, every day 12.00
noon–5.30 p.m. School tours by prior arrangement. Admission fee.

The short summer months during which the farm is open reflect the short but happy life-cycle of its inhabitants. In a humid hothouse at the rear of the farm you enter a mini-rainforest. Dodge the warm spray and try to find as many brilliantly coloured butterflies and moths as you can — and tot up how many stages of development you can spot. You can feed the adults on nectar and feel the silk on the cocoons of Giant Atlas Moths. In the main body of the building there are dead butterfly collections from all over the world, huge stick insect families, a python and some cuddly tarantulas and their dinners. You can ask *any* questions about insects and arachnids, learn about cultivating your own caterpillars and buy some gifts at the little shop.

Morel Children's Farm
Straffan, County Kildare
Tel: 628 8636
Entrance: turn right for Straffan off Naas by-pass; take left at
signposted T-junction before the village.
Open (daily): 10.30 a.m.–6.00 p.m.; during the school tour season,
families should come after 2.00 p.m. on schooldays. Admission fee.

It seems that all the rabbits that didn't make it to Australia came to Morel Farm: the long-haired, lop-eared and exotic rabbits. Here too you will find racoons and marmosets, as well as the more common goats, pigs, lambs, ducks, peafowl, Jersey calves, turkeys, guinea pigs and several dozens of assorted fowl. The goat pens and rabbit pens are open for visitors to wander through, and in the different seasons, young animals can be bottle-fed. There is a picnic area by a stream, complete with sandy beach, as well as a snack bar off the farmyard. Birthday parties are catered for (sausage and chips) and school tours can also be organised by prior arrangement. The farm is open all year round and it has a very leisurely atmosphere.

Glenroe Open Farm
Kilcoole, County Wicklow
Tel: 287 2288
Entrance: signposted from Greystones–Kilcoole and Dublin–Wicklow roads.
Open: April–September, Monday– Friday: 10.00 a.m.–5.00 p.m.;
weekends: 10.00 a.m.–6. p.m.; March and October: weekends only;
closed rest of year. Admission fee.

'Welcome to Glenroe' says the sign outside Kilcoole and yes, it is definitely the home of the TV soap where the entrance to Dinny's house is via the cabbage field. In fact if RTÉ is filming here you won't be let in. However, apart from a series of historic *Glenroe* photographs, Dinny's house is not hugely interesting and he really should get decorators into the bedrooms. What is really on offer is a friendly farm encounter with pigs and piglets, goats, donkeys, a horse, smart woolly lambs, deer and a 'free' range of different fowl and rabbits. There is also a little coffee shop and *Glenroe* souvenir shop.

Greenan Farm Museums and Maze
Greenan, County Wicklow
Tel: 0404-46000
Entrance: signposted from Rathdrum village and Rathdrum–Laragh road.
Open: May, June, September, Tuesday–Sunday and July–August every day: 10.00 a.m.–6.00 p.m.; October, Sundays only. Also open Bank Holidays and Easter weekend. Admission fee.

There's an observation post that gives you a view of the layout of the cypress maze, which has a pond at its centre and several bridges on the way. Resist the temptation to cheat, just go in and get lost — it's fun. There is a picnic and play area too, and the air here is really fragrant. For more serious pursuits there's a gigantic barn given over to field, farm and forge tools and transport of the past — the animal traps are true horrors. Further on, there's an original stone farmhouse which has links with the Rebellion of 1798 but is now maintained in nineteenth-century mode. Also here is a Bottle Museum where, among other ancient glass items, there are fizzy drinks bottles shaped like torpedoes. One of the cottages has tea-rooms and there's a delightful nature walk down by the little river, complete with tiny islands.

Annamoe Leisure Park and Trout Farm
Annamoe, County Wicklow
Tel: 0404-45470
Entrance: beside the bridge in Annamoe village.
Open: June–August daily: 10.30 a.m.–6.30 p.m.; May, September: weekends only. Admission fee.

A fun place to eat and get wet. There are picnic and barbecue facilities, and of course, the *in* thing to eat is the trout you have just caught in the dark pool (though the dice are rather loaded against the fish). Rods are available. There is also a large shallow pond with rafts and a fort, and three-seater canoes can also be hired. Bathing is permitted too in the fresh mountain water. Bring towels and dry clothes!

Clara-Lara Funpark
Laragh, County Wicklow
Tel: 0404-46161
Entrance: about three miles from Laragh on the Rathdrum road.
Open: May–September daily: 10.30 a.m.–6.00 p.m.
Admission fee plus extra fees for some facilities. Season tickets and group rates available.

If you go down to the woods between Laragh and Rathdrum you will have a Tarzan-fine day — just don't expect to be dry and clean afterwards. But, of course, that is the 'C-L' experience — assault courses, tree platforms, lots of water hazards including a docked pirate shop for smaller folk, rowing boats, karts, and more. You can picnic or bring food to barbecue. Take a break between the soakings and chasings and do the marked nature trail where you might see some of the creatures who are avoiding the Ghengis Khan humans.

Finwey Farm
Spink, Abbeyleix, County Laois
Tel: 0502-31958
Open to schools and individual family visits.
By appointment only.

This farm offers therapeutic treatment to children and adults with disabilities, experience of trauma or with other special needs. Visitors can take part in farm tasks, pet animals and, by arrangement, ride horses. There are also goats, hens, rabbits, calves, donkeys and horses, dogs and puppies. This is not a drop-in farm so you must make an appointment before your visit.

Four RDS-approved working Farms within striking distance of Dublin are:

Coolnakilly Farm, Glenealy/Ashford, County Wicklow
Tel: 0404-44610
Provides a tour, activities, clay pigeon shooting and archery. All year, by appointment only.

Young McDonald's Farm, Askamore, Gorey, County Wexford
Tel: 055-26312
Many animals, a tree walk, museum, tea-rooms. Easter–September, Monday–Saturday: 10.00 a.m.–6.00 p.m.; Sunday: 12.00 noon–6.00 p.m.

Ballylane Farm, New Ross, County Wexford
Tel: 051-425666
Orienteering course, tea-rooms, indoor picnic and barbecue facilities. May–September: 10.00 a.m.–6.00 p.m. Groups by appointment.

> **Tullyboy,** Boyle, County Roscommon
> Tel: 079-68031
> Deer, ostriches, Icelandic horses, museum, hand-milking and bottle-feeding in season. Easter–September, Monday–Saturday: 10.30 a.m.–6.00 p.m.; Sunday: 12.00 noon–6.00 p.m. Groups all year by appointment.
> Telephoning beforehand is recommended, for precise road instructions.

Other parks: Try following any of Dublin's linear river parks like the Ward River, starting at Howth Castle; the Tolka starting at Finglas, or the Dodder, starting at Donnybrook or Rathgar (see page 174).

Other gardens: *Houses, Gardens and Castles of Ireland* is a booklet featuring many more gardens. Ask for it in a Tourist Office. There's a Gardens Festival in Wicklow in June when many private gardens are open to the public. Check with Bray Heritage and Tourism Office. Tel: 282 8480.

Chapter 3

Shopping

This section is about spending money — yours in fact. It's a random and off-beat guide to shopping in Dublin, because I presume you already know where to get the bare necessities but are interested in cheap, unusual or extra-pleasant places to go. So, for instance, clothes shops are not included, but fancy dressing-up is. In addition, apart from truly specialist shops, this chapter only outlines those which are close to the city centre. Your local shopping centre may have nearly everything, but you can't beat a good lazy day in town browsing and wandering from shop to shop, and you certainly won't find the variety of odd-bod places in the suburbs as you will in the city centre. So, gather a gang of friends together some Saturday, collect your assets and head downtown. Bus is the best mode of transport for a shopping trip.

Ancestors

You can almost buy ancestors. If you like your family name and/or have relations visiting from America, a good place to go is an heraldic artist's shop. They have maps, crests, scrolls, histories, badges and songs. Try Heraldic Artists at 3 Nassau Street or Historic Families on Fleet Street.

A map of Ireland with family names on it is on sale in most book shops and, of course, the *crème de la crème* of heraldic places are the Heraldic Museum in Kildare Street and the Freemasons' Hall in Molesworth Street, both of which appear in the Chapter 1. For Genealogy proper go to the National Library for preliminary enquiries. They offer free tracking leaflets and a fee-paying service.

Arty-Crafty

Two good all-round art shops are O'Sullivan's Graphic Supplies in Grantham Street off Camden Street, and Kennedy's in Harcourt Street. They are for professionals so they are expensive. The Art and Hobby Shop on the top floor of the Stephen's Green Centre is good for younger people. Eason's second floor will tog out anyone who isn't too demanding with oils, poster paints, millions of markers and lots of types of paper. K & M Evans in Mary's Abbey off Capel Street do all kinds of well-priced art and craft materials, but you just *might* run into your teacher here. RPM Supplies at 50 Lower Dorset Street sell everything a potter or sculptor could need. Hey Doodle Doodle, upstairs in 14 Crown Alley, Temple Bar, let you paint, and then buy ceramics after they fire them for you. Pompei Paints at Leisureplex in Stillorgan also offer pottery sessions and parties. Daintree Specialist Paper Shop in Pleasants Place off Camden Street sell handmade jewel-coloured papers and stationery. Habitat in St Stephen's Green and Combridge's in South William Street sell picture frames cheaper than most. Arnott's in Henry Street has acres of bright poppy felt and miles and miles of raffia.

(For art classes see page 272.) Needlecraft at 27 Dawson Street has everything for serious craftspeople as well as starter tapestry kits and rainbow-coloured wools and silks.

Astrology

Not as a science mission, but for fun or curiosity, you could drop in on The House of Astrology at 3 Parliament Street. They sell items that could make good presents — scarves, cards, mottos, cards, charts and more.

Ballet

If you take up any kind of dance, or if you just like the gear, Dance World in Parnell Street will fit you out, in tights, shoes and tulle. Most department stores also stock leotards and dance tights. Irish dancing costumes, materials and shoes can be bought from Irish Dance Wear at 51 Mary Street. (For dance classes see pages 274–277.)

Bicycles

If you are buying a bike, make sure you get a good try-out first and, if you aren't comfortable, do not take the bike just because it looks good. A lot of people love racers, mountain bikes and BMX but if you don't feel comfortable on one (or the price is not right) try out the other reliables. Many shops sell second-hand bikes which means some kind of guarantee; the alternative is to try the evening papers or local papers.

A dynamo, carrier and pump are the best accessories to get. Saddle-bags and panniers can be very expensive, and you can always wear a rucksack or adapt a large sports bags instead. And get a good lock and chain. A combination lock is the least bother unless you have a rotten memory. Always lock the gear wheel and the frame to a fixed object and always in as public a place as possible. However, since the city centre is so full of professional thieves with equipment, after you have bought a bike, insure it at once. If your family has house contents insurance it's only a couple of pounds extra to get a bicycle mentioned in the policy. You can park your bike in complete safety in the city in Square Deal Cycleworks, Temple Lane (Tel: 679 0838).

Reliable bicycle stockists in the city are: McDonald's in Wexford Street, Harding's of Bachelors Walk, The Bike Store at 58 Lower Gardiner Street and Cycleways in Parnell Street. However it's often best to buy locally. Suburban dealers are just as good and may have a wider selection of second-hands or hire-purchase terms. Plus they will remember you better. Belfield Bike Shop in UCD do a good sale of their hire bikes when the season is over. Exotics like unicycles, tandems, child carrier vehicles and so on are available at Square Deal Cycleworks (see above).

For twilight or night cycling, you must be properly lit up; the best thing is to get your bicycle fitted with a good dynamo. Otherwise, front and back lights always have to be removed. You should get yourself kitted-out with armbands and/or belts of the reflective variety.

Hiring bicycles: Many shops have a special Rent-a-Bike scheme with daily and weekly rates. A deposit and proper identification are required. You can get a list of all the stockists who operate this scheme from Dublin Tourism in Andrew Street. An Óige (see page 320) do a very cheap 'bike plus hostel' voucher holiday for members.

Book Shops

There are book shops all round the city, so I will mention the ones that have second-hand departments first because these buy from you as well as sell to you. You won't make very much but you can get rid of any old books you no longer want, for a profit.

Nassau Street has Fred Hanna's (the second-hand section is downstairs) and, at the far end, in Clare Street, is Greene's. This is a beautiful shop with a book-thronged staircase and it has appeared in many films set in Dublin. You can try across the road in Duffy's of South Leinster Street. Chapters Book Shop in Middle Abbey Street also buy second-hand books. Temple Bar Square features a Book Fair every Sunday and every so often a Book Barrow Fair is announced in the papers; these are usually held in the Mansion House on Dawson Street. The Book Barrow fairs are a throwback to the days when the Liffey quays were full of book merchants selling their wares from barrows, like they still do in Paris. A Millennium Book-market on this theme is planned for a pedestrianised space on Grattan Bridge.

You will find books which are a little out of the common run at the following places: The Forbidden Planet on Crampton Quay (down from the Virgin Megastore) is given over to **comic books**. Old and new classics are here, along with model kits, figures, T-shirts and even books on how-to-draw-like-comic books. Sub-City, a cellar at 2 Exchequer Street, do similar stock, and Wow Comics in the Dún Laoghaire Shopping Centre specialise in TV series spin-offs. There is an **Irish language book shop** at 6 Harcourt Street. This has very cheap, gloriously illustrated picture books that will make younger members of the family very happy; you can also find them in Government Publications Office in Molesworth Street. Connolly Books in East Essex Street is for **politicos**. For **art books**, you will not do better than the National Gallery, Hugh Lane Gallery or IMMA shops. Cathach Books in Duke Street is an **antiquarian** book shop that is worth a peek; they show off their valuable first editions in the window, and also sell old maps and prints. Fancy reading TinTin in French, Estonian, Basque? Modern Language in Westland Row deals entirely in **foreign language books**. Linguaphone at 41 Upper Abbey Street sell many varieties of disc and video language courses. Murder Ink at 15 Dawson Street is devoted to **crime books** and the owner will be happy to make suggestions from the large stock of American editions.

Back to the main business. Every shopping centre has a book shop. In Dawson Street the big book department HQs, Hodges Figgis and Waterstone's, are open late every weekday evening and they are also open on Sundays. Eason's has a well-stocked computer department, children's department and a play area for small children. Nearly all city centre shops do bargain books; check out Eason's and Hodges Figgis in particular.

The Children's Book Festival is in October every year, with different happenings, writers in person and various competitions in all book shops that stock children's books.

Fancy Dress

For professional standard costumes and fancy dress try Clown Around in Clarendon Market (Tel: 677 5040), D.O.D. Fancy Dress (Tel: 873 5056), 15 Sackville Place or the Dublin Costume Company (Tel: 668 5200), at 16a Eastmoreland Lane, behind Baggot Street Hospital. They also stock stage make-up of every kind. Alternatively, you can make your own fancy dress costume out of bright bits and pieces. Second-hand clothes and curtains are the basics, and tinsel, sequins, gold and silver paint are the transformers.

For the basics try your nearest charity shop (suggestions: Simon Shop in Camden Street; Lifeboat Shop, Rathmines; Barnardo's, Liffey Street) or the smart retro-shops in the Temple Bar area. Mary Street and Capel Street have a great number of army surplus shops, with bits of uniforms and belts and equipment. Art and model shops have gold and silver paint. Indian shops sell exotic scarves and shawls which make great costumes. Try the Ilac Centre or Stephen's Green Shopping Centre.

For very classy things try Jenny Vander's in South Great George's Street Arcade. This shop has beautiful antique clothes, including children's clothes. Very dear, but good for ideas.

Any library will have books on costume — ask at the counter.

Food

Most of us eat wherever we happen to find ourselves, but nevertheless there are places worth going to on special occasions. (See also Chapter 4 — I-Spy Walks.) This list is only a small selection. All were in munching existence at time of publication but you should check for opening and closing hours of all but the very obvious. Booking is advised for centre-city restaurants in the evenings.

Burger, fries and milkshake freaks will already have their favourite marked out from the huge selection of McDonald's, Supermac's, Eddie Rocket's and Burger King eating dens. They offer great basic junk chomping all over town — you can't miss them. The Kylemore Café on O'Connell Street is good for basic fuel and cakes.

For slightly up-market **family junkets** try the Bad Ass Café (Tel: 679 5981) in Crown Alley, for pizzas and steaks, with wine for the ones who are old enough. Great view of passing Saturday craic and a flyover money system. Clery's store in O'Connell Street has a rooftop restaurant, though it's not open-air, alas. Go at a quiet time for a window-seat. Habitat restaurant also overlooks St Stephen's Green. Both of these establishments are open during store hours. Good for Sunday brunch are Elephant & Castle (Tel: 679 3121) in Temple Bar, and The Mermaid Café (Tel: 670 8236) at 69 Dame Street. The Chicago Pizza Pie Factory (Tel: 478 1233) beside the St Stephen's Green Shopping Centre and Captain America's Cookhouse (Tel: 671 5266) at 44 Grafton Street have good menus for under 12s.

Gallagher's Boxty House (Tel: 677 2762) at 20 Temple Bar, has plenty to offer on the menu apart from the boxty, or potato pancakes, but they are delicious. Kelly & Ping (Tel: 817 3840) in Duck Lane, Smithfield, do all kinds of

Asian dishes. Canaletto's (Tel: 667 0699) on Mespil Road, does both sandwiches by day and delicious mixed Irish and Italian meals at night. Da Vincenzo (Tel: 660 9906) at 133 Leeson Street Upper, does authentic Italian pizza. At The Mongolian Barbeque (Tel: 670 4154) at 7 Anglesea Street, you can mix your own food which is then cooked for you; excellent reductions for children also offered. Vegetarians can try Marks Bros (Tel: 677 1085) at 7 South Great George's Street, or Cornucopia (Tel: 677 7583) at 19 Wicklow Street. The Olive Tree is the restaurant in the Islamic Cultural Centre (Tel: 260 3740) at Roebuck Road, Clonskeagh. They serve Middle Eastern hot food and salads and delicious honeyed dessert at most inexpensive rates; open everyday except during Ramadan (a month-long fast the dates of which lie early in the year).

If you love **good fish and good chips** go to Beshoff's in Westmoreland Street or O'Connell Street — it's dearer than your local but is very good. Another good city chipper is Café Angelo's at 36 Wexford Street. Or go fishy on the city limits at Harry Ramsden's emporium on the Naas Road.

If you are looking for **Theme Restaurants** they are mostly American. Thunder Road (Tel: 679 4057) situated on Fleet Street, has a heavy biker image while Strike Four (Tel: 872 4325) in the Virgin Cinema Complex features American sports as well as food, and Planet Hollywood (Tel: 478 7827) in the Stephen's Green Shopping Centre, is starry-eyed. You can find a little bit of Paris by dropping into the Alliance Française coffee-shop on Kildare Street for some _pain au chocolat_. The Irish Film Centre has its own restaurant/bar with an interesting space and shop. Chief O'Neill's Hotel (Tel: 817 3838) in Smithfield, specialises in Irish traditional music, with the Ceol Music Centre behind it. The Odeon Bar in Harcourt Street, has nice lunches on weekdays and just happens to be in a converted railway station. The Winding Stair Bookshop on Bachelors Walk, and Hodges Figgis in Dawson Street, both combine books with food. Almost every gallery and museum location has its own tea-shop/restaurant, and the National Gallery is particularly recommended.

Bewley's Oriental Cafés are getting a special entry, because though they have changed in the last few years, they are still part of the nineteenth-century coffee-shop tradition — all dark wood, plush and aromatic. There are four in the city centre, on Grafton Street, Mary Street, Westmoreland Street and South Great George's Street. The Grafton Street Bewley's once had its own Museum and offers theatrical happenings on occasion. It has many floors and also features a lovely old-fashioned lift. Westmoreland Street has real coal fires in winter. Bewley's Cafés are probably best known for their luscious buns and cream cakes but you will find the makings of a four-course meal as well; also, their tea-caddies make cheap colourful presents, or small treasure chests.

The Powerscourt Townhouse Centre on South William Street, has, between the balcony, the basement and the ground floor, at least nine different eating places altogether — very nice to lounge in and gawk, and listen to live piano music.

Old-fashioned Afternoon Tea. The very thing to demand from an adoring relative with money and/or a car. Try the Conrad Hotel — very expensive and very classy, Powerscourt House in Enniskerry, County Wicklow, for the most beautiful view, or Hunter's Hotel in Ashford, County Wicklow, for charm.

More Food Ideas

Every Saturday there are two Dublin food markets with special offers. St Andrew's Resource Centre in Pearse Street houses an organic growers' co-op which sells vegetables, grains, herbs and flowers. After three free admissions you pay a small membership fee. It's Soviet-style in decor but the food is good and cheap. Much more showy — and expensive — is the open-air food market in

Meeting House Square, Temple Bar, where the food that food-writers write about wafts delicious smells around the area.

There are now numerous Asian restaurants in Dublin, but you could have a look at the raw materials in the Oriental Emporium at 25 South Great George's Street, which has lots of packaged treasures like watermelon seeds, fortune cookies and lily bulbs (and lots of other things you can only guess at). If your family likes eating Chinese bring them something from here — there are so many sauces and they are much cheaper than in ordinary shops. There's also the African Market at 168 Parnell Street. Similarly with the food store in the Islamic Cultural Centre in Clonskeagh — many delicious and exotic deals in food ideas.

Bretzels, the Jewish Bakery on Lennox Street, just off South Richmond Street, sells hot bagels on Sunday mornings. These are crusty chewy rolls meant to be eaten with butter and cream cheese. They also have delicious breads and gooey cakes, such as rum balls.

In season, you can pick your own strawberries and apples, and get huge amounts of them at a very cheap price — you can also stuff your face as well as the bags. Watch the papers (and road signs) for the ads. Baldonnel Orchard is one such place. It's an apple and plum orchard, and the Irish Air Corps hangs out nearby, so there's free plane-spotting thrown in. Take a right turn at the Roadstone factory on the Naas Road.

Strawberries are for the picking in June, in north County Dublin for the most part, but also from Lambert's Fruit Farm in Ticknock.

Finally, if you can't afford anything except what is in the home larder, you could try cooking Coddle. Perfect for after a cycling trip, and as Dublin as they come.

For Coddle, you need:

8 pork sausages
8 thick rashers, or ham pieces
4 large chopped onions or leeks
2 pounds of potatoes, peeled and sliced
2 pints of boiling water
salt and pepper
knob of butter; and parsley, if you like it.

Boil the sausages and rashers for five minutes in the water. Remove and keep the water. Put the meat into a casserole with the onions, potatoes and parsley. Season and add enough of the boiled water to cover. Put greaseproof paper on top and leave in a slow oven 200° F or 1/2 gas until everything is cooked. This takes about an hour, but feel with a fork to be sure. Serve hot with parsley and butter. This serves from one to eight persons depending on appetite. (If it doesn't work try a cookery course! See page 297.)

Games

Fantasy gamesters can slash and burn, gyre and gimbals in the two outlets of Games Workshops, at Unit 3, Lower Liffey Street, and Unit 249, Blanchardstown Shopping Centre. They have a full range of Warhammer creatures, weapons and accessories, as well as game zones.

Hair

Apart from cutting your own hair (and there's a book available on that), shearing can be expensive, especially if you want to keep your hair short. The following city centre hairdressers offer a cheap service if you come as a willing model to their apprentice classes, held mainly in the evenings. You still say exactly what it is you want, but you may not get it, of course (same really as in normal conditions). The cutting will be supervised, however, and it certainly will not be a 'Mother's Cut'. All enquiries were about a wash, cut and blow dry.

> Peter Mark, 36 Grafton Street. Tel: 671 4399
> Robert Chambers, 31 South Anne Street. Tel: 677 1323
> David Marshall Hairdressing School, 27 South Great
> George's Street. Tel: 677 0598
> Lunatic Fringe, 69 Grafton Street. Tel: 679 3766
> Toni and Guy, 52 Dame Street. Tel: 670 8747
> Hair Academy, Charlotte Way. Tel: 478 1119

For a fabulous old-timer barber's shop in the centre of town try the Regent Barber at 2 Lower Fownes Street.

These are some of the most well-established hair salons and have a large staff to run the apprentice class scheme. Others may run similar classes on a less formalised basis, so it's worth making enquiries in a place you like. These salons and others sell all the products you need for a daring hair appearance, from gel and mousse to glitter gel and hair make-up. For a simple, short-term colour effect, you can use cooking colouring, sold in any good supermarket or grocery. Special hair products can be found in various outlets in South Great George's Street Arcade, and you can also buy from a salon suppliers like Terrisales at 71 Middle Abbey Street.

Internet Cafés

Central surfing at Global Internet Café, 8 Lower O'Connell Street; Cyberia Internet Café, Temple Lane; Planet Cyber Café, 23 George's Street.

Joke Shops

Funny Biz is a long-established joke shop in South King Street, beside the Gaiety Theatre. It has got a dread display of masks, dog turds, dead rats, spiders, dead hands, as well as 12,000 other things (they say) and farting powder for those special occasions.

There is another riveting and ghastly Funny Biz emporium which is situated on D'Olier Street. Here you can get mock wounds, real skeleton make-up and a juke-box-full of cheap jokes and magic tricks.

Markets

The Hippo in the Dandelion Market
by Daniel Reardon

A serendipitous hippo,
Content and tubby on the table
Smiled at me in marble.
He was mine for a pound
Which was just about mine.

I milled around the market-place
Wanting his happy fatness
To roll upon my desk.
I clutched the crumpled note
And strode back to the stand.

All the junky jewellery and curios
Sparkled as before, but the hippo
Was gone — sold.
I sank in thin despair
And spent the pound on beer.

Sadly, the Dandelion Market is no more. But nowadays there is a variety of markets (see also Food). George's Street Arcade Market offer old music, retro-clothes, tasty food, tattoos, tarot readings and lots of other things, housed in a gorgeous Victorian Gothic redbrick 'container'. At weekends, Mother Redcap's, off Francis Street near Christ Church, is also full of bits and pieces. The Blackrock Market (Saturdays and Sundays), signposted off the main street, rambles over several houses and yards and has gimcrack shops, junk, books, records, toys, clothes, plants, food and a great buzz. The Blackberry Market on Lower Rathmines Road, is also a junk market and is a good place for old radios and appliances.

Then there are the centre-city shopping centres, which are really up-market markets.

The Ilac Centre has entrances on Henry Street, Moore Street and Parnell Street. It's shaped like a huge cross and in the heart of it is a cool fountain area. At one end there are bubble-lifts that crawl up like ladybirds to the car park levels. There are several restaurants and plenty of sit-down space, though the centre gets very crowded on Saturdays when lots of people decide to sit around. Most kinds of shops and stores are represented and some of them are mentioned separately here.

The Ilac Centre also has a wonderful library. It's the Central Library of the Corporation libraries and everyone is welcome. The children's library is crammed with really new books, lots of places to sit, a tape tree for listening to stories, and lots of toys for very small kids to play with. There are also lectures and videos for older people in the main library together with newspapers, magazines and listening areas for music (classical, folk and jazz). The computer resources are excellent. English and other language speakers can check out the language exchange timetable. It's a great place for a library and is well used.

The Powerscourt Townhouse Centre is a place to be taken to by someone with money and a generous heart. It's a handsome, luxurious market though it might not like to be called a market as it is so expensive.

You get to it from Grafton Street by going down the little alley-way called Johnson's Court, or by the main entrance on South William Street. These wide steps lead up to Powerscourt House, a beautiful eighteenth-century building, and the shopping centre is out the back, if you like, in the court and stable yard. There are three storeys of galleries overlooking the courtyard, all covered in so you can 'sit out' in all weathers.

The shops are a real mixture. On the ground area there are some cheap enough stalls, with toys, jewellery and gimmicks. Don't forget to try the flavoured ice-creams and pancakes on the ground floor too.

St Stephen's Green Centre is at that end of Grafton Street. This is a comfortable twentieth-century variation of an old indoor city market and it's always buzzing with action. Three galleries, lots of stairs and escalators and you still might miss the amazing glass clock in the middle! Apart from the dozens of conventional shops there are some little gems here, dealing in crafts and sports (see other categories). On the top floor is a mini-market corner with exotics like conjuring and juggling aids, bonsai trees, beads, cheap clothes and a clown shop. There's also a good ice-cream stall on the bottom floor.

The Square in Tallaght is a shopping centre with a difference — its pyramidal shape. It's also a real local meeting place. Inside there's a good mix of shops, stores and restaurants on different levels, but also a radio studio.

2FM broadcast from the Crow's Nest twice or three times a week, and you can hand requests directly into the studio. Above all this again is the UCI twelve-cinema complex which runs a Saturday morning club for children — see the papers for what is showing.

Moore Street has survived all the threats to murder it, and you will probably see why. Once you pass the topmost stalls you can buy the cheapest fruit and vegetables in the country. In summer you can buy buckets of strawberries and raspberries for the family for half nothing. The radio butcher shouldn't be missed for his sheer 'alive-alive-oh', and sometimes you will see fish, crab, lobster and cods' roe on sale in the open, like the old fish shambles.

For the Dublin Corporation **Fruit and Vegetable Market** proper, go down Henry Street, Mary Street and into Little Mary Street. The market — currently under-going a big clean-up — is housed in a redbrick Victorian custom-made building, a little like the old leopard houses in the Zoo. All round the door tops you can see carved fruit and animals and inside, mounds and crates of the real thing. Open very early every weekday morning, and you must buy in bulk. By the end of the day there are often bargains to be had — like the sixty-five daffodils I was once given *free*.

Dublin's **Bird Market** is a shadow of what it once was years ago when you could nearly buy an ostrich. It's in Peter Street, off Bride Street, opposite St Patrick's Park, every Sunday morning and starts at about 11.00 a.m. Canaries and budgies are the main tweeters, but sometimes wild birds like yellowhammers have been seen here. Birds used to be common centre-city pets as they took up very little room, cost hardly anything to feed, and reminded people of the country they could not get out to see. Sometimes sparrows used to be dyed to pass as exotics.

Model Shops

There are several specialist modelling shops. Modeller's Den in Aston Place, just behind Virgin Megastore, has remote-controlled aeroplanes and suchlike. Marks Models in Hawkins Street has a vast collection of cars, trains, rolling stock and landscaping, plastic model kits and scientific kits and games. They also do train repairs and offer a great selection of kits and ready-mades, plus accessories and materials.

For model soldier and fantasy game enthusiasts absolutely the best method is to make your own, and the excellent Prince August Moulds in County Cork operate a postal service as well as selling their kits through toy shops. You make the lead soldiers in a little frying pan (supplied) and then paint them however you like. Write for a catalogue to: Prince August Moulds, Kilnamartyra, Macroom, County Cork; Tel: 026-40222.

Music

Tower Records in Wicklow Street, Golden Discs (Grafton Arcade, Mary Street, Ilac Centre, Stephen's Green Centre), HMV (Grafton Street and Henry Street) and Virgin Megastore on Aston Quay, are all excellent **chart and album** release outlets. You can also find video and game stocks in most of these branches. There's a good selection of **Indie** and **Punk** at Road Records in Fade Street, off George's Street. Always try and have the release number when you are looking for something that is not in the charts. For **second-hand music and golden oldies** try Freebird on Eden Quay; Record Collector, basement of 30 Wicklow Street; or the stalls in the George's Street Arcade.

Claddagh Records in Cecilia Street behind the Central Bank, stock **Irish** and **folk** music from just about everywhere. Celtic Note on Nassau Street, offer mainstream Irish/Celtic music and accessories, and the shop at Ceol Traditional Music Centre in Smithfield is accessible also to passers-by.

Opus 2, 24 George's Street, have **classical** and **spoken arts** while Golden Discs, HMV and Virgin are also concert ticket stockists.

You will also get **sheet music** in Opus 2, at 24 George's Street, and in Walton's in North Frederick Street and George's Street.

Walton's is a dream emporium for anyone who is lucky enough to be buying any class of musical instrument. Some people go along every weekend and drool over the range of guitars, but there's everything from concertinas to concert harps behind the lovely old façade. Better still, if you fancy yourself on the jazz clarinet or reveille-ing the neighbourhood on a trumpet, did you know, (a) that these woodwind and brass instruments are horrendously expensive and, (b) that you can rent one before you decide to buy? A make-up-your-mind-is-this-your-life period of three months rental is operated by Educational Music Services Limited, 22 Mountjoy Square (Tel: 872 5292). It is a very popular scheme.

For anything at all, from a triangle to a bagpipes, try Goodwin's the pawnbrokers halfway up Capel Street, or Charles Byrne in Stephen Street. They have an amazing collection, and every instrument must really have a story to tell.

The Dublin Corporation Music Library is in the Ilac Centre library. You pay a low annual fee for your borrower's card and they stock tapes and CDs in the following categories: classical, folk, jazz, spoken arts and musicals. You can borrow sheet music too and learn-to-play-type books. (Details on how to get involved in music begin on page 284.)

'Odd' Shops

Everyone can probably draw up a list of shops that deserve to be seen or patronised and this is mine.

Read's the newsagents in Nassau Street. They stock folders, paper, pens and art materials cheaper than just about anywhere else and they have a fine selection of fancy pens.

Grattan's Stores actually looks like the oldest shop in Dublin. It's on Essex Street West, just down from the Viking Adventure, and is a lovely old Dublin corner shop. Let's hope it will survive there.

Another charming oldster is the **Frederick Gallery** on South Frederick Street, included here because of its lovely Old Curiosity Shop curved window. It is a small art gallery.

Definitely not PC to say, it but an old-fashioned tobacconist's shop is a good stock house of cheap presents for poor pariahs who smoke. Try **Fox's** at the end of Grafton Street. Amazing pipes and tobacco that fell off a pirate ship, perfumed snuff, or coloured cigarettes (Sobranies in bright pinks and purples) make good choices, and there are also some lovely wooden boxes.

SWALK in Hibernian Way is a stationery shop with complete charm and lots of stuffed toy animals.

The Ark's shop in Eustace Street sells tiny writing items, mugs and jigsaws, all on Ark themes.

There is at least one old-fashioned sweet-shop with glass-jar displays of real story-book sweets. Have a look at **Kavanagh's** in Aungier Street and buy satin cushions, wine gums and acid drops by the bagful.

Past Times in Wicklow Street stock reproduction medieval, Celtic, Art Nouveau and Victorian clothes, jewellery, miniatures and knick-knacks. They also have kitchen stuff, books and unusual music.

Designyard on Essex Street East stocks changing exhibitions of jewellery and craftwork, which are certainly worth admiring. But how about the shop's design itself? Underneath it flows the legendary Poddle river so you will find this traced on the floor in a shimmering mosaic. Its four metalwork gates represent the cities of Madrid, Vienna, New York — and Dublin.

Dublin's answer to New York's Tiffany's is **Weir's**, on the corner of Grafton Street and Wicklow Street. It's a jewellery, glass and china shop and, not so great outside, inside it's a real treat — huge, with glass cases full of valuables, and massive tickings from massive clocks. You have to hold your breath in case you knock anything over. It's really quite decadent looking, though there are small, reasonably priced items here too, if you look.

Parties and Celebrations

Well, what do you like to do? Home parties with balloons, magic, animals, disco and so on, can easily be master-minded by taking a look at the large **Entertainers** entry in the Golden Pages. Similarly **Party Planners** or **Event Organisers** give you a list of people who hire out party equipment of all kinds (bouncing castles, shoe houses and other play equipment).

Outside the Home

Indoors: McDonald's do parties in all of their restaurants — by arrangement. Play and adventure centres generally offer a party service with full meal and about an hour of rocketing and bouncing on whatever sliding, climbing and squeegy equipment they have. Be sure to book well in advance for weekends. Try: Giraffes, Coolmine Industrial Estate (Tel: 820 5526). Laser adventure games combined with bowling are a big draw and Leisureplex Centres at Stillorgan (Tel: 288 1656), Coolock (Tel: 848 5722), Tallaght (Tel: 459 9411), and Blanchardstown (Tel: 822 3030) do parties of all sizes complete with meal. They also have Zoo play areas for younger guests. Dawson's Family Amusements on the Esplanade in Bray (Tel: 286 0974) do parties for children up to 12 years old, comprising food and frolicking on a variety of amusements. If your party is a small and 'surfy' lot, you could book lines in a cyber café (see Internet Cafés). Hey Doodle Doodle (Tel: 672 7382) in Crown Alley (see Arty Crafty above), offer parties where everyone paints their own pieces of ceramic. Pompei Paints (Tel: 288 1656) at Leisureplex in Stillorgan also offer pottery sessions and parties. Paint & Party (Tel: 831 3708) at Artane Castle shopping centre offer a similar service, with plaster work as well as ceramics. The Lambert Puppet Theatre combine a puppet show in their mews theatre in Monkstown with a home-cooked party meal at weekends (Tel: 280 0974). In the Virgin Cinema Complex you could combine either a giant IMAX film (Tel: 817 4200), or Virtual Reality Rides (Tel: 872 4692), with a party meal in the Strike Four Restaurant (Tel: 872 4325). Indoor karting for groups is available at Kylemore Karting (Tel: 626 1444) off the Naas Road (with meal combo at Harry Ramsden's) and at Kart City, Santry (Tel: 842 6322) on Saturdays, meal provided.

Outdoors: Many children's farms can arrange parties or provide room for your own party provender. Highly recommended for a summer party (see pages 107). Parties can be arranged in the Zoo — you don't have to be a member (Tel: 677 1425). Fort Lucan (Tel: 628 0166) at Westmanstown, Lucan, has a full range of wild outdoor fun activities. Outdoor and indoor sports activities are laid on with party meal in Spawell Leisure Centre, Templeogue (Tel: 490 4401).

Very active, pretty expensive and certainly memorable are two watery options. Surfdock in Grand Canal Harbour (Tel: 668 3945) will do a session of windsurfing, canoeing and sailing followed by food for groups. Dublin Bay Sea Thrill do a 40-minute splash express tour from Dún Laoghaire harbour. You must hire the whole ten-seater boat and waterproofs are provided (but not food). Not a bad idea for two families to try. If you have a summer party how about a picnic on Ireland's Eye (see page 205) or a climb up Bray Head? Extremely active and tough (and reasonably elderly) teenagers could alternatively try paintball game parties. Paintball Pursuit (Tel: 843 3510) or Splatoon (Tel: 295 9373) have all the works. In the city, with a smallish party you could take a horse-carriage ride from St Stephen's Green and proceed in a stately manner to a burger-joint party. You could also book everyone in on one of the special Tours (see pages 210–221), from air (expensive!) to open-top bus, and take in a meal at the nearest food outlet — that *would* be different. Or alternatively, take one of the Iarnród Éireann family day-breaks — they are super value — and have your party out of town (see page 218).

Pet Shops

Pet shops are rare enough in Dublin, and they don't, quite rightly, keep puppies or kittens. Mice, birds, fish, hamsters, gerbils and all their food and accessories are kept though, and these shops can be interesting places. Tighter controls have been passed so that the trade in large exotic birds and other species is dying out. You are advised to deal locally, but if you are in town, City Pets on Marlborough Place, Wackers Pet Shop on Parnell Street, and the Dublin Pet Stores on Capel Street (established in 1845 — what *did* they keep then? You could ask), are good general stores, while Pet Shop Superstore, in Stillorgan Industrial Park, is a huge establishment with a lot of rabbits and guinea pigs, snakes and odd beasties, as well as all the accessories, and an undersea world of fish. (See more fish at National Sealife Centre, page 41.) If you have a long-haired dog or cat and have fallen behind in grooming, look under 'Pet Grooming' in the Golden Pages for your nearest outlet — it's quite an expensive service, so stock up on those brushes and combs.

Meanwhile, if you have a sick pet, free treatment is available in the Veterinary College clinic on Shelbourne Road, Ballsbridge. The clinic is open weekdays all year from 9.30 a.m. to 1.00 p.m., but you must make an appointment (Tel: 668 7988). It will shortly move to UCD, Belfield premises. Cats should be brought in baskets or zip-up bags. Your dog won't be able to bite the vet — the College provides muzzles to stop him.

Apart from the listed veterinary surgeons there are several animal clinics that offer treatment at reduced cost.

The Blue Cross has a mobile dispensary (Tel: 497 1985 for details). St Francis Dispensary at 163 Church Street, just off the quays, operates a clinic three nights a week, Monday, Wednesday and Friday, 7.00 p.m. to 9.00 p.m. (Tel: 872 0113). DSPCA have clinics in Tallaght and Ballymun (Tel: 493 5502). The Cat Protection League does Trojan work in rescuing sick and stray cats and they will give you any information, or settle you with a new pet cat. They can also arrange visits to schools (Tel: 671 5509). (For ways of getting involved with animals see pages 306–326.)

Photographs and Posters

One-hour photo shops will enlarge and mount your photographs and they can also rescue old prints that have no negatives. You can visit the National Photographic Archive and the Gallery of Photography, both in Meeting House Square, Temple Bar, where there are exhibitions of historic and modern photographs, with photography books, reproductions and postcards on sale. They also have posters, cards, books and camera magazines. The Irish Historical Picture Company on Lower Ormond Quay have a huge collection of period photographs, sorted by town and county — they make excellent presents.

Cinemania beside the Irish Film Centre on Eustace Street specialises in movie posters and photographs (and toys) and the IFC itself has a good cinema selection in its shop.

The Dublin Tourism Centre on Andrew Street sell posters, maps and images and you can pick up quite an amount of free publicity fodder here too. For general posters, either paper, framed or block mounted, try We Frame It on Dawson Street or Athena in the Stephen's Green Centre. They both have good selections. The UNICEF shop on Ormond Quay has posters (cheap), beautiful cards, diaries and calendars that would brighten up the dullest room. The National Gallery, the Municipal Gallery and the IMMA have excellent selections of posters and cards from their own collections and abroad. Cinemas and film distributors will sometimes give away advertising posters, as will travel agencies (especially at holiday fairs) and some embassies. It all depends on the way you ask and the way things are with them.

Room Decoration

There comes a stage when doing up your room (or part of it) becomes pretty essential. Here are some ideas ranging from very expensive to zilch. Department stores have all the basics and the big sales are in January and July.

Furniture: Cheerful bunks, beds and wardrobes can be seen in Habitat on St Stephen's Green and Bob Bushell on City Quay. Arnott's on Henry Street and Classic Furniture outlets are agents for gorgeous up-market bunks-cum-sofa or work stations; you can find cheaper models in Atlantic Home Care or Texas Home Care outlets. The best way to learn about storage space is to examine a boat or a caravan and work out your own ideas. You could also pay a visit to Storage Solutions which is at 222 Harold's Cross Road. Orange-boxes for box shelf-making (sand, paint with bright colours and glue together) can be got free or for a few pence if you bring a persuasive person to the Corporation Fruit Market.

Computer desks come in all qualities and shapes. Try Compustore outlets — they often have special deals because they are more interested in selling hard and software than timber ware.

For really interesting furniture and furnishings ideas go along to Crafts Council of Ireland at Designyard in East Essex Street. Their computer system lets you call up images in every craft imaginable; you can study them close up, see prices and outlets. Not *everything* costs the earth — you would be surprised.

Paint: On that computer above you might also discover artists who paint *trompe l'œil* images on walls just like the house-owners of Pompeii. Or you could try it yourself —

easy to paint over if it goes wrong. The Stencil Shop is on Johnson's Court off Grafton Street; you can also learn to make your own from any decorating book. For the widest range of paint colours try the Irish-made Colourtrend, which operates in an old workhouse in Celbridge, and also sells its products in many hardware outlets.

Cages/aquaria for fish, gerbils and other animals: Pet Shop Superstore in Stillorgan Industrial Park does a good range of both.

Pictures, wall-hangings, kites, fans and so on: (See Photographs and Posters in this section.) For kites see Toy Shops — kites make great wall decorations. Oxfam in South King Street have a good range of room decorations and any trip to the top floors of the Stephen's Green Shopping Centre will reveal lots of interesting bits and pieces.

Lighting: Roches Stores outlets and Habitat have the cheapest and best selections. For ultra-modern lighting — and other 'techno-craft' items — try Haus on Crow Street, Temple Bar, especially during their sales.

Large Stuffed Toys: Any department toy store, SWALK on Hibernian Way, the Zoo shop, The Dolls' Hospital on George's Street, and of course, if you are a good marksperson, any funfair stall.

Plants: Try a bottle or bean sprout garden, or a window box. Growing exotic plants from fruit pips is fun and it does work. This guide was re-edited in the shade of a mango plant. Plant your lemon, orange, mango (or whatever) seed in a pot of compost, water, cover with plastic wrap and leave in a warm, light place. Keep it moist. It should sprout within weeks. If not, try again. It works, honestly.

Sports

Department stores and shopping centre supermarkets usually stock good sports gear and equipment. But for

nitty-gritties you need special shops. Here are some which
are located in the city.

The Scout Shop at 146 Capel Street, welcomes non-
scouts also. Camping gear, knives, uniforms, belts, badges
are all here. Bramac's on Liffey Street is a really interesting
shop. They stock camping equipment, anoraks, belts,
knitted hats, ropes, tartan shirts, warm sweaters — mostly
cheaper than anywhere else. Elvery's (who have an
elephant as their shop sign) of Suffolk Street and the Great
Outdoors of Chatham Street, off Grafton Street, are
palaces of sports equipment. You can buy everything from
a snowmobile to full diving gear here, and no one minds
you just having a look. The sports clothes though are
rather dear in these shops — best bought in a big store.
Patagonia on Exchequer Street stocks expensive sports and
leisurewear but they do have good sales.

Champion Sports have numerous outlets; as well as
clothes they specialise in blade and board equipment. The
Soccer Shop on South Great George's Street and Soccer
City, Crampton Quay, tog every fan and player out, while
Arnott's has a dedicated Manchester United store. Motor-
racing fans can try Pitstop on Lower Liffey Street, Formula
Plus in the Blanchardstown Shopping Centre, or the
Chequered Flag at 101 Terenure Road North.

Fisherfolk will be fair bait for Rory's Fishing Tackle on
Fleet Street or Watts on Ormond Quay, who also stock
archery equipment.

Horsey people can buy their gear in good department
stores or in a range of out-of-town outlets (check Riding
Clothing in the Golden Pages). But many people might like
to drop in to Holmestead Saddlery Superstore in Kill,
County Kildare, to admire this special craft, since the old
saddlery shop in Poolbeg Street has sadly closed.

Stamps/Coins

Stamp collectors can go to the Philatelic Office in the GPO
for Irish stamps and also to order first-day issues. The office

runs the Voyager club for young people. Cathedral Stamps at 78 Marlborough Street sell all kinds of souvenir and specialist stamps and accessories (Tel: 878 6384). Whyte's at 30 Marlborough Street, trade in coins and medals. There's also a fine collection of Viking coinage and tokens in the National Museum on Kildare Street. You might also visit Loughshinney (see Beaches) and see if you can discover any Roman coins there; many remains have been found in this area. Small dingy antique shops and second-hand booksellers often have coins, old stamp albums and old postcards. **Stampa** is the annual autumn fair for philatelists; it is advertised in the papers.

Toy Shops

Toys, like books, are sold everywhere, but the specialist shops are the best. Chain toy shops like Smyths, Supertoys and Toymaster have many outlets in the suburbs. However, don't forget that big supermarkets often have a huge stock of well-known brands, cheaper than anywhere else. Virgin Megastore on Aston Quay is good on board games and the latest film and television spin-offs. Comic book stores (see Books above) sell a wide range of models and games from super-smart TV series, as well as golden oldies. The Early Learning Centre at 3 Henry Street (beside Arnotts), has a huge range of toys for babies and younger children, as well as art materials, musical toys and kits of all kinds.

The Art and Hobby Shop at the top of the Stephen's Green Centre is especially good for 'crafty' toys and kits. The Dolls' Hospital is at 62 South Great George's Street and, exactly as its name implies, it's where missing eyes and arms, bald patches, voice-boxes and so on are taken care of whenever possible. Teddies are also treated. But that's not all — it's also a dolls' clothes and a specialist doll's house shop. You can buy Irish-made wooden houses or, better still, get someone nifty to make you one and save your money for the furniture. Everything is to scale — one inch equals one foot in our world and you can get things like chandeliers with real bulbs, washing machines that spin, drop-leaf tables, bunks, cots, potties, Welsh dressers and so on. If you think the stuff is magical, which it is, then look at the 'collectors' furniture. This is aimed at adults who collect miniatures — *perfect* ones.

Mark's Models on Hawkins Street feature fantasy toys and models as well as kits and boat, train and plane stock. Very cheap toys — suitable as presents for small brothers and sisters, or party stuff — can be bought in pound shops or walk around stores like Hector Grey's on Liffey Street.

Nimble Fingers in Stillorgan is obviously not a city shop, but it has got toys and equipment you can't buy in other places — trampolines and kit bags of building bricks, wooden dolls' houses and miles of bedroom friezes, for example. Also available there are good baby toys, marbles, paints and some old-fashioned cheap toys.

For hand-crafted wooden horses and toys try the computer catalogue at Crafts Council of Ireland, Designyard, East Essex Street.

YOU

I have called this the 'You' entry because it's a list of places to buy things with Yourself on them.

T-shirts: T-shirt Print of the Ilac Centre and Stephen's Green Centre, or Apprentice T-shirt Print of Stephen's Green Centre, will print your name or whatever you like on a T-shirt or sweatshirt.

Mugs, plates: Go to Hey Doodle Doodle of Crown Alley, Temple Bar, paint your own ceramics and they will fire them for you. The firing takes a couple of days.

Identity bracelets: Most jewellers or specialist counters in department stores engrave bracelets and tags.

Stationery: Personalised stationery is a luxury if you don't have a computer artwork package. There are coin machines in shopping centres to print name cards and stationery. But you could try DIY with....

Rubber Name Stamps: The Rubber Stamp Co., Capel Street. Just walk in and they will do one for you. Read's of Nassau Street also supply them.

Video and Computer Games

You won't find hardware outlets listed here — that really is up to you. For hiring consoles and games your local video shop is the first stop.

Diskovery on Lower Liffey Street have a good stock of educational software and games. On the same street Gamesworld stock new and second-hand games. Game Ltd, at 7 Grafton Street, and Electronics Boutique at 2 Dawson Street, both have a large selection of games. Try Virgin Megastore on Aston Quay for main-movers and Peat's of Parnell Street have excellent stock, plus the hardware and the expertise.

i-Spy Walks

Sunday is a good day for family walks. However, many places in Temple Bar, for instance, may be closed, so Saturday might be a better choice.

The Georgian Walk with Statues is a walk through eighteenth-century 'Celtic Tiger' Dublin, with a park trail, and a museum at the end that sums up the original lifestyle which existed in these parts of the city. Many of the sites in Medieval Dublin are covered in the Museums chapter, but if you actually walk according to the map, you can plot for yourself the tiny size of Viking-Norman Dublin. Finally, the Temple Bar Walk. Some Dublin people think that the Temple Bar area is just for tourists and that all the bars and eating-houses combine to mean unnecessary hassle. Believe me, it's an exhilarating place to walk and is packed with sights. Nowhere else in Dublin will you find this pattern of narrow streets in good working order; and that is why it's so full of street life, good, middling and bad. *Do* get to know it — you would if you were in a foreign city.

If you would like to do a walking tour with the help of experts, there are several guided routes to choose from (see page 318).

Dublin is very, very old — but you need to be a bit of a detective to find out the way it looked 200 years ago, not to mention 900 years ago or before that again. The oldest human remains found date to about 5000 BC. Some ancient campers left their midden, or rubbish dump, behind them on Dalkey Island back then (some things never change), while the oldest centre-city find dates from about 1300 BC — a tomb discovered in Suffolk Street near the Dublin Tourism office. About a thousand years later a little village grew up around the Liffey at its shallowest part, where a ford of branches or hurdles was laid across. When the village grew bigger and more important — though not as important as the settlements in Meath, where the High King lived — the four great chariot roads of Celtic Ireland met in Dublin.

Once St Patrick (and quite a few others) had successfully converted the Celts to Christianity, Dublin acquired some churches and monasteries and it became quite a bit bigger. Viking Scandinavians were able to smell Celtic Tiger Mark One because they came, saw, and conquered Dublin in the ninth century. With help — and hindrance — from the natives they turned it into an important Viking city over the next two centuries. Dublin Vikings had a great slave market (do the Dublin Viking Adventure and find out) and sent slaves as currency throughout Europe. But what goes around comes around. When Henry II's French-speaking Norman knights settled in the city after 1170 they eventually banished the Vikings north of the Liffey. The new inhabitants then drew up their own plans and began to engineer the first stone city of Dublin.

The map over the page shows the size of medieval Dublin, which was, of course, a walled city. At the six main street entrances there was a gate, and at its fullest walled extent there were thirty-two watchtowers. There was an inner wall too, and that is still standing on Cook Street. The cooks were kept outside the inner walls because with their pots and pans and fires they were considered a hazard.

MEDIEVAL DUBLIN

1 Cook Street medieval gate to the city. Walk up the steps to St Audoen's Church.

2 Christ Church Cathedral. It was built in 1172, perhaps earlier.   Look out for Strongbow's tomb. Boy pretender king crowned here in 1487. (Mummified cat in crypt; great website on the Net.)

3 Dublin Castle, with its Black Tower.

4 St Patrick's Cathedral. Dates from 1192. The Poddle used to flood both the cathedral and Patrick Street. Now the river is all underground. Look out for the stone from St Patrick's Well. Listen for choirboys at Evensong; they go to school across the road.

5 This is the site of the very oldest part of Dublin — the Ford of the Hurdles.

6 St Michan's Church. Go to the crypt and look at the leathery hand of the Crusader. There are preserved bodies here.

7 St Mary's Chapter House, Meeting House Lane. This has a 6-foot drop and very musty old air inside. Here is where Silken Thomas threw his sword on the table and started a rebellion. (He was executed in 1537.)

(You will find details on opening hours for these sites in the Museums and Buildings chapters.)

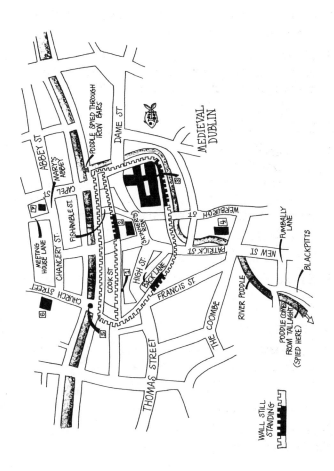

MEDIEVAL DUBLIN

ABBEY ST

PODDLE SPIED THROUGH IRON BARS

DAME ST

MARY'S ABBEY

FISHAMBLE ST

CAPEL ST

CHANCERY ST

MEETING HOUSE LANE

CHURCH STREET

COOK ST

HIGH ST

SKINNER'S ROW

BACK LANE

FRANCIS ST

THOMAS STREET

THE COOMBE

WERBURGH ST

PATRICK ST

NEW ST

RIVER PODDLE

FUMBALLY LANE

BLACKPITTS

PODDLE COMES FROM TALLAGHT (SPIED HERE)

WALL STILL STANDING

Ten Dublin Street names no longer in use:

Crooked Staff	Hell
Little Boater Lane	Pudding Row
World's End Lane	Wormwood Gate
Paradise Street	Dirty Lane
Salutation Alley	Gallows Hill

Ten Dublin Street names still in use:

Misery Hill	Winetavern Street
Duck Lane	Lemon Street
Golden Lane	Observatory Lane
Fumbally Lane	Engine Alley
Harmony Row	Carman's Hall

Dublin was this size in 1200 AD — when it started to grow the first 'suburbs' were called 'Liberties' and were attached to the guardianship of certain saints. Then it grew more ... and more ...

Even though it's hard to pick out the medieval features without a lot of poring over books, some things do give this part of Dublin away for what it is. The hills, for one. Nowhere else in modern Dublin city are there found these up-and-down streets. The first settlers, and then the Danes, built their settlements to be nice and safe on top of the hill. The narrow winding streets are another giveaway — though some of their colourful names like Cutpurse Lane and Skinners Row have gone. However, Fishamble Street is still there, it was the location of the ancient fish market, just up from the river. Another giveaway is the drop you have to make when you enter any of the medieval buildings marked on the map. Ground level goes up about one foot every century.

Medieval Dublin was noisy, busy, dark inside the dwellings (no windows, rush candles), and very smelly. Plague came to the city many times before and after the terrible Black Death year of 1348. For ordinary people, life was much the same as in any city in Europe. The weather was worse than, say, the weather in Florence, but people everywhere worked hard, ate less than we do, went to church more than we do and had fun whenever they could. This could be marching with their guilds, going on a hunt outside the city walls, or walking to the common to see someone even more unfortunate than themselves being punished. And drinking a *lot* of ale. People did their washing and took their drinking water, not from the Liffey, but from a river called the Poddle. Can you see it on the map? It was their lifeline, even though it sometimes overflowed and flooded their houses beyond repair. Now the Poddle has been driven underground and most Dubliners never think about it. You can see it in two places now: where it empties into the Liffey at Wellington Quay, and at the end of the Dublin Castle tour, down in the Undercroft; here you find the pale and dank Poddle lapping around the old wall of Dublin. You can trace it on old maps, and today, in the suburbs, you can find traces of it out towards its source in the Tallaght/Walkinstown area. It's also above ground for quite a bit after Harold's Cross. Meanwhile, when you walk over the ancient streets of Medieval Dublin, remember that many are built on water.

> *Dublin — One Thousand Years of Wood Quay* by Jonathan Bardon and Stephen Conlin (Blackstaff Press): a picture book with explanatory text which offers great assistance in picturing this part of the city at different periods.

The Temple Bar Walk

The starting tape for this walk lies between any two of the Bank of Ireland's giant columns in Foster Place. However, you could not actually tie a tape from one to the other because these columns are *engaged* — that is, joined to the wall — unlike the free-standing ones further on. It's quiet here (on a Sunday anyway!) and leafy, so you can take your bearings without being jostled.

You can explore the Bank/Old Parliament building on a weekday (see page 59) but right now try to find a fossil or a shell in the columns. They are made of Portland stone, from the part of England that was once covered by warm seas. Ichthyosaurs swam in them. The street that faces you, Dame Street, is swimming in banks and other kinds of money-houses. It was one of the first of the Wide Streets, designed in 1769, by — surprise, surprise — the Wide Streets Commission. They called it Dame Street after a dam gate that had steered the River Poddle around the medieval part of city. The Poddle, though small, was, and is, tough — it takes its Weetabix — and you can see it emerge into the Liffey further on.

Directly opposite Foster Place, up Church Lane, is where the Vikings were reckoned to have had their **Thingmote**, or 'Thingmound' — a mound said to be 40 feet high and 224 feet all round, which they used as an official meeting place. Meddlesome King Henry II met some Irish chieftains on it when he visited in 1171 after his Norman knights had done their invasion work. It was flattened for landfill when Trinity College was built. There were slash-and-burn developers around in the sixteenth century too.

Ten places that still feel their age:

Ship Street, originally Sheep Street, behind Dublin Castle

Iveagh Gardens

Collins Barrack Square

St Mary's Abbey

Christ Church Cathedral Crypt

The South Wall and Poolbeg Lighthouse

Johnson's Court, off Grafton Street

Dublin City Wall walk to St Audoen's

Tailors' Hall courtyard

Henrietta Street entrance to King's Inns

Turn right off Dame Street and head down **Anglesea Street**. Now you are in the Temple Bar area. The streets here are narrow, and many of them have cute first names, like Sycamore or Crow, or skinny last names like Alley, Lane or Row. When developers in ruffs first began to build here in the early 1600s they put up some warehouses and 'ship-shops' for the dock trade by the river; but after Dame Street appeared and real people began to live here in big houses with long gardens, they needed proper shops. A later development were the McDonald's of the day — newfangled chocolate and coffee shops. Some of them became far more notorious than any of the ale-houses. There were quite a few little theatres around here in the eighteenth century also. Nowadays you can eat and drink, go the theatre and buy just about everything here — just like old times. The area acted as a set for the making of the Tom Cruise film, *Far and Away*, pretending to be old Boston. There are still a few of the cutpurse guild around — be careful!

Try and spot the beautiful shopfronts with carved bay windows owned by the AIB and a solicitor. Not so smart outside, but deadly inside, is the Stock Exchange. Alas, they do not admit curious people anymore, not even shareholders — only traders and brokers. This building dates from 1878, after the great Irish railway shares boom in 1844 and before the great Irish bicycle shares boom in 1895. This last bonanza was connected to the airy invention of pneumatic tyres by Mr Dunlop. He had his first factory in Stephen Street, just where the new Dunnes Stores emporium is being built. Turn left into **Cope Street** which continues on past the back of the great layer-cake slab that is the Central Bank (a popular weekend skateboarding venue). Turn into **Crown Alley**. Anywhere along here you can fit yourself out in retro-chic clothes, beads, buy music — very old and very new — or just enjoy the buzz; it's never quiet. Look out for the old warehouse sign 'Domestic, Colonial and Foreign Removals'.

Do you see the Bad Ass Café? Not only did singer Sinead O'Connor carry plates around in here, as the Hot Press Rock Trail plaque will tell you, but Rachel Joynt, a sculptor with a great sense of humour, has commemorated the actual Bad Ass right there on the path with little golden hoofprints. See? Keep your eyes peeled for many of Rachel's pavement sculptures along Crown Alley, Temple Bar and Merchants' Arch — they celebrate tools and trades.

Walk past The Bad Ass Café and on to **Temple Bar** itself which is called after a seventeenth-century property owner, not after a temple. To your right is the Palm Tree seat if you want a desert island sit-down. Just opposite this is one of the area's oldest shops — Rory's Fishing Tackle, which also stretches down the little street called Asdill's Row. Peeking through the greenery here there is an old apartment block that strangely manages to look like it got swapped with a Florida motel. If you want to breathe more of this kind of atmosphere you can go and peer into the Thunderoad Café which is further on down the road in Fleet Street — it's full of Harley-Davidson 'vroom vroom' stuff.

Come back and go through **Merchants' Arch.** From here you can cross the graceful Ha'penny Bridge for nothing — if it was before 1919 you would have to dig in your pockets for that halfpenny toll charge. Take a look at the extremely skinny tall house facing you on the right. Can it be real? Look at the river — green and soupy but not smelly anymore. Mullet and seals have been spotted in this part of the Liffey — try your luck from the middle of the bridge. You can step onto the Millennium Boardwalk from here: by night the lighting is spectacular.

Turn right, along the **Square**. There are always temporary exhibitions of street art on display, from tractors to Christmas decorations. What do you think of today's model? Look at the lovely old barber's shop, the Regent. Opposite is the Temple Bar Gallery and Studios — free entry for all kinds of contemporary displays, through the atrium and upstairs. This is a great place for free brochures, flyers and way-out postcards. Again, look at the street. If you are lucky you will see odd lights flashing on and off at your feet — these are set off by people using lifts and loos in the Studios.

Walk up **Temple Lane** (on old maps it's visible as Dirty Lane), twist left and into **Crow Street.** At its bottom, where Cecilia House is, once stood the legendary Crow Street Theatre, the largest in Dublin and built to be as big as any in London. It started out pure and arty but changed into a small amphitheatre and ended up having indoor pony races. It lasted from 1758 to 1819, and went out of business after a night of rioting known as the Crow Street Riots. You can see a picture of the races during the video at No. 29 Merrion Square (see page 60).

Crow Street is now famous for its Green House — you can see the other side of it on Temple Lane. When its foundations were built a pagan Hiberno-Viking burial site was discovered. Now the apartment complex draws its heat from the earth's core and among other things it celebrates bicycles — see how its balconies are made? It has two wonderful doors that are really works of art. The tree door is by Remco de Fouw; the far door with its stuffed layers is by Maud Cotter and it's called 'Absolute Jellies Make Singing Sounds'. On weekdays you can go into the modern furniture shop called Haus to get a better look at the Green House. Up Temple Lane there are more bikes at the Square Wheel Cycleworks. They call themselves 'Ireland's No. 1 Subterranean Bikeshop'. You can park bikes here for a fee.

Cross Temple Lane into tiny **Curved Street.** This is a spanking new street and its tenants are just as new. On your left is Arthouse — where the art comes via electronic means. Specialised computer techniques can be learnt here, there is an internet café and there are regular family Open Days during the year. Look at its differently shaped

windows — why so, do you think? On the right is Temple
Bar Music Centre. Recording goes on here (see page 286)
and it's also a concert venue at nights and sometimes on
afternoons.

You should now be standing on **Eustace Street** facing
The Ark. Perhaps one of The Ark's animals facing out has
its eyes on you — the parrot-bright creatures include a
unicorn, fish, bird and snail. The Ark is Europe's first (and
so far only) cultural centre for children. What happens
here is theatre, music, art workshops and much more,
during the week for schools, by arrangement, and at
weekends for the public (details on page 270). But The Ark
wasn't just a cute choice of name. The building, with its
fine tall windows, used to be a Presbyterian school. The
tradition was that the only toy the children were allowed
play with on a Sunday was a Noah's ark, because that
featured in the Book of Genesis. From the story of Noah
come today's welcoming Ark animals, and in the shop
inside you can buy any number of mugs, T-shirts, jigsaws,
pencils and so on, all based on Noah's seaworthy boat.
The Ark's small theatre is curvy and made of Irish oak, it's
'arky', and, even more magical, it can open out onto
Meeting House Square behind, so that a much larger
audience can see plays when weather and show permit.

However, before you go into the square there are other
places to see on Eustace Street. Up towards Dame Street,
on the side of The Ark you will find the Irish Film Centre
with its film reel sculpted into the street. Walk down the
illuminated strip and you are in a pleasant space with a bar
and restaurant, shop and the entrance to two arthouse
cinemas. Upstairs are the offices of different Irish film
organisations. The cinema space used actually belonged to
the Society of Friends, or Quakers, who still have a
meeting house next door. They have been here for a long
time — since 1692 — although thirty years earlier the first
two Quaker women who made a public address in Dublin
were thrown in jail.

Beside the IFC there's a shop called Cinemania which sells everything devoted to movies — great for presents. Down at the far end of Eustace Street there's a round well shaft which was discovered during renovations — no drinks available today though. At this stage, you should pass the Temple Bar Information Centre — have a check to see if anything special is happening in the area.

Take any turn into **Meeting House Square**. This is a people-friendly spot — no traffic of any kind except roadie vans leaving musicians off, or indeed leaving vegetables off (not necessarily the same thing!) This space has an organic produce market every Saturday; it also hosts regular concerts and on summer weekend nights there are free showings of classic movies in the square. Tickets are available from the Information Centre. There are also outdoor chess games and chess classes during the summer, and a circus at weekends.

On one side the Gaiety School of Acting overlooks the square. It's a good home for it, because this area was the flourishing theatre quarter of the city in the eighteenth century and a significant number of Irish actors and actresses, managers and playwrights, went to London from here and became famous. Photography is another art that is getting a look in here — you will find the Gallery of Photography, the DIT School of Photography and the National Photo Archive surrounding the square. Go on through to Sycamore Street. Up on **Sycamore Street** is the stage door for the Olympia Theatre — underneath flows the Poddle river, heading full steam ahead for the Liffey.

Continue down **Essex Street East** (it's a continuation of Temple Bar). The Project Theatre with its new look is one of the cool small theatres that changed Dublin audiences for ever in the 1970s, 1980s and 1990s. Across the road is the Clarence Hotel, once stuffy and *nice*, now superchic and expensive, because it now belongs to U2. The Connolly book shop is a good, old-fashioned 'lefty' shop; capitalists will need vaccinations. Close by is the very narrow Crane Lane — you can go through for a really medieval feel. Crane Lane was the site of one of the first synagogues in Dublin. See if you can spot the smart gold dolphin carved on the one-time Dolphin Hotel?

Go back to Essex Street, just as it enters **Parliament Street**. On your right is The Porter House, a pub which makes its own beer — look up at the ledges and hatches on each level for lowering grain. Down towards the river is the unique shopfront called the Sunlight Chambers. You know the tough household Sunlight soap? This place was theirs — they used to own an entire suburb near Liverpool. Around the facade, in two layers, runs a ceramic strip showing men working hard and women washing their dirty things for them — ha! (The same company moved into washing powders and now have smart TV ads — this is the early version!) This lovely and unusual front has emerged sparkling clean and proper with the many years of city grime now removed.

Parliament Street leads up to the City Hall. This classical building straddles the hill climbing towards the very earliest part of the city. This was where official grandees and early speculators hung out when it was the Royal Exchange. It became the Corporation headquarters — though they have now moved into the Civic Offices nearby — and it's still open to the public on weekdays. If it's open go in to see the dome, the round room and the statue of Daniel O'Connell wearing a toga (he did not really dress like this, of course, but he did have his first public meeting here in 1800). You can also attend Corporation meetings here (see page 226).

There are some interesting shops on Parliament Street. Read's the cutlers is reckoned to be the oldest shop in Dublin (1670) though it has been bought over by the pub which took its name. They plan to maintain the sword and knife shop as a museum (it remained closed at time of writing). The House of Astrology is also on this street, if you like that sort of thing, and several buildings along here sport the gable-fronted top storeys that gives them the name 'Dutch Billies'. Check them out — you could imagine them by a canal in Amsterdam. And watch out for the modern version further on, on Fishamble Street.

But this tour continues straight across and into **Essex Street West**. Facing is a real old-style Dublin corner shop, Grattan's Stores. Let it be preserved! You might buy something here out of respect, and take a break. Outside Grattan's is one of the stones that shows where the walled city's original gates stood; see if you can spot others. Across the road is a very new development, built on top of a recently excavated medieval and Viking site. Only that was not all the archaeologists found. Underneath all the Danish DIY they found what seems to have been an Anglo-Saxon house. Whole chapters of history and rousing songs may have to be re-written.

Next, swing down into **Lower Exchange Street,** which becomes **Blind Quay** (because it did not actually face onto the river). See the round apartment tower — it's built in honour of the old gate-tower here called Isolde's Tower. You will end up down on the quays proper from where you can see the front — only now it's the back — of the Dublin Viking Adventure (see page 76). This was a church, before that it was the very famous Smock Alley Theatre, and it looked very much the same outside then as the way you see it today. Of course, then it did not have a wonderful sculpted Viking boat, made by Betty Maguire, outside on the path ... sit down here and have a rest.

Walk up **Fishamble Street**. Imagine it lined with stinky fishy stalls, baskets and creels, and saltwater splashed everywhere. That is what it looked like for hundreds of years — fish were landed and sold here from at least the 1300s and it was a principal street from the port of Dublin up to the city of Dublin (not far). The quay on your right is called Wood Quay — it was built on marshy ground fenced in with strong wood supports. But it's most famous because of the sad and hopeless campaign in the 1970s to save the area as a rare excavation site. Instead everything was dug up and the Corporation built their shiny show-off offices. You can visit these on weekdays.

Watch for more pavement sculptures outside the offices — Viking combs and knives, spears and so on. A little park is planned on the left, near the site that Handel's glorious 'Hallelujah!' Christmas chorus was first heard. You can see the plaque: 'Messiah: April 13 1741'. To commemorate the event there's a free performance here in the open every Christmas.

Christ Church is on your right (see page 54), and Dublinia is further up (see page 75). There was once a little passage called Hell nearby, leading out of Christ Church Lane. Maybe it was the Hill of Dublin that had driven voyagers mad — anyway you are on the great ridge of old Dublin town now. From here turn into **Lord Edward Street** and cross the road onto the junction of **Castle Street** and **Werburgh Street**. **St Werburgh's,** the stern-looking newly polished church facing the chip shop had its tall spire chopped off after 1798 in case rebels used it to spy on the Castle. It's famous for holding the body of Lord Edward Fitzgerald — and also that of his killer, Major Sirr. Those guns in front are not guns, they are early fire-fighting equipment; churches were where early firemen mustered. St Werburgh? An Anglo-Saxon female saint and princess.

Turn down in Castle Street. On your left, No. 4 is the headquarters of Dublin Civic Trust in what was a very old shoemakers' shop. On weekdays you can go in and learn about architectural and conservation plans in Dublin. Next door is a timber remnant from the days of timbered beam houses (think English Tudor) — it's the only trace of these kind of buildings left in Dublin. The little lane with the gates is close to where Jonathan Swift was born though no trace of the actual house remains. Further down watch out for the little bridge newly constructed to cross what is now an imaginary moat, but was once a very deep one. You could take time out here to sit in the Castle's elegant Dubhlinn Park built over the Poddle's black pool. Alternatively, back onto **Dame Street**, another tiny watery park is the Millennium park on your right with its three stone ladies who are actually supposed to be Wood, Metal and Stone — one out of three isn't bad. Look left at the house that has a delightful and puzzling inscription (clue: it's not indignant) 'Sick and Indigent Roomkeepers' Society'. Count the chimney pots and think of all the poor maids and chimney boys who had to keep the flues and grates clean. You are now approaching **South Great George's Street**. End of tour — time for food! There are lots of restaurants on this street, but, if it's Sunday, why not have a really interesting food treat in the Good World Chinese restaurant — they do *dim sum* (plus all other kinds of Chinese dishes) and it's packed with many Dublin Chinese people. On the other hand, you could try Yamamori for Japanese noodles. Back in Temple Bar there are dozens of restaurants, some of which are covered in the Shopping chapter of this guide.

Georgian Walk with Statues and Park

This walk is a bit of a treasure hunt, really. Sometime after we began painting animals on the walls of caves, humans started making statues — and we have never stopped since. Central Dublin has hundreds of sculptures old and new, funny and po-faced. This walk tells you where some of them are. It also takes you through the best-preserved Georgian square in the city. Here the eighteenth-century townhouse (the original owners had country houses too, you can bet on it) architecture is tall and elegant and seemingly all the same — until you spot the different details. You will be able to explore the inside of one house when you are finished walking.

Ten odd or gruesome things that happened in Dublin:

In 1900 a steam train shot through its buffers and came through the outer walls of Harcourt Street station, looking like a Magritte picture

Payment was made to a Great Angel, a Small Angel and a Dragon for services rendered to St Patrick's in 1509 (They were actors in a miracle play)

A suggested recipe for roast child was published in Dublin in 1729. This was the infamous Modest Proposal of Jonathan Swift

In 1784 Dublin's first aerial passenger — a cat — took off by balloon for the Isle of Man, followed months later by a human, Richard Crosbie, who only made it to Clontarf

A horseshoe spark ignited a pile of gunpowder by the Liffey docks in 1596. 120 people were blown up

The first camel arrived in Dublin in 1105, a gift for the High King from the King of Scotland

Ringsend boasted its own floating chapel in 1832, with room for 400 worshippers, some of whom preferred to pray in the rigging

The Liffey froze over for two months in 1338 and in 1739. Carnivals took place on the ice

In 1197 the city of Dublin was excommunicated by the Pope who was quarreling with King John

In 1773 a cook was sentenced to be boiled alive in St Stephen's Green for poisoning several persons

Begin on the Grand Canal bank between Leeson Street and Baggot Street, down near the lock gates on the north side. You can cross on the narrow passageways — see how the gates work? On the south side there is a jetty for canal boat moorings. Sit beside the thrush-brown man who is taking up a lot of space on one of the benches, but mind his hat! This statue is of Patrick Kavanagh, a poet who loved this canal and wrote about it. John Coll is the sculptor.

Go over Baggot Street (it used to lead to the public gallows) and stay by the canal until you come to Upper Mount Street. The church in the middle of the road is called the Peppercannister — you can figure out why yourself. It was built so the smart people round about did not have to travel into town on a Sunday. Classical concerts are held here sometimes. By now you can see the next statue. The little girl swinging on rope out of the lamp post was made by Derek Fitzsimons for the Dublin Millennium in 1988 to celebrate all the street-games and street-children of Dublin. A little further on, by the side of the church is a house used as an office building. See the poised little figure on top of the porch? She's called Birdy and she was made by Rowan Gillespie.

Birdy is certainly related to another statue that you can detour to see before reaching Merrion Square park — if you want to see a real hero. Go further down the canal until you come to the last bridge. The tall building facing on your left is called Treasury Building — see the little climber (also by Rowan Gillespie) halfway up the huge wall of the building? Cat burglar or nude Everest-climber, this statue really appeals to commuters using this route into town because it's the most inquired-after sculpture in Dublin. It's called 'Aspiration'. The building itself was once a glory spot (or hell-hole) of the 1916 rebellion when insurgents were trapped here, in Boland's Mill, under the leadership of Éamon de Valéra. This road was also once famous because its builder grew Jerusalem artichokes along here.

Backtrack up to Merrion Square. The park belonged, as all these Square gardens did, to the owners of the houses around it who let their children and dogs play here. It's a beautiful park that has lots of trails and is not at all straightforward. Here is what you have to find:

- **the grassy knoll** — looks smooth enough to roll on ...
- **the bog oak garden** with the big head of the South American liberator Bernardo O'Higgins — a gift from the people of Chile
- **Tribute Head** by the English sculptor Elizabeth Frink, given to the park by Amnesty International when Nelson Mandela was still in jail in South Africa
- **the tiny white flower garden** facing the National Maternity Hospital, with a poem by Eavan Boland — this commemorates all little babies who do not live
- **bust of Michael Collins**, the freedom fighter (he has been spotted on occasion with a smoking cigarette in his mouth)
- **lady with a harp** — she's Éire of course (by Jerome Connor)
- **a tragic trio called 'Victims'** — an anti-war group by Andrew O'Connor

> • **the playwright Oscar Wilde**, by Danny Osborne — this one is hard to miss because, (a) people are always climbing up and posing with him, (b) it is brightly coloured, (c) it is near the entrance closest to town, (d) it is near the playground. It also faces number 1 Merrion Square which was Oscar Wilde's parents' house (see page 81).

All these sculptures are very different in style. The Chilean hero is like a Roman emperor, the victims like a religious group. Do you think they are all in their best positions? Would you like to know how sculptures are cast? (See page 234.) Would you like to try it out yourself? (See page 272.) Take time out to look at any sculptures anywhere you come across them. For more trails see the book list.

Now — you deserve a break. Cross to No. 29 — where Upper Mount Street meets Merrion Square, diagonally opposite from Oscar. This house is open as a museum of a Georgian house interior. Read about it on page 60. You can eat here, or in the National Gallery restaurant, or walk over to Grafton Street and avail of one of its burger outlets.

Ten places outside the city for a special occasion Sunday lunch:

All of the places listed below are chosen because they combine good value and choice for a set lunch price, have children's menus or serve half-portions, and are located in or near interesting surroundings, with parking. For these reasons booking is essential.

Deer Park Hotel, Howth. Past the Castle and towards the golf course. (Tel: 832 2624)

Malahide Castle Restaurant, Malahide Castle. (Tel: 846 3027)

Portmarnock Hotel: Links Brasserie, Strand Road. (Tel: 846 0611)

The Corn Loft, Julianstown, County Meath. (Tel: 041-9829133)

The Buttergate Restaurant, Millmount, Drogheda. (Tel: 041-9834759)

Finnstown House Hotel, Lucan. (Tel: 628 0644)

Killakee Restaurant, Killakee Road, Rathfarnham. (Tel: 493 2645)

Fitzpatrick's Castle, Killiney, Dublin. (Tel: 284 0700)

Roundwood Inn, Roundwood, County Wicklow (Tel: 281 8107)

Hunters Hotel, Rathnew, County Wicklow. (Tel: 0404-40106)

Chapter 5

Rivers and Canals

The outings in this chapter have been designed so that you can walk some, cycle some, or take a car to a starter point and carry on by foot or bike. Brave people might do the full canal trips by bike in a day — they are about 13 miles one way. The Liffey trip is divided into sections and some of it is notional — having been written before certain new developments, like the Millennium Liffey Boardwalk and the Spencer Dock Development, were in place. The Liffey is no stranger to new designs however. It has been changing ever since humans first threw their hurdles across it and it is well able for the twenty-first century.

River Trips

You may have a river flowing through your back yard or, better still, underneath your floorboards. However, such rivers are not included here — they are your own, private rivers and you can trace them to their sources yourself and write your own guide/s. The Poddle river is referred to several times elsewhere in this book, so it isn't here either. Neither will you find any of Dublin's lost rivers in here — such as the Steine or the Pill. Sadly, a lost river is not in the same league as the Blue Nile.

The Liffey — Central and North

This tour offers:

a)   *a short walk from the Viking era, to the rich eighteenth century, to modern moneybags.*

b)   *a car trip to the deep sea docks.*

The very first observation of this trip can be made any time you are walking down D'Olier Street in the direction of Trinity College. That little bit of shrubbery in front of the Garda station shows where the southern bank of the Liffey was when Dublin was Danish. The Vikings beached and put up a Long Stone to show that they had claimed the place. (The American plaque on the moon is similar if rather more tactful.) The Long Stone lasted until the 1790s. Now there's a sculpture on the site and a pub down to the left called The Longstone. Back in Viking times people went oyster-fishing here when the tide was out — it was a seaside area then.

Dublin city has been creeping further down and over the original river bank ever since, until the mud-green Liffey you see now is a tame beast flowing between nice strong walls. It's still tidal all the way to Watling Bridge, by Guinness's brewery, which is really quite far into the city. Old photographs of Dublin show sailing ships' masts as far up as O'Connell Bridge. But three bridges have since been built and they have pushed any shipping business further down to the mouth of the river.

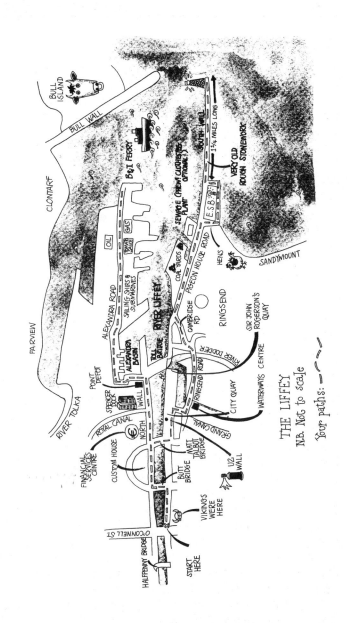

THE LIFFEY
N.B. Not to scale

Your paths: ~ ~ ~

Start your tour proper at **Custom House Quay**. If you have time you can visit the Custom House Visitors Centre (see page 66). Liberty Hall, the little piece of Manhattan on your left, was built in 1965. It's the home of many trade unions, just like the first Liberty Hall which was burnt down in 1916.

Londoner James Gandon designed the Custom House, and its construction lasted from 1781 to 1791. The people who were supposed to benefit from the new Custom House, tradesmen and merchants, were furious because it seemed to them at too great a distance from the city — it was outside 'Burgherland'. So they hired a mob to fill in the foundation trenches. The weather turned out grand and sunny so the mob gave up and swam in the trenches instead. However, Gandon carried a sword whenever he came to visit the site — just in case.

The Custom House is built of granite and Portland stone and cost about half a million pounds — an awful lot in those days. It was burnt out in 1921 but the outside was mostly unharmed. So you can still see the river gods' heads on the frieze. The word 'custom' then also meant imports and exports (as it still does now) and cattle were big business; look out for the friendly bulls' heads over the centre pillars. At the back of the Custom House are four statues representing Europe, Asia, Africa and America, but nothing, not even a kangaroo, from Australia, which was then, officially, only three years old.

Cross carefully over to the river side of the Financial Services Centre, just past the Custom House. On both sides of the river great glassy blocks of banks are 'moored' here just like the Viking longships — and for exactly the same reasons. But the real docks have left lots of traces.

Just look at the ancient mechanical hauling monster that straddles the road. Everything from tea to bananas, bacon to spices, Irish oak to Italian marble were loaded or unloaded along both sides of the river. Turn in by the triumphal arch on your left — an original gateway — and you will see the lock that once allowed boats into George's Dock and, further on, into the Inner Dock. Now these docks are great watery spaces surrounded by offices and apartments, populated by small cute seagulls eating from financial wizards' outdoor lunches. In summer it's a very pleasant place to sit out on benches, or stroll. It's not exactly Venice, or even Amsterdam, but it certainly has a marine quality. The handsome bars are called Harbourmaster's Bar and Fisherman's Wharf.

The great long low building that stretches alongside George's Dock, parallel to the river is, for the moment, called Stack A. Once it was a tobacco store and in 1856, it hosted one of the biggest parties ever held in Dublin, welcoming over 3,600 soldiers home from the Crimean War, with a slap-up dinner. It's a fine piece of industrial architecture and perhaps by the time you are reading this it will have become the museum and exhibition space for which it has been set aside.

Further down the river bank, North Wall Road, is Spencer Dock, another monster space under the management of Dublin Docklands Development Authority. In 1999 it had more cranes than any other site in Ireland has ever had. The rest of this trip is recommended as a car trip only (unless the Spencer people include a cycle-track). It's an odd little trip, taking in the deep sea docks. Continue past The Point Depot. This huge concert/theatre building was developed from warehouses. It has its own heli-pad for rock stars now; it used to have a running goods-railway.

Turn left at the roundabout and head down for the docks. There are two entrances, one is at Alexandra Road and the other is a few hundred yards up from this, on the same side — you can take either. Once you get past the custom police you will have one of the weirdest trips possible in Dublin. Everywhere there are oil tanks, gas tanks, warning notices — it's like a radioactive settlement on the moon. Not at all pretty but you can get an unusual

view of the city ticking over. At the end you can see the
two arms of Dublin port stretched out — the North Bull
Wall with its starboard green lighthouse trying to touch the
port-red Poolbeg lighthouse on the South Wall.

The ferries leave from here, and further back towards
the city, at Alexandra Basin, are the docks for visiting
monsters. Navy ships, submarines and sail training ships
from many nations make occasional courtesy calls and
some have conducted tours. These are advertised in the
papers, though it's usually the sailors in uniform around
the city centre that are the giveaway. Head back the
same way that you came. The custom police will
probably wave you through, but then again you could be
a smuggler....

The Liffey — South Wall

This trip starts at the south side of the Matt Talbot Bridge,
facing the City Arts Centre. Continue on down the
dockside — be careful, the traffic is fast here because this
is a southside shortcut. This district is called City Quay.
All the pubs along the quays traditionally had special
licences to open at seven o'clock in the morning for the
people who worked on the docks. Look out for one
called Dockers, behind it is Windmill Lane. Go down
here to make the pilgrimage to the U2 Wall. For years
fans have been writing strange and wonderful messages
on the walls beside Windmill recording studios, first
serious home of the Dublin band. Have a read and add a
bit of your own if you have the equipment. Fishing and
dredger boats and sometimes the odd navy ship, moor
along here by Sir John Rogerson's Quay, called after the
man who built its walls. It was once a very busy quayside;
ship's biscuit was baked along here and there were wine
shops and food shops.

The very tip of the quay is where the tiny Liffey
pedestrian ferry made its triangular trip for six hundred
years, between 1386 and 1984. Then the powers that be

zapped it and built the East Link toll bridge downriver instead. This bridge is free for walkers and cyclists but cars have to pay. A toll may be a nice medieval notion but the former ferry that only cost 10p was nicer again. What *is* fun is to be nearby when the bridge is raised for shipping. It all happens in less than five minutes.

Go round the Grand Canal Basin (see Windsurfing, page 313) onto Ringsend Road and into Ringsend village. On the way are huge dilapidated warehouses and factories, museum pieces that show how busy the river and canal traffic once was. On your right is the Waterways Visitors Centre that will tell you everything you need to know about the canals (see page 38).

Turn left at Ringsend village into Thorncastle Street and right into Cambridge Road and then go on to Pigeonhouse Road. Ringsend village used to be a small fishing village cut off from the city of Dublin by the marshes round the mouth of the Dodder. In the 1600s, however, a pier was built out along where you walk at this part of the tour, and all the ships which used to dock in Dalkey harbour landed here. Unfortunately Oliver Cromwell was in one of them, in August 1649. The giant double candy-stick in front of you, the Pigeonhouse or Poolbeg power station, was not called after a flock of homing pigeons, but after an enterprising gentleman named Mr Pidgeon (though the spelling isn't the same). He built a refreshment place on the pier for travellers and day-trippers who wanted to see the South Wall being built. It was quite a journey out here across the Dodder slobs from Dublin. This had to be done in a special, tough vehicle called a Ringsend Carr.

Pigeonhouse Road is now chopped into several lengths. One piece, taken at the roundabout, bends back towards the city and leads past old coastguard cottages to the Poolbeg yacht club. Another is found by following the signs for the South Port and taking a left turn. You can hardly see the Liffey here anymore because there are so many industrial outcrops and containers in the way.

However, you can see many boats or ships on the move, and you will see more later. Also you might see the number 1 bus, not a common sight for Dubliners these days; it goes to the power station. You come to the sewage treatment plant which is a very smelly area — the gulls love it though. There's not so much for them in the Pigeonhouse military fort which you actually pass through. You can still see the remains of the walls and some of the garrison houses are still lived in. The soldiers who lived here were scavengers themselves, most notably in the 1790s. Unfortunate locals were press-ganged on several occasions and taken on board ship to fight in destinations abroad. Ringsend Robin Hoods rescued quite a few of them in hold-ups.

Ahead of you from here are the gates of the power station and in its grounds you can see the original handsome Pigeonhouse Hotel. School groups can visit the station (see Joining In, page 232) but right now go round it, past the landfill park on your right called the Irishtown Nature Park, past the rocks, past three beaches (that is three at low tide; two the rest of the time) and on to the start of the South Wall proper.

Going out on the wall is an experience not to be missed. It's a tiny 'road' that goes two miles right out to the Poolbeg lighthouse in the middle of Dublin Bay, the most isolated part of the city. This Wall has been here since 1761 and was built in order to deepen Dublin's harbour. The enormous flagstones are virtually impossible for bikes and really the only way is to walk out. The journey seems more like a boat ride than a walk, with a panoramic view of the city and port. You will see all sorts of sea birds — cormorants, terns and oystercatchers to name but a few. There's also excellent seafishing from the rocks for mackerel, bass, eel and sea-trout. There's even an heroic swimming club out here, called the Half Moon. *Do not* go out on a rough day, and always come back the way you went!

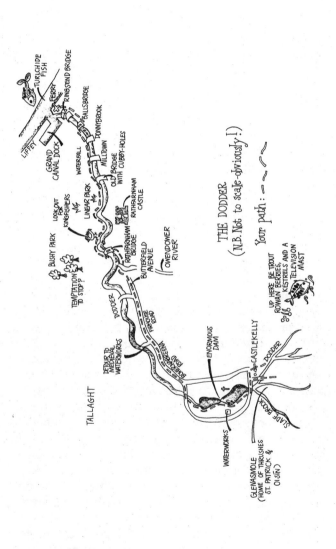

THE DODDER
(N.B. Not to scale–obviously!)

Your path: ～～

TURLOUGHIDE FISH
RINGSEND BRIDGE
FERRY
LIFFEY
GRAND CANAL DOCK
BALLSBRIDGE
WATERFALL
DONNYBROOK
MILLTOWN
OLD BRIDGE WITH CUBBY-HOLES
LOOK OUT FOR KINGFISHERS
BUSHY PARK
LINEAR PARK
RATHFARNHAM CASTLE
TEMPTATION TO STOP?
RATHFARNHAM BRIDGE
BUTTERFIELD AVENUE
OWENDOWER RIVER
DODDER
UP HERE BE TROUT ROWAN BERRIES, KESTRELS AND A TELEVISION MAST
DETOUR TO MEDIEVAL WATERWORKS
BOHERNABREENA ROAD
ENORMOUS DAM
CASTLEKELLY
TALLAGHT
DODDER
SLADE BROOK
WATERWORKS
GLENASMOLE (HOME OF THRUSHES ST. PATRICK & OISÍN)

The Dodder

This trip takes you from the mouth of the Dodder river to
its source in the Dublin mountains (a distance of roughly
15 miles), so whatever else you do, bring *food* and *boots*.
You will need our map or a better Ordnance Survey one
(O.S. 16/50): It's really worth going the whole way,
because if you ever get stuck with a bore who has climbed
Everest or traced the Nile to its source, the Dodder trip
could be your best attack.

There is a meeting of the waters of the Liffey, the Grand
Canal and the Dodder and that is your starting point. You
cross Ringsend Bridge (straight out from Pearse Street) and
go left down Thorncastle Street to see this H_2O junction.
The Grand Canal docks are just opposite. There's a tale
that during a great medieval famine in 1331, monstrous
fish called Turlchides, between 30 and 40 feet long, turned
up right here on the Dodder. Presumably Ringsend
fishermen caught them and brought them to be carved
into Turlchideburgers on Fishamble Street.

What is no fishy tale is that the Dodder in those days
was much wider and shallower, making a marshland out of
the area. Ringsend Carrs, bringing passengers and parcels
from the Pigeonhouse docks, used to splash merrily
through the mire before any bridges were built. When
they were finally constructed, the Dodder bridges had a
habit of floating out to sea in rough weather. Even now, in
spells of bad weather, the Dodder gets a mean swell on it.

Take the south bank (left, if that is any help) from
Ringsend to Ballsbridge, which will bring you under the
railway and past Lansdowne rugby grounds. Near the
bridge at Ballsbridge and further up river at Herbert Park
you will see some of the small, pretty, redbrick cottages
that are found all over Dublin 4. They were built over 100
years ago as part of the Pembroke estate.

Cross over the bridge at Ballsbridge to the north bank
and go past the pompous swell of apartments and hotel

complex. Before this development, Johnston Mooney and O'Brien had a bakery here and before the bakery there was a calico works, turning out the stuff for making small girls' and housemaids' pinafores.

Continue on up by Herbert Park. Near Donnybrook bridge is Bective sports grounds, once the site of the Great Mad Crazy Donnybrook Fair, which gave a lot of people sore heads every August from 1204 onwards. The noise was too much for one sensible Victorian lion in 1846; he escaped and rolled around like a puppy in the Dodder before being captured again.

Cross at the bridge. You can either go up Beaver Row on the south bank, a pretty country-type road, or if you want to mess with water take the path on the north side, by crossing the iron footbridge. You can get down to the first of the Dodder weirs here, and there's an accessible weedy island. Good in very dry weather for climbing on and getting up close to the duck families that are learning to swim; in wet weather the weir looks spectacular.

At Clonskeagh take either bank to Milltown. On this stretch of river from Clonskeagh as far as Old Bawn in Tallaght there used to be fifty mills and factories using Dodder water power. There were flour mills, iron works, woollen mills, cotton and saw mills. The more you can get right down to the banks, the more of the stubs of these old mills, and their mill races, you will find. You can plot them on your own map of the Dodder. The good news is, despite the collection of trash and plastic bags that floodwaters leave on the banks and shrubs, the Dodder is far less polluted now than it was in the nineteenth century. Recent surveys have found otter spraints this far down the river. That would be some prize, spotting an otter!

Milltown has two bridges. The old one, a medieval one, doesn't lead anywhere particular except across the river, but it's in perfect shape and has a pedestrian cubbyhole where in bygone days you dived for cover if a 'Hell's Angel' dogcart tried to ram you. There are actually three bridges if you count the huge railway viaduct — the Nine Arches which once carried the Harcourt Line. Soon it will carry the southern branch of the LUAS light railway.

Go up the hill by the Dropping Well pub, and turn left at the top, down the curvy old road with its clock-house and back to the river again. This is a beautiful stretch of the Dodder Linear Park as far as Bushy Park at Rathfarnham. Here the habitats of river birds begin in earnest though you can spot kingfishers, herons and water hen as far down as Donnybrook and Ballsbridge. On the road alongside, one of the old gates to Rathfarnham Castle sits in the middle of nowhere. The original castle was built because Rathfarnham wasn't at all a safe place to live. Dublin and Wicklow chieftains operated a Patriotic Front with Bonny and Clyde-type raids on the Pale, and one of their chief haunts was Rathfarnham. However, there's only one ghost on record here, a retriever that drowned in a pond, and if you want to look for it, go ahead. The Castle is well worth a visit (see page 51).

You can criss-cross the river on bridges and stepping-stones all along the way to Rathfarnham Bridge. Fishing is popular here — check with the Dodder Angling Association (see Angling, page 310). Cross over Rathfarnham Bridge and go on as before. The Owendower River joins the Dodder here, and the Linear Park ends at the next bridge but you can carry on from there. Bushy Park, on the right, is a handsome park, but for river tracking purposes your first ordeal is on the left, on the south bank. It involves following the river instead of the comfy road. There is a track which leaves you out at Kilvere on Butterfield Avenue. Then you can wheel down the hill, straight through the next crossroads and along Firhouse Road. The river hugs the road for a bit then swings back behind the GAA grounds (there's a path for investigation). It's a goodish way to the next glimpse of water but it's easy cycling along the cycle-track. Of course if you had big waders, you wouldn't have to leave the river at all, but deep water lies ahead anyway, as you will discover.

The road is being built up to take the Southern Cross section of the M50. Stay straight. At Morton's pub there's a little housing estate called Mount Carmel. Go round the back and you will see another interesting Dodder waterfall with a footbridge across it. At one time you could see a small stream here (it was dry on my last visit). Only it wasn't a stream. Right here, in 1244, the Sheriff of Dublin said 'Dig' and they dug. They dug right across the fields to Tallaght and made a channel between the Dodder and the Poddle. You could see it take off here with its ancient stonework and strange sluice-works and you could follow its course on a map. The reason for it was that there simply was not enough water in Dublin for everyone to have their yearly scrub. The city kept growing and the poor little Poddle did its best, but it just couldn't cope with the demand. This little artificial stream — called the City Watercourse — made an enormous difference, and everyone was happy for another 500 years.

Back to the tour and on to Old Bawn. Old Bawn was famous for its Old Bawn House, on the right, where, it is said, coaches with headless horses and horsemen drop by regularly and deposit an archbishop (with a head) who makes a quick tour of the premises he built here in 1630, and then they all 'head' off again. Out in the back of Old Bawn House, by the river, there were some grim executions in 1816. You can see the mantelpiece from poor Old Bawn House in the 1916 room in the National Museum, and a hoary old thing it is too.

Off again down Bohernabreena Road to the Bridge. The Dodder is very strong here, full of bounce and vigour, coming out of the Bohernabreena reservoir. The entrance to the reservoir and waterworks is just over the bridge. Officially you are required to have a visitor's pass; in practice Dublin Corporation are not unwelcoming to tidy, environmentally-minded people.

If you get in, keep to the right or west side of the lakes. You aren't allowed to swim in them but you can fly-fish. There are two rather enormous dams — well, reasonably enormous — complete with streams, pipes and gurglings everywhere. These waterworks were built in 1883, then — as with the City Watercourse — a sign of expanding Dublin. There's a grassy slope down from the dam that is heaven to roll down, no matter how silly this looks.

The whole river valley looks like a little piece of Canada, especially in autumn, but as far as stories go it was one of the first places in Ireland to be inhabited. The valley is called Glenasmole, the Valley of the Thrushes — and if you believe everything in print, well, whistle a certain tune and Fionn Mac Cumhail and Oisín and the rest of the pack will come bounding out of the bushes. Bohernabreena was a magic fort with gorgeous food, and Glenasmole was one of their favourite pads, and indeed, as far as Oisín was concerned, it was nothing less than Texas. Oisín met St Patrick who had a very mean housekeeper. The housekeeper served them scraps rather than a meal. Oisín was highly insulted and lamented his Glenasmole where, he claimed, the rowan berries were bigger than bread rolls, the ivy was bigger again, and the blackbirds were the size of St Patrick's roast beef dinner. You can check out his claim for yourself. He did not mention the cheeky black-and-white dippers who hang out near the curtain of water between the lakes. And he had never heard of the purple rhododendron that blooms here in late spring.

If you have waited until now to eat, you have done the right thing. That done, you are fortified for the mountainy part of the Dodder exploration. Continue along the reservoir path out the far end of the valley. Take the Castlekelly road and keep going up. On the right is Kippure mountain. On the other side of it the Liffey rises, then takes a much more roundabout route to meet up again with its mountain twin, the Dodder. Now if you look at the OS map you will see the problem, which has been carefully kept from you up to now.

Which is the *real* Dodder? Does it matter? I followed the middle stream, Cot Brook, upriver by shingle pools, rowan trees and gold (it looked like) in the river bed. And, yes, I did see the stream pop out of the bog, just like the books say, quite near to the television mast. But be warned, it's at least a two-hour trek from the road up and back, so if you want to leave this journey until another day don't feel ashamed. You can drive all the way to this point the next time. *Do not* go up on a foggy day — you could easily get lost. Be careful of green boggy bits and *always* keep by the stream. Most important, always travel in a group, and *make sure* you have told several people exactly where you are going.

The Canals

The northside of Dublin has the Royal Canal and the southside has the Grand Canal — in this they are equal. However, the southside had its first (in 1779), then the northside stole the old blueprints of the Grand Canal and plotted the Royal Canal from them. But because the two waterways were so close to each other all the way to the Shannon, neither of them could get an upper edge on the market of passengers and goods. Each had its big barges pulled along — this was before steam, remember — by horses. If you have read *The Wind in the Willows* it is all in there. The last straw for the canals, and one that saved umpteen tow-horses' backs, was the advent of the railways.

But as everyone who crosses either of the canals on their way to town knows, they are far from dead, what with fishing, canoeing, swimming (illegal) in summer and the war between the dumpers and the cleaner-uppers. Since most of us have a right-angled relationship with the canals it is no harm to try a parallel one for a change, and travel along the towpaths. You can take a car to a highlighted bridge/road and walk part of the way or better

still travel by bike if you want to cover all the ground at
once. It's best not to pick a day after a run of rainy
weather unless you have wellingtons, chains on your
wheels and an extraordinarily sunny temper. Pick a good
dry day — farther up the canals these towpaths are still
what most roads once were — dirt-tracks.

A smart move would be to visit the Waterways
Centre (see page 38) before going on the canal
trips. Doing it afterwards might be a Plan B.

Part of the Millennium water celebrations-to-be,
include the building of a 5-km cycle-track along the
Grand Canal.

The Grand Canal

Get right down to where the Grand Canal enters the Liffey,
going down Sir John Rogerson's Quay until you can go no
further. The canal docks are a splendid place, with strange
outlets, strong sea-locks and a great open-dock harbour
that gets used for boat building, windsurfing and canoeing.
When the docks were opened here in 1796 up to 100,000
people came to celebrate. Now, a lot of new building is
happening around here, with tall apartments shooting up
like mushrooms. But Grand Canal Dock needs some more
imaginative input before it can become a busy waterside,
full of small workshops, houseboats, restaurants, and
children's facilities, as in the very popular Camden Docks
in London. You could write to Dublin Corporation or any
of the Dublin 4 TDs to ask why this is not happening yet.

Meanwhile the canal may not look its prettiest — but
don't be put off, it has covered a distance of 80-odd miles
from the River Shannon to get here. The grimy buildings
along the way are among Dublin's oldest industrial ones
and the canal dock area was the centre of the Dublin gas
industry. If you come along Hanover Quay you will pass a
street called Misery Hill (though some miserable git has

stolen the sign), which was once a leper colony, and afterwards a gallows place. If you stare down at the middle of the wide bridge (Pearse Street) you can see that at one time it could be raised — the joints are still there.

Cross over and up Grand Canal Quay. Floating on your left is the Waterways Centre — a must-do, but not right now.

Leave the docks part of the Grand Canal and travel up on the north, or right-hand side. This part of the canal, from Ringsend to Rialto, was really an afterthought. It's called the Circular Line and you can see why if you look at it on a map, though when travelling up the canal, walking or cycling, it seems as straight as a ruler.

You come up towards Baggot Street and Leeson Street bridges. You meet your first lock with its prim notice 'Not for Public Use'. There are thirty-six locks between Ringsend and the Shannon, with the canal ascending to its highest point at Robertstown, County Kildare, and levelling or descending after that. You may see the water-levels being changed in the locks; there's a greater chance of doing so in summer when cruisers use the canal.

Lock-keepers had a hard enough time in the early days — if a dead dog floated past they had to fish it out and bury it in their own gardens. As well as that they were each provided with a halbert to cope with vandals or patriotic saboteurs. There was plenty of that, especially outside the city; canal banks were broken open and boats smashed, as the miserable shareholders of the Grand Canal Company watching their stocks fluctuating for real. But the lock-keepers were also supposed to guard against simpler kinds of behaviour. Swimming or washing in the canal brought a fine of £1.2s.9d., and if your dog did the same, well, eleven shillings was the wet money due. The canal was opened over 200 years ago, in February 1779 to be exact, and in those days that was pretty hefty money. Needless to say, offenders were not easily caught.

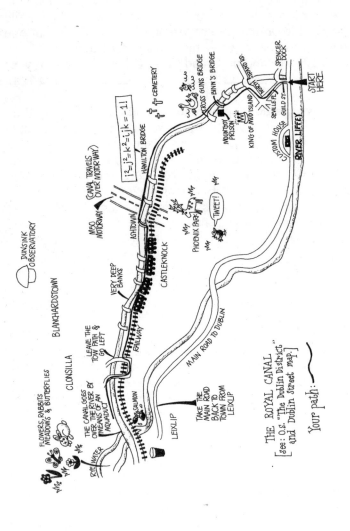

DUNSINK
OBSERVATORY

BLANCHARDSTOWN

CLONSILLA

FLOWERS, RABBITS
MEADOWS & BUTTERFLIES

THE CANAL GOES
OVER THE RIVER BY
MEANS OF AN
AQUADUCT

RYE WATER

LEIXLIP

SALMON

TAKE THE
MAIN ROAD
BACK TO
TOWN FROM
LEIXLIP

LEAVE THE
TOW PATH &
GO LEFT

RAILWAY

VERY DEEP
BANKS

CASTLEKNOCK

MAIN ROAD TO DUBLIN

PHOENIX PARK

TWEET!

ASHTOWN

M50
MOTORWAY

(CANAL TRAVELS
OVER MOTORWAY)

$i^2 \cdot j^2 = k^2 = i \cdot j \cdot k = -1!$

HAMILTON BRIDGE

CEMETERY

CROSS GUNS BRIDGE

BINN'S BRIDGE

MOUNTJOY
PRISON

KING OF MUD ISLAND

CUSTOM HOUSE

SEVILLE PL.

GUILD ST.

NORTH STRAND RD.

SPENCER
DOCK

START
HERE

RIVER LIFFEY

THE ROYAL CANAL
[see: O.S. "The Dublin District"
and Dublin street map]

Your path:

Most boat-handlers operate the locks themselves these days. There's a special 'key' that opens the sluices in the top lock. This lets the water through to fill the bottom so that it becomes level. A load of hand power is needed to push the gates open and the boats can then pass up or down. If there is a number of boats passing each other the operation takes quite a while, but nobody expects speed on the canals.

Go up the picture-bookish stretch of canal between Mount Street and Leeson Street. Patrick Kavanagh the poet, whose statue seat is by Baggot Street lock-gates, wrote lovingly of the place. He probably knew by name the goats that were once tethered here, on long iron chains.

On up to Charlemont bridge and Portobello. The handsome dark green building, picked out in white, was once one of the Grand Canal Grand Hotels, with its own harbour — now the grassy spot. There were four other hotels, at Sallins, Robertstown, Tullamore and Shannon Harbour. Even though stagecoaches were quicker, eighteenth- and nineteenth-century passengers liked the comfort and tranquillity of canal travel. It certainly was no candidate for speed warfare, not even for a water rat race. Early speeds averaged 2 mph, settled later at 4 mph, and when fly boats (narrower, with more frequent changes of horse) were introduced, a dazzling 9 mph was reached. (No one nowadays can imagine just how many horses were around in pre-engine days, but as a general rule, it was impossible to walk 100 yards without tripping over several horses. Even when you were on a boat.)

If you intend to follow the canal trail further, here at Portobello is a good place to get some supplies because you will need them. Canal passengers had mainly mutton and spud stews, kept on the boil in huge cauldrons. The boats — their seats were filled with chopped hay — were capable of carrying '15 uncrinolined passengers'.

Shake an 'uncrinolined' leg there and continue on the north bank, past the Institute of Education and up

Portobello Road, full of tiny redbrick cottages, up to
Clanbrassil Street bridge, where it's all change to the south
bank. Stay on that side until further notice.

When you come to Suir Road bridge, you will see a
green space on your right that is actually a dead canal.
This was the straight and narrow branch that once led into
the heart of the city — to the Grand Canal Basin, Basin
Lane and the Pipes. The Pipes of course led to Guinness's
brewery; Guinness were the last commercial users of the
canal, with barges afloat until 1950.

Continue on a comfortable towpath up Davitt Road —
at the next bridge there's a very cute and easily spotted
lock-house with its own footbridge. Change over to the
other side of the canal at this point. Between here and
Killeen's humpy bridge there are often several friendly and
curious wandering horses. You are approaching the
newest bridge (though it completely ignores the canal)
where the giant M50 road roars overhead.

Bridges are few from now on, so be sure you want to go
on once you have passed one — there's no accessible
road from the towpath along this stretch. This route
conducts you as far as Hazelhatch (in County Kildare) but
you can drop off at two points: Clondalkin (Ninth
Lock/Newlands Road), or the twelfth lock on the Lucan
Road. On a fine autumn day you cannot beat this section
of the canal and there are millions of juicy unclaimed
blackberries for the picking.

Clondalkin and Ballyfermot were villages far from the
centre of activities in canal-travelling days. Passengers
would have felt that they were in very rural settings by
now as they travelled further west. It can still feel that way
as you walk along the bank of the canal from here. There
are canal water filter beds for Guinness's brewery on the
north bank before Clondalkin — after Clondalkin,
whatever you do, don't take the north bank (on a bike at
any rate). It may look more tempting but after the locks
there is a dead end.

It's quite a stretch up to the twelfth lock (you will know it by the old pub) and here the advice changes. Cross *now* to the north bank, go down by the mill and the pub, squeeze your bike past the gate, and you are into the wildest and loveliest stretch of the canal as far as Hazelhatch. The twelfth lock and Hazelhatch have several moored houseboats which give them an air of watery business. You will pass under a handsome derelict bridge at Gollierstown. Nearby were limestone quarries which were used in the construction of the canal. Remember, *quarries are dangerous places because they can subside.* There are many waterbirds to be seen here, herons and moorhens abound. There's a prickly stretch just before Hazelhatch which you have to grin and bear, and then you arrive. A grand total of 13 miles from Ringsend that would have taken you 3½ hours in a horse-drawn canal boat. How long did it take you?

You can return the same way. If that doesn't seem like a good idea, turn left to Celbridge/Lucan, or right to Newcastle/Clondalkin, from where the main roads lead to town.

Fish you can find in the canals: Carp, Tench, Roach, Bream, Rudd, Perch, Eel and the dread Pike.

The Royal Canal

This trip from start to furthest point is approximately 13 miles. However, returning by the main road is shorter. The Royal Canal has had a bad deal — even today it's not fully boatworthy although it has much restored and it has got certain advantages over the Grand:

1. You get out of the city much more quickly.

2. It has got more character.

3. Its M50 meeting point is more exciting.

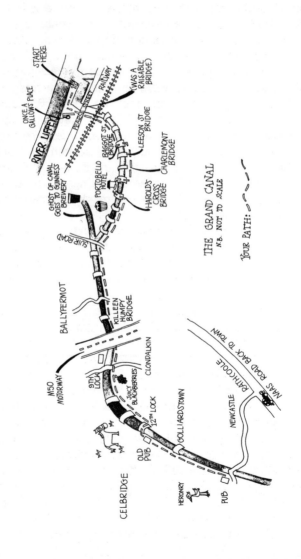

THE GRAND CANAL
N.B. NOT TO SCALE

YOUR PATH: ~ ~ ~

START HERE

ONCE A GALLOWS PLACE

RIVER LIFFEY

PEARSE STREET

RAILWAY

(WAS A RAISABLE BRIDGE.)

BAGGOT ST BRIDGE

LEESON ST BRIDGE

CHARLEMONT BRIDGE

PORTOBELLO HOTEL

GHOST OF CANAL GOES TO GUINNESS BREWERY

HAROLD'S CROSS BRIDGE

SUIR ROAD

BALLYFERMOT

KILLEEN HUMPY BRIDGE

M50 MOTORWAY

9TH LOCK

JUICY BLACKBERRIES

CLONDALKIN

12TH LOCK

GOLLIARDSTOWN

NEWCASTLE

RATH COOLE

NAAS ROAD BACK TO TOWN

CELBRIDGE

HERONRY

PUB

OLD PUB

Just for a starter peek take the north quays, past the Custom House down to Spencer Dock where the Royal Canal joins the Liffey without benefit of any fancy sea-docks. Take the time to marvel at the building around here — the Spencer Dock development is pure Hong Kong style. However, it does mean that you can't follow the canal from here. Further up, the GAA are building a brand new Canal End stand at Croke Park, which will cantilever itself over the canal and railway. Until all the works are complete the canal waterway cannot be properly restored; so this tour proper starts at Binns' Bridge at Drumcondra.

Here is what you miss up to this point: between Ballybough and the Liffey the canal looks dead fishy — sometimes you have to stare right down to see if there's any water left at all. But even before the canal was built this place was a bit off. North Strand was literally a strand once and this part of the city — up to the next road at Ballybough — was known as Mud Island. Gangsters, smugglers and con men of the pimpliest kind lived in rows of cabins here, in a flea-loud glade. There was even a king of Mud Island, a kind of Fagin character, and if you got the thumbs down from him you would shortly be found in a Mud Island dustbin. When some of the sea was reclaimed and new roads built in the eighteenth century, it was goodbye Mud Island. More recently the great new Cusack Stand in Croke Park said hello — it's visible for miles.

On the way up to Binns' Bridge at Drumcondra you might see, as I did, several rats swimming about. Whatever you feel about rats, they certainly don't look as unsavoury in the open, and they are wonderful swimmers, like tiny beavers. Binns' Bridge has a fine, clear nameplate on it — most of the other bridges' names are difficult to read, but almost all of them are called after directors of the Royal Canal Company. Mr Binns was the one allegedly responsible for stealing the plans of the Grand Canal. However, it took a long time to get the canal going — you see '1795' on this bridge but it wasn't finished until 1817, and it never saw anything like the amount of business that was evident on the Grand Canal.

After Binns' Bridge continue on the left or south bank. You can really feel the climb along the Royal, which of course is why the locks are so deep. It will be good to see it fully open again — it has been closed to through navigation, except for get-around canoes, since 1961.

The enormous place on your left is Mountjoy Prison. Brendan Behan's song, 'The Auld Triangle' commemorates both the bridge and the canal. Around the jail runs a ditch of water which turns it into a fortressy-looking place.

Past Mountjoy there is another dead canal to match the Grand Canal's one. This grassy bank goes all the way down to Broadstone Railway Station, which is dead too, come to think of it. Passengers for boats to Mullingar got on here (if they had dogs and were willing to pay, a first-class service was laid on for the beasts). If you go across the North Circular Road, in search of a place called Royal Canal Bank, you *will* find water — a kind of secret pond with resident waterbirds. Ironically, this was part of a waterworks, and nothing to do with the canal.

Continue on across the big bridge, Cross Guns Bridge, and down the towpath again. Mills old and new have settled in here for the duration; as indeed have certain others — in Glasnevin or Prospect cemetery away to the right with its imitation round tower which was built as Daniel O'Connell's monument (see page 88).

It's very pleasant from here on with the trains trundling by to Galway and you whizzing by on your bike or your legs. (You know how to whizz don't you?) A swan family or two, complete with elegant cygnets, can usually be found outside some cottages here on the towpath and they are usually grateful for scraps; but throw from a safe distance! Mostly the path goes under the humpy bridges and lets the roads go by overhead. Look out for Hamilton's bridge, or Broomebridge — it's clearly marked on the far side. A scholar indeed was William Rowan Hamilton.

While most people would be digesting their rice crispies on the way to work, his brain was digesting higher mathematics. Going under this bridge one morning in 1843 on his way to Dunsink Observatory he said 'Eureka!' and came out with: $i^2 = j^2 = k^2 = ijk = -1$. Whatever that means, apparently it's VI (Very Important) and known as a QE (Quaternion Equation); it is carved on the bridge.

You are on the south bank after Ashtown (which is also a good starter point for a walk or cycle) and the canal becomes very beautiful indeed. That is after the Royal's M50 experience which is much more dramatic than the Grand's. If you are walking or cycling you will find it, but if you are driving, travel along the Navan Road to the M50 roundabout. Go round it a few times and underneath you will see the canal being carried over the motorway, along with the railway. Magic! To get down there yourself, take the turn for Blanchardstown Village, turn in by Talbot Downs and the Castleknock Inn and park. You will find Talbot Bridge here; go back towards the city and suddenly you find yourself snug and safe but surrounded by the amazing spaghetti road complex.

The next stretch of Royal that *must* be walked (and I mean walked: it is too dangerous to cycle) is the stretch between Coolmine Road and Porterstown Road (both points of entry) that tries to find Australia. This stretch had to be dug through solid rock; it was known as the Deep Sinking and you will find the rock coming through the towpath. You can imagine the length of rope that the poor horses needed in order to tow their boats. Be very careful — especially if it's muddy. (Note to OPW/Dúchas: this section of the path should be paved for safety.) At Porterstown you will see a plaque erected to an unfortunate sixteen people who drowned here in 1845 when their barge struck rock and sank. Don't miss the tall building standing spookily by the north bank just here; it was a school, and judging by its appearance, it has lots of stories to tell.

The north path continues past Clonsilla to the north and Lucan to the south. After Collins Bridge there's a boat slip managed by the Royal Canal Amenity Group; if canoeing is your thing, they are worth talking to. You are now in County Kildare and can continue the rest of the way to Rye Valley which is where this trip ends.

This is how you know Rye Valley. It is a bit like the riddle of the duck's egg, going over water and under water. The water (canal) goes over the water (the Rye) by way of a water bridge or aqueduct. These weren't easy to make, believe me, even if Roman aqueducts were in mass production all over Europe. Far below you see the Rye sparkling in its own valley, and you can scramble down to the waterfall if you like. This area used bring walkers out into the Rye water-meadows which were a botanist's dream — full of wild flowers every spring and summer;

purple valerian, tickly teasel, smelly lady's bedstraw, guelder roses, and grass of Parnassus were some of the delicately-coloured flowers on show here. It should have been declared an environmental park but it's now a camp. At least houses haven't been built here yet, so maybe some of the seeds will survive.

At the next bridge, Louisa Bridge, leave the canal and turn left back into Leixlip (unless you want to take the train, the station is beside the bridge). Leixlip is the name the Vikings gave to this stretch of country. Lax-hlaup means salmon leap, which is what the fish had to do here if they wanted to get upriver and spawn.

The small Church of Ireland on the main street is over 1,000 years old and was part of a fort in those days. Say hello to the face on the tower — it has been around long enough.

The graveyard here is nice and old too, and across the river is Leixlip Castle, owned by a member of the Guinness family, which is all right because the first Guinness brewery was next door to the church in what is now the parking lot. In those old days Guinness wasn't brown and creamy, it was common old pale ale. The story goes that one day the head brewer fell asleep and burnt the day's quota of ingredients for the pale ale. He fed it to the locals who kept coming back for more of the lovely burnt stuff.

If you go to the end of the parking lot you will see the Leixlip Castle Folly facing you. Someone has painted a strange lady with a lute on one window eternally singing to the Liffey at Leixlip.

Time to head homewards now. Look out for the drainpipe house at the end of the village. If you take the main road back be careful — best to cycle on the path. Or you can take the road for Clonsilla, Blanchardstown and the Phoenix Park — which is signposted all the way.

beaches, islands, a barbecue and birds

Why is Dublin like Rio de Janeiro? Because there are sandy beaches a few miles out from the city centre. As a general rule beaches on the northside of Dublin are the better beaches, sandy and clean. They do get crowded though, and southside beaches have other things to recommend them. So you or your family might be interested in breaking out of old Sunday traditions and trying some new beach to explore.

There are three (well, two and a half) islands to be visited, one with its own king, birds to be noted and a recipe for a very easy beach barbecue — if you don't already have one.

Beaches

Howth

Buses: 31, 31A (for Sutton) from Lower Abbey Street; DART.

You won't be the first person to discover Howth. Ptolemy, the fourth-century Roman cartographer, put it on his map of the world as the island of Edros. It is a peninsula, Sutton Cross being where Howth almost becomes an island. The Fianna were supposed to love the place and the Danes certainly did. The great thing about Howth is that it has a variety of faces. In parts, it is as wild as Connemara, while in others, it is among the poshest places in Dublin. But at the bottom of it all Howth is a fishing village.

Balscadden Beach

— just past the harbour where the bus comes in. This is a small rather stony beach, but it is on the first leg of the climb to the summit, so if it is a warm day and you are going up, this is the only accessible beach for you on this trip.

Sutton Beach

— is on the other side of Howth facing south. This beach is sandy but very very shallow and there are lots of waders here, a spillover from Bull Island. You can explore the rocks — good pools too — and go right up to the Martello Tower. After this the Irish Sea currents open up so do not attempt to go further.

Howth Harbour and Marina

—there's a fishing fleet here and if you have the right manner or face, or whatever it takes, you might get taken on board a trawler for a look. It's a matter of asking questions and this just takes a bit of nerve. In the mornings (weekdays) you can buy really fresh fish down here. There is also good fishing off the end of the pier for mackerel and pollack. Ireland's Eye is the island facing you and there *are* boat trips (see Islands, page 205).

Howth Head

A proper cliff walk round Howth could take a whole day. You start the climb after Balscadden Bay. The road turns into a path and it's very easy to follow. On a clear day you can see the Mourne Mountains in County Down. But keep your eyes on the path and watch your dog if you have one. *Do not* go cliff climbing, it is extremely dangerous and there have been too many accidents already. Below you will see Puck's Rock, a huge rock split in two. Legend has it that a devil fell here when St Nessan waved a Bible at him. Further on is Casana rock, a proper caterwauling rock covered with seabirds. In May/July this part of the climb is covered with sea pinks and campions and is very beautiful. Do not pick them unless you live on a sea rock yourself. In 1855 the *Queen Victoria*, a steamboat, hit the rocks here in the middle of a snowstorm. On the inland side of the path are old quarries and lead mines.

As you reach the Summit, down a slope, you will see the Baily Lighthouse which guards the northern entrance to Dublin Bay. It was the last manned lighthouse in Ireland. At the Summit there are all sorts of things you can do. You can give up and catch a bus down — into the village. Or you can walk down about 50 yards towards the Summit Inn and over the road you will see some yellow bollards guarding the entrance to a grassy track. This is where the old Howth tram used to roll back down to the harbour. It was dismantled by CIÉ in 1959 but is now restored in the Transport Museum at Howth Castle. You can follow the track down.

If you want to go all the way to Sutton Strand, follow one of the paths towards the lighthouse and you will find a trail leading away to the right. There are more dramatic cliff-drops and in one place you can actually see how sand

is made. Then catch the 31A bus back to town or explore
the right-of-way paths around the Ben of Howth — this is
the hill area to your left as you face the village. It's wild
heathland and can be used as a good practice area for
mountain walking. If you can get a map all the better, as
the golf course seems to be expanding daily — you won't
get lost but you might get hit by a ball.

Portmarnock/Malahide

Buses: 32, 32A from Lower Abbey Street. Train from Connolly Station,
or DART to Sutton and take a feeder bus. Route: As for Howth, but
turn before Sutton at Baldoyle Road and continue straight on.

Portmarnock is Dublin city's nicest, nearest, beach —
which you could tell anyway from its being called Velvet
Strand. There are miles of strand, slight surf, breakwaters
and sometimes donkey rides in summer. There's a small
fair on the beach, and a crazy skyscraper Martello tower.
The far end, near the golf course, is quieter and has
glorious dune flowers in late spring. In 1930 and 1932 tiny
planes took off from the strand to make the first, and then
the first solo, flight east/west across the Atlantic.

If you follow the beach round the curve to Malahide
you leave some of the crowds behind — it gets rockier,
and the beach is not so perfect. But it's interesting to
explore because, (a) it leads to the Malahide estuary
which is always different and full of boat life and, (b) you
can hunt for fossils in the stretch of pale brown broken
stones. Also, much nearer to Malahide itself (near the
toilets) you will find coral fossils, and brachiopods fixed
in limestone rocks. They can be traced, if you are a fossil
freak.

Malahide was a port town in medieval times. After the
Dublin–Drogheda railway opened in 1844 it became a
seaside 'watering place' complete with promenades and
military bands. Malahide Castle and grounds are well
worth a visit (see page 50) as is St Doulagh's miniature
abbey (see page 57).

Donabate/Portrane

Bus: 33B from Eden Quay. Train from Connolly Station. Route: Swords Road and signposted turn.

Donabate is a wonderful beach with miles of dunes. It *is* that bit far away and a trip there needs an early start. Portrane is just beyond Donabate, on the same bus route. You go through Donabate, keeping left. You can stay with the Blue Flag sandy beach at the head of the village or, for the caves, take the right turn by the sea and go to the end, to the Martello tower. These little shingle beaches are *not* for bathing; they aren't particularly attractive either, but *when the tide is fully out and only then*, you can go down and explore the caves. Because the sea fills them at high tide, you will find sea anemones clinging like wine gums to the cave walls and roofs. You will also find white shreds, hanging spookily and bat-like from the roof. Examine this find carefully — it's what Nature has made out of human nature. The cliff path walk to Donabate carries a safety warning. Just in front of this beach a tragic shipwrecking happened in 1854 and 347 people drowned. Do not go here without adult supervision and *always* remember the tides. The island is Lambay, which is not within reach of ordinary mortals (see Islands, page 206).

Thanks to the dunes these beaches are ideal for barbecues on summer evenings. Here is a very simple **barbecue menu** that works well for everywhere.

> Bring (for ten people) 3 lb of sausages; 10 buttered bread rolls; 10 tomatoes; tomato ketchup; 2 large onions (optional); 1 packet of margarine for frying; apples; chocolate biscuits; minerals; frying pan (large); and at least *one* knife.
>
> Everything should fit into four rucksacks which can be shared around. For the fire, either cheat and bring a camping stove, or bring matches, firelighters and newspapers. Choose a sheltered dune area. Find flat stones from someone else's barbecue and make a square hearth that your frying pan will sit on. Collect twigs, paper rubbish and any driftwood from along the beach and build a fire. When the fire is well lit and glowing, melt the margarine in the pan and fry the sausages and tomatoes. Stick them in the buttered rolls with sauce and some raw onion. It's very fast and the food will be gorgeous. You can keep the fire going for warmth if you have collected enough fuel, but make sure the sparks are completely extinguished before you go and clear away any mess that wasn't burnt.

Loughshinney

Bus: 33 from Eden Quay — very rarely goes via Loughshinney so this should really be a car or bike trip. Route: Swords — turn for Lusk and follow Loughshinney signpost. Or is it Lough Shinney? I've seen both!

Loughshinney is more difficult to find than Rush or Skerries, which you can also visit on the 33 bus route, but it's a scaled-down and interesting place that you could get very attached to; and not *too* many people know about it.

There's a perfect miniature harbour and a safe beach that very small children adore; and because it's all quite small the water heats quickly, like a rock pool. The houses come right down to the beach and their gardens rise in a higgledy-piggledy sort of way. There are great rock pools beyond the harbour and the cliffs look like moon cliffs. There was a geological crusher phase in the distant past which helped to produce these Ryvita-like rock formations. On the walk to the left you pass by earthworks of an ancient promontory fort — you have to imagine the aerial view. Recently Roman remains were found near here and since then there have been arguments about whether the Romans arrived in Ireland. Probably some did, the way Irish people turn up everywhere.

The **Southside Beaches** start very near the city, at Sandymount, and go all the way down to the bottom of Ireland. However, this book stops at Bray, or almost. The DART from Pearse Station will take you to all of these beaches and they can also be reached by bus.

Sandymount Strand

Buses: 2 or 3 from Townsend Street; DART.

This is a huge strand, great for walks with dogs, for castle building and beachcombing, but not for swimming. When the tide is out, you have to walk miles to the shoreline; when it's in, you can see all manner of unpleasantness floating around. On the beach you can go in to see the old sea baths, looking a bit decayed now, like an old Moorish fort. It used have a long wooden pier going out to it and separate pools for gentlemen and ladies. From the Martello tower up to Merrion Gates used to be a high-class bathing area in the last century, with rows of brightly painted bathing boxes. All along the stretch of strand from Sandymount to Blackrock you can see the overflow of waders from Bull Island, as well as people shell-fishing or worm-digging. If you like cockles and lugworms, away you go. Good advice is not to eat the cockles, however, just to save the shells.

Booterstown

Buses: 7A, 8, 45; DART.

There is a tiny bird sanctuary between the road and the railway along this stretch of the coast. It's a miniature slob with a causeway for viewing, although drainage is threatening it. A noticeboard with portraits of the inhabitants will tell you what to look out for, but the resident heron can often be seen from the bus. Booterstown Common often houses circuses, at different times of the year. Camels have been seen grazing wild on the football pitch. Again, this is not a beach for swimming, rather for activities such as walking, digging and riding.

This coast road to Blackrock, believe it or not, used to be a favourite carriage drive for wealthy Dublin families in the eighteenth century, and, naturally enough, it came to be patronised by highwaymen, the real kind, with masks and pistols. Letters to the papers about road conditions were even juicier in those days — and they even had groups of vigilantes set up to patrol the road from Baggot Street to Blackrock.

Blackrock

Buses: 7A, 8, 45; DART.

In the middle ages, there was a road from Poolbeg to Blackrock which stretched across the sands. The mayor and Corporation of medieval Dublin established the boundary of the city along this road. They would throw a javelin out as far as they could to mark the outer limits of their franchise. The Blackrock franchise or boundary stone can still be seen on the main street outside the Central Café.

Take the beach from Blackrock towards Seapoint. You will find it difficult to go all the way because a rather mean individual has closed off access where the old Seapoint Baths used to be. However, there's a jewel of a little beach with beautiful shells along here and you will pass some strange little temple-like structures and a tiny lookalike of Nero's baths. They were built in 1834 by the railway company for the Earl of Cloncurry as compensation for building the railway to Dún Laoghaire through the Earl's property. Unfortunately, the building of the railway marked the end of Blackrock as a fashionable resort of the eighteenth century!

Seapoint

Buses: 4, 7A, 8; DART.

Go through Blackrock, take the Coast Road, then about a quarter of a mile down Seapoint Avenue you will find an excellent swimming area, designated a Blue Flag beach in 1999. The water is deep around the rocks at high tide, but there's an ordinary slope from the strand. Canoeing is another option here (see Joining In, page 311). The rocky stretch on the left has plenty of cormorants, turnstones and gull types who moved in when the baths closed. Napoleon may not have come to grief at the Martello tower here but, incredible as it seems, all along the stretch where people paddle, there's a long history of horrible ship-wrecks. The building of the railway got rid of the worst of the rocks.

Dún Laoghaire Harbour

Buses: 7A, 8, 46A; DART.

If you go to Dún Laoghaire on the train you are following the line of the first railway ever built in Ireland. It was built in 1834. Then it was called the Dublin–Kingstown railway and it was made to stop at the West Pier and come no further because people were afraid it might run amok in the town. (See page 218 for the guided DART tour.)

The best way to see the harbour is to go straight out on to one of the piers. The first one is the West Pier. The piers are quite different both in appearance and in clientele and you can develop a pet favourite. The West Pier is on the

Dublin side of the harbour. It's wilder and quieter, with long grass, and much frequented by fishermen and dogs. It's a fair walk out one pier and back but from the end you can see Dublin Bay curved round like a billhook. The lighthouses at the ends of the piers are unmanned. You can also see the two lightships moored in the harbour, one is a relief ship and the other is used by sea scouts for training. Near the West Pier is the Coal Quay; it's part of the original Dún Laoghaire harbour, having been built in 1767. Fishing trawlers now put up here, and there's always maintenance work going on — hence the several ships' chandlers on the main street of the town. On the far side of the West Pier, outside the harbour walls is the windsurfing area and car park.

The East Pier is past the yacht clubs, the Mail Boat jetty and lifeboats. It's the entertainment pier — the bandstand is still in use during the summer. The seaward side of the pier is a rocky embankment which can be climbed on or fished from (for codling, bass and eel). A Millennium Way is planned for this route over to Sandycove. Meanwhile, examine the sea baths here which are opposite the People's Park and are now closed. They were built for Victorian bathers and boasted all the niceties sure to satisfy even 'the most fastidious invalid'. Seaweed baths, and separate tanks for ladies and gentlemen were listed among the perks. Now Dún Laoghaire Corporation is seeking a creative idea for the baths. If you have one contact them!

It's worth leaving the seafront and going uptown to see the shops. The Dún Laoghaire shopping centre has a great variety of shops while the newer Bloomfield Centre on George's Street hides a little treasure, an oratory built by the Dominican nuns which is a marvel of Celtic art (see page 58). All kinds of shops nestle in the streets of the town; note the ships' chandlers. Dún Laoghaire also has the Maritime Museum (see page 41) and as well as its charming People's Park.

Sandycove beach is easily seen from Dún Laoghaire and used to be considered a beach suitable for women and children, while the deep swimming place round the corner under the tower was the 'Forty-foot — gentlemen only'. That's what it says. The beach is *very* small but children seem to love it. You can go into the Martello tower here because it's the James Joyce museum (see page 71).

Dalkey

Bus: 8; DART. Route: Dún Laoghaire, Sandycove, Dalkey.

Dalkey is about 2½ miles from Dún Laoghaire. It's not really a beachy place, more one for watching boats or messing about in them. This boating tradition goes back to the days when it was Dublin's trading port — from about 1200 AD–1600. There are two small harbours, Bullock and Coliemore.

The first harbour, Bullock harbour, is before the town. It has a fine busy-boat atmosphere in summer and there is a marine emporium on the old stone quay. A fine dynasty of fishermen's cats live regally on the quayside. Rowing boats and outboard-engined boats can be hired in good summer weather. Rock from Dalkey quarry used to be shipped out from here, and there are huge rocks behind the sea wall to be explored. If you catch a fish you no longer have to give one to the castle behind — which used to be the fee the Cistercian monks who lived there charged for fishing the waters.

Coliemore harbour (through the village and down Coliemore Road) is the old port of Dalkey — though it was a pretty rough place, the cargo was unloaded onto rocks which were called Salt Rock, Corn Rock and Coal Rock. The obvious place to head for is the island, there are boat trips in the summer. Dalkey village is a pretty place and because it was Dublin's port it once had seven castles — Goat's Castle is now the Dalkey Heritage Centre (see page 52).

You can walk to or from Dún Laoghaire to Dalkey by a special path called 'The Metals'. When the rock for Dún Laoghaire harbour was being quarried in Dalkey, between 1817 and 1867, it was whizzed down in trucks on metal tracks. The full ones going down pulled the empty ones going back — a proper funicular railway. 'The Metals' starts beside the railway on the waterfront in Dún Laoghaire.

Killiney

Bus: 59 from Dún Laoghaire station; DART. Route: Dalkey, Coliemore Road, Vico Road.

Killiney has several beach locations. The train leaves you at the main beach while the walk up the Vico Road is wonderful with rocks and sea, distant boats and strawberry-pink houses which overhang the cliffs. There's an entrance to the right which will bring you up to the hill park. Steps on the left will take you down to the White Rock bathing place — for good swimmers only. There's a small beach past the railway bridge which is the place to come in winter to watch storms and spray. To the left of the footbridge is Decco's cave, called after an Italian who used to live in it. It was originally the opening to a lead mine in Killiney Hill.

The main beach is very long, a bit stony, but good for swimming and shore fishing. There are some grassy dunes and mounds. You could travel alongside the railway track all the way to Bray from here.

Bray

Bus: 45 from Poolbeg Street; DART. Route: Donnybrook, Stillorgan, Foxrock, Shankill, Bray.

Bray has a pretty awful beach, but then again it has got Bray Head, which was made to be climbed, as well as several amusement palaces and the National Sealife Centre (see page 41).

The promenade on Bray seafront is a very old-fashioned affair. It goes well with all of the hotels and guest-houses facing it. In Victorian Dublin, Bray was the place to come on your half-day off per month if you were 'in service'. That is how the amusements grew up — and there are still dodgems, ghost trains, palm-reading, fish and chips, candy floss and one-armed bandits.

Bray Head is not a difficult climb but the vegetation changes — from blackberries and ferns to a pine glade, to rock — making it seem like a little Alp. You can see Wales on a clear day from here, and you can nearly always see some of the Wicklow mountains. The walk to Greystones is four miles — if you are tempted.

Alternatively, you can follow the track by the railway. The construction of the track through solid rock is a smallish marvel though it put an end to Bray smugglers who had an 'Ali Baba' cavern underneath, known as the Brandy Hole.

Islands

All coastlines have islands and Dublin's is no exception. Exploring an island, picnicking in what might well be a smuggler's cove, looking for all the different kinds of flora and fauna that flourish away from the car pollution and the citizenry, is a real thrill that can be yours on any good spring or summer's day. The 'half-island' qualifies for winter visits as well. There are three and a half islands on this agenda. The first two are perfect specimens. Bring warm clothes, no matter how hot it is, and food.

Dalkey Island

Ferries go to the island from Coliemore Harbour. No regular service or boatman — ask a fisherman. Price by arrangement.

There are rowing boats for hire at the harbour, but you would need to have an excellent adult oarsperson — though the island looks very close this is deceptive, because you have to travel diagonally against the cross-currents. So the best advice is to stick to the ferry.

Once you land on the rocky shore you are under the jurisdiction of 'His Facetious Majesty, King of Dalkey, Emperor of the Muglins, Prince of the Holy Island of Magee, Elector of Lambay and Ireland's Eye, Defender of His Own Faith and Respector of all Others, and Sovereign of the Lobster and the Periwinkle'. The King of Dalkey is quite benign however, and there's no customs so you are free to range all over the island. Dalkey is the site where the oldest recorded Dubliners have been noted. A midden or refuse dump from 5000 BC has been excavated here. There are lots of rabbits and a population of beautiful wild goats that look just like Icelandic sweaters, grey and brown and shaggy. There's a ruined seventh-century church that belonged to St Begnat once but is now the goats' shelter. At one end of the island is an old magazine fort, which like the nearby Martello tower was built to keep a weather eye out for Napoleon. The story goes that the soldiers were forgotten about after Napoleon was defeated at Waterloo, and they stayed on Dalkey Island for forty years waiting for a French invasion. The rocks out to sea are the Muglins and in 1766 two pirates were executed and their bodies chained to the Muglins as an example.

Ireland's Eye

Ireland's Eye is reached by ferry from Howth Harbour. Boats leave in summer regularly, or on demand, from a signposted stage on the further pier. Last return boat leaves the island about 6.00 p.m. It's not cheap, so plan on making a full day trip. Bring all food and drink — there's no shop on the island.

Ireland's Eye is bigger than Dalkey Island, but it's a democracy and does not have any goats. It has cliffs with lots of seabirds, like Howth, and the same cautions apply to these areas. Gannets have successfully begun to breed here. This is a fantastic thing to happen in any capital city territory. *Do not go cliff climbing or egg collecting.* There was a time when goshawks used to breed here — they were a falconer's bread-and-butter sort of hawk. Centuries ago too, the old reliable ruined church (St Nessan's) and Martello tower were built. St Nessan's was always being broken up by pirates, so in the end it was abandoned. Pirates may or may not have used the caves on the eastern end of the island; seals don't, they apparently prefer Lambay. The centre of the island is carpeted in bracken, jungly but surmountable (and an excellent toilet facility). Don't spend too long in the bracken — its spores are bad for you. On the side facing Howth there's a beach that is quite pleasant to swim from; it's also a good place from where to watch the weekend sailors.

Lambay Island

Lambay Island is really here under false pretences. It is privately owned, but *very, very* occasionally permission has been granted for interested groups (like a naturalists' club) to visit. It's situated north of Ireland's Eye, just out from Rush, and has an extraordinarily rich wild life including a population of seals.

Bull Island and Dollymount Beach

Bus: 30 from Lower Abbey Street.

Bull Island is the half-island on the list. It really is an island, but there's a wooden causeway at one end, and a bona fide road at the other, so most visitors don't feel like intrepid explorers. Yet Bull Island has got more wildlife in its little toe, so to speak, than many an Atlantic run-wild, run-free beach. It also has the most popular beach in Dublin, Dollymount beach, and a golf course, the Royal Dublin.

It's a completely artificial island. Get off at the wooden causeway, walk over, and you see the Bull Wall stretching ahead with a lighthouse at the end. The wall was built in 1825 (with some help from Captain Bligh of the mutinous *Bounty* — see also the Maritime Museum, page 41) to make a deep channel going up into Dublin port. A sandbank built up behind the wall, and the bigger it got the more things grew there — until finally there was the Amazing Tale of the Bull Island Mouse.

The Bull Island Mouse was discovered and found to be pale and sandy, unlike field mice or sober dark Dublin house mice. So just about when Charles Darwin published his *Origin of Species*, the Bull Island mouse was trotted on as a witness for Darwin — to prove that animals did adapt and evolve to survive. It was all very exciting.

The beach is just to the left of the wall and stretches for 3 miles. It isn't peaceful, but it's a very good sandy beach, with dunes all along. The sea water is cleaner than at Sandymount, which is also near to the city centre, but do not expect great things of it.

The marvellous thing about the Bull is the horde of birds that do not care in the least that they are surrounded by city rather than water. So, if you want to go nature-spotting, face in to land, rather than out to sea. Take wellingtons, an anorak, a pocket bird book and a pair of binoculars, if you can get them. If you come in on the bona fide road (nearer to Howth) you can acclimatise yourself by dropping in at the Interpretative Centre at the roundabout. It's open from 10.00 a.m. to 4.30 p.m. The video will show you what to look out for; the display boards will give you the Identi-kit details from lowly worm to lofty lark. You will get an idea why the Island was created a UNESCO biosphere.

However, if you come in on the causeway, or you want practice before theory, turn left at the Sea Scouts boat-shed on the Bull Wall, just after the cottages. Among the birds you will see walking about on the salt-marsh are curlews, dunlins, herons, knots, plovers, red- and green-shanks, sanderlings, turnstones. These waders are just crazy about their mudpie diet, but in order that they won't fight over the same worm, notice how they all have varied leg lengths for wading at different depths and different length bills for digging in different layers.

Out on the water you will see geese from Greenland (in winter), swans and an assortment of ducks. On land larks and pippits are very common, and you might see a short-eared owl, kestrels (spot the kestrel and bat nesting boxes on the telephone poles), sparrowhawks, merlins, or the fabled peregrine falcon, who *has* been spotted, no doubt watching the golf like a hawk as well he might, in case the golfers encroach into the wild territory that belongs to Dubliners.

On land you might also be lucky enough to see a hare (some of whom cross over the mud at low tide in autumn). They are shy and should not be introduced to your dog. The Irish Seal Sanctuary often release healed seals into the wild from here — see notices in the newspapers for this. You might also see a wolf spider, a cuckoo-spit bug, a snail-killing fly, a spider-hunting wasp, a dune-robber fly or a hairy woodlouse. And if you don't think you could see any of these creatures, but would like to, why not go on a field trip with a club? (See page 326.)

We didn't include a chapter on Dublin 'mountains' because the book would have been impossibly long if we had tackled the huge range of walks and climbs within striking distance. And it has been done very well by somebody else. Let someone in the family buy a copy of *This Way Up!* and *Hill Walkers' Wicklow* by David Herman (both published by Shanksmare), or *Easy Walks near Dublin* by Joss Lynam (Gill & Macmillan), available from all good bookshops. The second book has twenty-four climbs, all with maps, times and distances. Mr Lynam mentions which climbs are not suitable for dog company (sheep), which need waterproof clothing, which are easy, which are Himalayan. But the Golden Rule is: always travel in company and tell someone where you intend to go.

Chapter 7

Walking, talking, Cycling, flying, Sailing and trotting dublin

This is a guide to some of the many ways in which you can travel around the city and its surrounds in the company of experts. Even though this book is based on the idea of people getting to know Dublin under their own steam, any one of these tours would make an interesting day trip. Some would make excellent birthday presents. Of course you have to pay for it and the following tour suggestions vary greatly in price. If you are entertaining visitors from abroad, they would probably love to try one of these tours; and if you *are* those persons from abroad — well, this list is for you. All are correct for this edition but be aware that this is a changeable business. Telephoning is a must to check on prices, length of tour in time and distance, and availability. Dublin Tourism office in Suffolk Street stock brochures on many of the tours below.

This list includes only those day trips and tours from Dublin where transport is included. The Excursions chapter (page 248) lists suggested tours outside Dublin where you fill your own petrol tank, saddle your own horse, bike et cetera.

Walking Tours

Historical Walking Tours of Dublin
Tel: 878 0227
Begins at Trinity College. October–April, Friday, Saturday, Sunday: 12.00 noon; May–September, daily: 11.00 a.m., 12.00 noon and 3.00 p.m. Theme: historical.

Walk Macabre
by the Trapeze Theatre Company
Tel: 605 776/087-245 6542
Meet at Grafton Street gates of Stephen's Green. 7.30 p.m. when the tour is operating during the summer — you must telephone. Theme: spooky and supernatural.

The Zozimus Experience
Tel: 661 8646/087-222 9992
Begins at Dublin Castle. Evenings all year round, by appointment. Theme: medieval, murder and mystery.

1916 Rebellion Tour
Tel: 676 2493
Begins at 23 Wicklow Street (International Bar). mid-May–September, Tuesday–Saturday: 11.30 a.m. Theme: it's in the name; copy of 1916 Proclamation included. Children free.

The Rock & Stroll Trail
Tel: 878 3345
Begins at The Hot Press Irish Music Hall of Fame, 57 Middle Abbey Street. Summertime only. Booking required, telephone for details. Theme: the many haunts of the rockers. Drink, Hot Press magazine and marker for signing the U2 wall, all included.

Ten street items to spot in the city:

Two matching gargoyles on top of the Dublin Brewing Company on North King Street

The Cowardly Lion on top of Newman House portal, 86 St Stephen's Green

The date 5618 carved in the Jewish cemetery in Richmond Road, Drumcondra. It translates into 1857 AD

The mysterious masonic markings on the archway, inside and outside, of Ranelagh Gardens

The *Gulliver's Travels* plaques on the apartments in Bride Street and Golden Lane: Jonathan Swift was born in the area

All Dublin's remaining lions and unicorns — how many are there? Start the count with the particularly fetching pair at the top of Henrietta Street

The *Ouzel* plaque at No. 9 Dame Street beside the Central Bank; the *Ouzel* was a Dublin merchant ship that was captured by pirates in 1695, crew and ship sailed back unharmed in 1700 and its pirate booty was turned to charitable use

The billiard-playing monkeys and other animals carved on the window frames of the Alliance Française building in Kildare Street, a former gentleman's club

The taximen's altar in the centre mall of O'Connell Street

The tombstones in Jervis Street Park, once the graveyard for St Mary's Church. They are now attached to the park walls like stamps

Trinity College Walking Tours

Begin at front gate of College. April–October, Monday–Sunday:
between 10.00 a.m.–3.30p.m.
Admission to Long Library and Book of Kells included. Enquiries at
porter's office. Under 12s free.

Theme: Trinity College.

Glasnevin Cemetery Tour

Tel: 830 1133
Begins at main gates of the Cemetery. Wednesdays and Fridays:
2.30 p.m. Free.

Theme: historical, biographical, sculptural.

The Dublin Literary Pub Crawl

Tel: 454 0228
Begins at The Duke bar in Duke Street and is obviously not for the
very young. Easter–October, nightly: 7.30 p.m.; Sunday: 12 noon;
November–Easter, Thursday–Sunday: 7.30 p.m.; Sunday: 12.00 noon.

Actors act out scenes from writers' books; drinks are had
at different places. Theme: writers, their works and lives.

Temple Bar Walks

Tel: 677 2255
Guided walks for school groups, art and architectural
students by arrangement with Temple Bar Properties.

DIY audio-tape tours

Blueroad Tape Tours, Pye Centre, Dundrum
Tel: 269 2129

Audio Tours Ireland

7–9 Aston Quay
Tel: 670 5266
Tapes and maps can be bought or hired from either of the
above organisations.

Joyce Walk

Dedicated Joyceans can do the 'following in the steps of
Joyce's hero Leopold Bloom' tour. Begin at Independent

Newspapers on Middle Abbey Street, go around by O'Connell Street, Westmoreland Street, College Green, Grafton Street, Lemon Street, Dawson Street, Molesworth Street to the National Library on Kildare Street. Robin Buick's fourteen themed pavement sculptures are there to help you follow the trail. Each year on Bloomsday, 16 June, there are several Joycean walks and entertainments.

Botanic Gardens
Tel: 837 4388
Guided tours of the Botanic Gardens are available for groups, by prior arrangement only; there is a small fee charged.

Wildlife Walks
These are open to all and are led by experts. They are advertised at regular intervals by organisations like Birdwatch Ireland or An Óige. (See page 325 for details of wildlife organisations.)

During Heritage Week (first week in September) Dúchas organise many free walking events in the forests, parks and gardens under their management. Details of these events are announced in newspapers or you can telephone 647 3000 for information.

Bus Tours
There are several companies offering open-top bus tours of the city. Different deals are reflected in prices; some include admissions or offer discounts, some are strictly convenience transport. Children's fares offer a fair reduction.

Dublin Bus
Tel: 873 4222
Tours operate daily all year round.

Dublin City Hop-on/Hop-off
(Eleven main sites of the city)
Daily Ticket lasts all day, from 9.30 a.m. First stop is Dublin Bus HQ,
59 O'Connell Street.

Grand Dublin Tour
This is a longer and fully guided tour of the city. 10.15 a.m., 2.15 p.m.

Coast and Castle Tour
Tours of Dublin's coastline
*North Coast Tour (and entrance to Malahide Castle): 10.00 a.m. South
Coast Tour (via seaside and Wicklow mountains): 11.00 a.m. and
2.00 p.m.*

'The World's only Ghost Bus'
Tel: 703 3029
*Bodysnatching, Dracula, wake and so on. Easter to October, Friday,
Saturday, Sunday: 7.30 p.m. start from Dublin Bus HQ.*

All the above leave from 59 Upper O'Connell Street

Guide Friday
Tel: 676 5377
*The Dublin Tour guided hop-on hop-off bus. Good discounts. Begins on
O'Connell Street (black and gold buses).*

Irish City Tours
Tel: 458 0054
*The Old Dublin Tour hop-on hop-off bus (eleven stops). Discounts.
Dracula Trail and North Coast Tour (Guided): 10.00 a.m.
South Coast Tour (Guided): 2.00 p.m.*

All begin at 14 Upper O'Connell Street. Frequency may
vary in winter.

Mary Gibbons Tours
Tel: 460 4464/087-688 9985
*These tours are historically and archaeologically based, with an expert
guide. Expensive, but with considerable reductions for children.*

Dublin City Tour

The Boyne Valley
— including admission to Newgrange.

Powerscourt and Glendalough
— including admissions.

Full-day combinations of the above also available. Different pick-up points, including Dublin Tourism Centre.

Gray Line
Tel: 670 8822/605 7705

Dublin Panoramic City Tour hop-on hop-off

Newgrange half-day tour plus admission
Monday and Tuesday: 10.00 a.m.; Thursday and Saturday: 2.30 p.m.

Glendalough half-day tour
Tuesday: 2.45 p.m.; Thursday and Saturday: 10.00 a.m.

Glendalough, Wicklow mountains and lakes
— full day. Friday: 10.00 a.m.; Sunday: 10.30 a.m.

All the above leave from 14 Upper O'Connell Street

Bus Éireann day tours
Tel: 836 6111

Glendalough and Wicklow

Newgrange and Boyne Valley

Kilkenny and Nore Valley

'Glenroe', 'Ballykissangel' and Wicklow Mountains

Russborough House and Powerscourt

River Barrow cruise and Waterford Crystal

Oriel Trail through County Louth

Mountains of Mourne

Check on seasonal availability for each tour.

Bus Éireann also do tours to:

Wales

Ffestiniog railway and Llechwedd Slate Caverns
Snowdon mountain railway and Caernarfon Castle
Summer only.

England

Blackpool illuminations — try the highest roller-coaster in the world!
Saturdays only in September. Admissions included.

Wild Wicklow Tour

Tel: *280 1899*
Off the beaten track in small coaches. April–October, Thursday–Sunday. Different pick-up points.

Over the Top and into the West
Tel: 838 6128
A full-day tour of Wicklow mountains, lakes and waterfalls. Monday–
Sunday: 9.45 a.m. Tour begins at Dublin Tourism.

St Kevin's Bus
Tel: 281 8119
Not a tour bus, but in operation since 1927, the St Kevin's Bus is a
daily service to beautiful Glendalough. Daily: 11.30 a.m. from the
College of Surgeons on St Stephen's Green; returns 4.15 p.m.

Legendary Tours
Tel: 668 6335
These are by mini-bus when numbers mount up, more often in the
operator's car. Richard Marsh takes his tours to the Boyne Valley,
Louth and Wicklow, each tour reflecting a different strand of Irish
mythology, which he retells. Expensive because intensive.

Train Tours

DART tours

Views Unlimited
Tel: 285 6121
Guided tours on the DART suburban line from Bray to
Howth, or to city centre. Part of this line was Ireland's first
railway. Picnics and end-of-tour admissions to sites can be
organised for groups. Activity sheets for children. Prices
are extremely reasonable. By arrangement only.

Iarnrod Éireann Day-breaks
Tel: 836 6222
There are ten destinations, with prices ranging from £35.00
to £60.00 covering travel and admissions for two adults and
up to four children. Choose between Fota Wildlife Park,
Cork; Lakes of Killarney by water bus; Ulster Folk and
Transport Museum; Bunratty Castle and Folk Park; the Hunt
Museum, Limerick; Westport House, Westport; Corrib
Cruise, Galway; Cobh and the Queenstown Experience,

County Cork; Enniscorthy and 1798 in County Wexford; King House and Boyle, County Roscommon. Most trips operate between April and October.

Boat Tours

Dublin Bay Sea Thrill
Tel: 260 0949
A powerboat zoom across the bay. Ten-seater boats must be hired by same group. Waterproofs provided. Begins at East Pier, Dún Laoghaire.

Ireland's Eye Boat Rides
Tel: 087-678211
Howth Harbour to the island of Ireland's Eye.

Dalkey Island
Summertime. Enquiries at Coliemore Harbour, Dalkey.

Galway Hooker Sailing — Lambay Island
Tel: 843 0340
Half or full day trips around the island. In season only, by appointment with Fingal Traditional Sailing, Rush.

Galway Hooker Sailing — Blessington Lakes
Tel: 045–865092
Trips on the Blessington Lakes, County Wicklow. Trips begin at Blessington Lakes Adventure Centre.

Irish Ferries
Tel: 661 0511

and

Stena Line
Tel: 204 7777

Bargain day trips on the high-speed ferries to Holyhead. Most people stock up on cheap alcohol but the town is there to be explored (beautiful church) and buses can be taken around Anglesey Island.

Bike Tours

Dublin Bike Tour
Tel: 679 0899
Bikes are provided, routes use back streets to main attractions. April–October, daily: 10.00 a.m; 2.00 p.m. Also Dublin at dawn, Saturdays: 6.00 a.m! Booking essential.

Activity Tours

Adventure Activities
Tel: 668 8047
Rock climbing Dublin. Monday: 4.30 p.m.; Thursday: 10.00 a.m. and 7.00 p.m. Equipment and refreshments supplied. Bus from Dublin Tourism to Dalkey Quarry for climbing session.
Also Walking in Wicklow. Easy and difficult options. Wednesday, Friday, Saturday: 10.00 a.m. Outdoor gear required. Refreshments included. Bus from Dublin Tourism to mountain site.

Cultúr Beo
Tel: 459 9159
Walking and monument spotting in the Dublin Hills. Buses from different pick-up points on Sundays and Wednesdays. Tours can also be devised to suit groups.

Horse Carriage
You pick a carriage or cab at the top of Grafton Street any fine day. Check out various prices — the destination is your choice.

Limousine

Limousine Company Ltd
Tel: 872 3003

The Limousine Company
Tel: 843 9055
Well, why not?

Air Tours

First Flight Aviation
Tel: 890 0222

Fixed wing and helicopter rides of different types and lengths. As at 1999 the price of the cheapest plane ride is £35.00, while the cheapest helicopter ride is £60.00. The aerial tours can be of Dublin and surrounds, or can include Wicklow or the Boyne Valley.

inside jobs

This is a short list of places that will let you in and show you how they work. Some of the publicly-owned places here might have fitted just as well in to the Museums chapter but there is a slight distinction.

Remember these points: (1) Most of these places will only take organised groups, and sometimes they specify how many, so you may have to work it through a school, a club, or a summer project; (2) people may be working when you get there, so don't do anything to get in their way. Keep any questions for the guide who is showing you around; (3) if you do get stuck in the machinery, remember I had nothing to do with it.

I have listed first the public (or public-funded) organisations that are part of the running of the country — and which are open to all, though sometimes needing a bit of postal homework beforehand. Individuals or families are welcome in these places. After that, the list is definitely one for groups by arrangement, and details are briefer. Some may also require a fee.

Áras an Uachtaráin
The President's Residence
Phoenix Park, Dublin 8
Tel: 670 9155 (Information)
Entrance: via Phoenix Park Visitors' Centre. Guided tour, Saturdays only: 9.40 a.m.–4.20 p.m. Admission free.

You must get here early because places on the tours are limited and tickets are allocated on a first-come first-served basis — no bookings taken. It is very good value with free bus through the manned front gates and an audio-visual introduction to the history of Áras an Uachtaráin. It started life as a glorified gamekeeper's residence when the park was a precious and royal deer park and was later done over in White House-style by the GPO's neo-classical architect, Francis Johnston, after the 1801 Act of Union. Then the house's glory days began — its banquets and balls and presentations — because it became the residence of the Vice-Regent, the English Crown's chief representative in Ireland. One VR, Earl Spencer (an ancestor of Princess Diana), saw two of his staff murdered — the notorious Phoenix Park murders committed by the Invincibles gang. After Irish independence the house became, first, the Lord Lieutenant's home and finally, in 1937, the presidential residence. You will see different traces of the eight presidents as you tour the house — well, just the public and council-of-state rooms, plus the president's study, the most personal of the rooms. Sadly, Áras an Uachtaráin is nothing as splendid as many big houses in the country and it probably never was. The rooms are much smaller than you would expect and some of the rather nice ceilings were taken from other houses, while the pictures and the colours are rather gloomy. However, there is a very splendid *Aesop's Fables* plaster-work ceiling. Nevertheless, Áras an Uachtaráin is set in a location that more than makes up for any shortcomings of its interior — there is a cinemascope view all the way to the mountains as well as all those magnificent park trees with their squirrels and birds. And it is very pleasant, as a citizen, to tour the home of the First Citizen, as a welcome guest. Who knows, one day it could be you issuing the invitations.

Government Buildings and the Taoiseach's Office
Merrion Street, Dublin 2

What could have more hubbub and bustle than the seat of government, cabinet chambers and the Taoiseach's Office? Government Buildings are open to the public on Saturdays when the weekdays' work is done. The huge complex was once the science and engineering part of UCD — that is why there are famous scientist statues around — but in 1990 it was restored, using the finest Irish oak, beech and sycamore, by Irish craftspeople, with each conference room having a different style. Along the corridors hangs a superb collection of modern Irish art. Downstairs there is a gigantic state-of-the-art press theatre, and yes, you do climb the beautiful curved stairs to enter the Taoiseach's office. Breathe in that powerful air! There is a private lift with the helicopter pad one way and the powerful Merc stationed at the other. Admission is by ticket only and in groups of sixteen only, with four tours every hour between 10.30 a.m. and 4.45 p.m. (closed between 12.45 p.m. and 1.30 p.m.) Tickets are available only from the National Gallery, down the road, and they are free.

Dáil Éireann
Kildare Street, Dublin 2
Tel: 618 3333

You can see how Irish democracy works by visiting the
Dáil. It sits on Tuesdays at 2.30 p.m. and Wednesdays,
Thursdays and Fridays at 10.00 a.m. and most frequently
during the months from January to July so this is the best
time to plan your visit for. You can write to any of your
TDs at Dáil Éireann (find out their names in your local
library), or more simply you can arrive at the Dáil, give the
porters your TD's name, and if all goes well you will be
escorted into the Visitors' Gallery and be given the printed
proceedings of the day. If you can arrange a group, family
or otherwise, so much the better.

The more faces you can recognise, the more interesting
it is to look into the debating chamber. Whether the
speeches are stimulating or not, whether there is a full
house or not, are matters of chance. Take time to look
around and observe the strict format of Government and
Opposition, ministers, spokesmen, frontbenchers, back-
benchers and, above them all, the authoritative figure of
the Cathaoirleach or Chairman. The press gallery is usually
full, and you can check your own story against the Dáil
reports in the papers and on the radio. The Senate
chamber, a small, ornate hall at the other end of Leinster
House, may also be visited. Leinster House is usually a hive
of activity with sirens and bells sounding for Divisions and
Quorums. The more you are interested in politics and
personalities, the more exciting you will find it.

Oh, and the House. It was built by the Earl of Kildare as
a home for his teenage bride, and became Leinster House
when he became Duke of Leinster. Later on it became the
home of the Royal Dublin Society before this organisation
moved out to its current location in Ballsbridge. If Leinster
House reminds you of anything else, it might just be the
White House. George Washington employed an Irish
architect who took Leinster House as his model.

Dublin Corporation
City Hall, Dame Street, Dublin 2
Tel: 672 2222

Meetings are held in City Hall on the first Monday of every month. There will no public access until City Hall is renovated fully. Normally, you can get tickets to attend these meetings by telephoning or writing to Dublin Corporation and asking for the names and addresses of your local city councillors; contact one of them and explain why you want to attend. Each councillor has two tickets to give away for each meeting. Ask for the agenda of the meeting when you get there.

Mayor, aldermen (this really means old men) and councillors will be there running the city for you like clockwork by telling the Corporation what to do with its bin lorries, shovels and library-fine money. It could be a new road, a set of swings, or, in very lucky times, swag to go to a street theatre group, that is up for discussion on the agenda. Whatever the subject matter, you will carry away a feeling of how the city is ticking over and growing all around you.

They argue a lot, these same councillors because, (a) each has his/her own area to paint red before everybody else gets in on the act and, (b) because, just as in the Dáil, they all belong to different political parties. So it is pretty lively down in the Council chambers and, unlike the Dáil, you are only a few feet away from the gladiators. They don't wear fancy robes any more — ermine is definitely out — but the mayor does wear a chain and keeps order.

> Corporation meetings will be suspended to the public while interior renovation of City Hall is taking place (to be finished by 2000).
> The same procedure applies to Fingal and Dún Laoghaire/Rathdown County Councils. Apply for tickets from local councillors.

Law Courts

You can visit them around Dublin and see how Irish justice works. Everyone has seen court scenes in films and on television. The real thing is different in many ways. I do not recommend visits to all of the courts and, indeed, you may have to be with an adult to gain admission from the Clerk of the Court or the garda on door duty.

The big courts — the Supreme, the High and the Circuit — all sit in the Four Courts proper. They hear the criminal cases and the big civil cases and sometimes have juries. They sit during the law terms which are roughly the same as school terms and hearings start at 11.00 a.m. and 2.30 p.m. (the morning sessions are the most lively). There is nothing going on during August and September or during Christmas and Easter holidays. The Legal Diary is the daily paper which shows what cases are on in which courtroom on that day. It is doubtful that you would be allowed in. The District Court, round the east side of the Four Courts in Chancery Lane, may be more accessible. Here lone judges sit handing out verdicts on more minor matters. This court sits all year round except for August and sessions start at 10.30 a.m. You can slip into the pews during sessions and leave without any bother. There are district courts at Bray, Dundrum, Dún Laoghaire, Howth, Kilmainham, Lucan, Rathfarnham and Swords which you can visit. Look up Part One of the telephone directory under Courts and telephone the office for the district court which you wish to visit, to make sure when it is sitting. **Tribunals** take place in special chambers of Dublin Castle across the river. If one is sitting — and they are semi-permanent, it seems — it will be open to all.

National Archives

Bishop Street
Tel: 407 2300
Entrance: office building, St Patrick's Cathedral end of Street.
Open: Monday–Friday: 10.00 a.m.–5.00 p.m.

This is where most of the documents that keep modern historians happy are stored (others are in the Four Courts;

some are restricted by government — the ones that would make historians _really_ happy). As well as government department records, all the useful sources for tracing family history, plus prison records, trades union archives and so on are kept here. You would probably need expert advice on how to discover the details you want, though anyone is allowed in to try for themselves. Fill out a form for a temporary ticket, deposit your belongings in a locker and go up in the lift. The Thom's street directories here go back to the 1820s and they always make fascinating reading, recording who or what lived in your house years ago.

Royal Irish Academy
19 Dawson Street, Dublin 2
Tel: 676 2570
Entrance: beside the Mansion House.
Open: Monday–Friday: 10.30 a.m.–5.00 p.m.

This handsome Georgian townhouse is the place to visit to see a real working academic library, complete with gallery. The Academy was founded in 1785 to promote 'the study of science, polite literature and antiquities' and its gentlemen (ladies came later) went out and dug up many of the treasures which are now in the National Museum, as well as compiling dictionaries of Irish and, during the rebellion year of 1798, working out early telegraph systems for security. One of the Academy's priceless treasures is _Lebor na hUidre_, the Book of the Dun Cow, which is the oldest existing manuscript in Irish. The public are welcome to look inside the reading and meeting rooms, buy any of the publications and can make enquiries from the friendly staff.

Civic Offices
Wood Quay
Tel: 672 2222
Entrance: several approaches.
Open: 9.30 a.m.–5.00 p.m.

Worth a peek to see what is inside the great glass hives built on top of a Viking harbour. The views are excellent

— as they should be because the offices stole a lot of the views themselves, especially those of Christ Church. City plans are on view here so that ordinary people can check what developments are in store for them. You can pass by the tropical trees in full growth and into the non-tropical little Civic Park where there is a concrete bandstand area and seating rows —music is played here regularly in summer. The historical goodies of the Corporation — charter, mace, chain book and so on are in City Hall. Corporation meetings also take place in City Hall. The Viking story is told, (a) in the National Museum, (b) in Dublinia and, (c) in the Viking Adventure Centre, but if you walk the perimeter of the Offices watch for the pavement sculptures of Viking belongings. The dark history of these offices is that they were built on the Wood Quay archaeological site, despite the vigorous protests by great numbers of Dubliners who were opposed to building on the ancient site.

Central Bank
Dame Street
Tel: 671 6666
Entrance: from the front Plaza.
Open: 9.30 a.m.–3.00 p.m.

The hated/loved money chest of the Central Bank was never intended to be for public use, only for government departments paying their bills, cashing their EU grants, or paying off the national debt. But until Euros are in full swing there is an order which allows any citizen who has European foreign currency — it must be paper not coin — to cash this into Irish currency without paying commission as they would in an ordinary bank. You are escorted by a guard (as if you were a prospective bank robber) up to the change floor and then back down again. Not much of an experience maybe, but it saves money, and it will soon be gone for ever, so why not gather up your pesetas and marks and step past the skaters.

Army/Air Corps
The Army Equitation School
McKee Barracks, Blackhorse Avenue, Dublin 7
Tel: 804 6000
The school sometimes shows interested groups around the stables and showjumping training ground. Special arrangements must be made and the group would really have to be concerned with horses in some way. Your first query should be in writing.

Army Visits can also be made by schools to the **Curragh Training Camp**, in Kildare. Telephone the Defence Forces Press Office: 804 2000. The Defence Forces' **Military Archives** in Cathal Brugha Barracks can be studied with special permission. Apply in writing.

The Air Corps at Casement Air Base, Baldonnel, do a very popular tour for schools, covering the history of military aviation right down to everyday maintenance work. By prior arrangement only. Contact the Flight Commander, in writing, at the Administration Wing, Casement Air Base, Baldonnel, Dublin 22.

Dunsink Observatory
Castleknock
Tel: 838 7911
Open: October–March (i.e. autumn and winter when the nights are long), the first and third Wednesday of each month: 8.00 p.m.–10.00 p.m. You need tickets which you can get by sending a stamped, addressed envelope to the Secretary at Dunsink Observatory, Castleknock, County Dublin. School groups can arrange day visits, but obviously they miss the stars. Bus: 40C from Parnell Street to Finglas South at the bottom of Dunsink Lane, half a mile from the observatory. Admission free.

By night the observatory looks like a strange temple, by day very odd indeed, like the beloved folly of a mushroom grower. It is about 4 miles from the city as the crow flies, along the Royal Canal, and when it was founded in 1783, students and professors used to walk the distance —

notably William Rowan Hamilton who suddenly penetrated a higher mathematical mystery while passing under one of the canal bridges (see page 189). Beaufort, who invented the scale for measuring wind speeds and gave new meaning to the life of weather forecasters, worked here for a while when he was 14 years of age and his entries may be seen in the record books. (See page 291 for astronomy clubs.) Dunsink Observatory itself has been undergoing some extensive renovations and it's intended that it have a wider science education role for young people.

The Meteorological Service
Glasnevin
Tel: 806 4200
Weatherfolk are very busy so tours of this fantastic building are *not* regular events. Only small school groups (no more than 10 in number) who are deeply interested should even think of applying — but you might be lucky. The 1979 building looks like an Inca temple but the Incas would have sacrificed all their gold to have the satellite technology that beams good and bad news to the forecasters who then beam it onto our television screens. Make a trial application (groups only, not individuals), in writing to the Head of General Forecasting, Meteorological Office, Glasnevin, Dublin 9.

ENFO
Information on the Environment
17 St Andrew Street, Dublin 2
Tel: 679 3144/1890-200191
Open: Monday–Saturday: 10.00 a.m.–5.00 p.m.

Definitely a place for projects. ENFO is a pleasant walk-in resource centre crammed with leaflets on all aspects of the environment in this country. You can ask questions, use the library, watch videos, look at exhibitions and experiment with the computer software, which include re-designing the globe and the oceans. School groups are

welcome but should book; individuals can just drop by.
Their website is hugely informative (see page 339).

Dublin Fire Brigade

Guided tours of local fire stations for school groups are
available by prior arrangement. A request should be put in
writing to the Chief Fire Officer, Dublin Fire Brigade
Training School, Malahide Road, Dublin 3 — Tel: 833 8313.
You can also contact your local fire station.

The ESB

This is one organisation which can definitely shed light on
what actually happens underneath the tall chimneys of a
power station. Poolbeg Station arranges group tours by
appointment. (You have to be over 14 years of age.) Apply
to Poolbeg Power Station, Ringsend — Tel: 668 5300.

The Islamic Cultural Centre

Roebuck Road, Clonskeagh
Tel: 260 3740

Over 7,000 Muslims live in Ireland, and the majority of
them are based in Dublin. The distinctive architecture of
the city's principal mosque and surrounding complex
stands out among its neighbouring suburban houses, and
intrigues passers-by. Visitors are welcome. Tours of the
mosque and facilities are by arrangement only and the
excellent restaurant and shop are open to all except during
the winter fast of Ramadan.

The Centre has five distinctive blocks: the mosque with
its unique dome and minaret, administration, sports
complex, living quarters and school annex. The Dublin
community claim that this is the most integrated Islamic
centre in Europe. Over 200 children attend the ten-
teacher school, which is like any Irish primary school
except that Arabic language and script and Islamic
religious practice are taught. The mosque and the other
blocks are carefully oriented towards Mecca, the holy site
of Islam thousands of miles away in Saudi Arabia. Under

the dome — and under the enormous Waterford glass chandelier — men kneel on a specially gridded, green (for Ireland) carpet and pray five times a day. Women pray on a separate balcony, but visitors of both sexes are permitted onto the mosque floor except during prayers. The Centre has a library but most of its handsome books are in Arabic; for research purposes you can ask for information booklets from the offices. Classes in Arabic are held at certain times of the year. Schools are very welcome to book guided tours and the Centre also runs open days with exhibitions throughout the year.

The Abbey Theatre
Lower Abbey Street, Dublin 1
Tel: 874 8741

Groups (by arrangement only) are shown around the Abbey Theatre during the day. You can see the inside, backstage, wardrobe and dressing rooms, as well as the Concorde-like lighting control room, and perhaps the odd famous face. Write or telephone the Abbey Theatre's Press Officer.

Black Church Print Studio
4 Temple Bar, Dublin 2
Tel: 677 3629

Occasionally, small groups may be shown around this studio's lithographic and silk screen works and camera room. The fruits of the trade are on display in the Original Print Gallery below.

Ganly and Craigie's Cattle Market
Ashbourne, County Meath
Tel: 835 0208

Weather depending, there are weekly marts here, usually on Tuesday afternoons. You can just walk right into the Cattle Market, and see a special sort of auction at work. Not everybody's taste, but it is a good smelly spectacle. You have to resist the calves however. This is a bidding mart and the game is to see who is bidding and how. The auctioneers never hesitate so be careful not to scratch your nose, or you'll never know who'll be sharing the top bunk tonight. It's a good idea to wear wellingtons and jeans, for obvious reasons. The bus to Slane from Busáras will leave you at Ashbourne.

The Dublin Art Foundry
3A Rostrevor Terrace, Dublin 2
Tel: 676 0690

This foundry is where sculptors get their work cast. Huge and small sculptures are made amidst a tremendous noise of bronze. It's down near Grand Canal Basin. Groups of fewer than ten people should telephone for an appointment.

If you would like to see one of the oldest crafts still practised you should drop in at a **FORGE**. The smithy at Dunboyne, just beyond Blanchardstown, is over 200 years old. The fire is worked by a pump now, but the anvil, the nails, and certainly the horses are the same as ever. Racehorses get light aluminium shoes, workhorses (very few of those guys) get clodhoppers.

The Irish Times
31 Westmoreland Street, Dublin 2
Tel: 679 2022

This newspaper has an ongoing working relationship with schools and shows small groups around its premises — by arrangement only. Write or telephone the Production Manager for further information. A newspaper office is an immensely exciting place, with people, stories and machines working at strange hours of the day. New technology has changed the buzz but the end product still gets born in a whirl. For contrast visit the National Print Museum (see page 38).

Avoca Copper Mines
Avoca, County Wicklow
Tel: 045–866 400
Overground guided tour, fee-paying and by prior arrangement. Free tours on Heritage Day.

Nick Coy is a mineralogist who knows every single cubic inch of the geology, prehistory, economics, medicine, engineering and social history of this mine, from the Phoenicians onwards. He takes interested parties (schools very welcome) over the ground and engine rooms, though until more money is invested, going down a shaft is not possible. During the Industrial Revolution this mine kept busy with pyrites — fool's gold — as well as with copper and zinc, and up to 1,000 carts per day arrived at Arklow harbour laden with export minerals. It had a railway, and yes, children did work in these mines.

The National Concert Hall,
Earlsfort Terrace, Dublin 2
Tel: 475 1666
Tours of the hall and its various rooms, plus a guided tour of neighbouring Iveagh Gardens, take place during Heritage Week.

I would be delighted to hear from any other organisations who will show visitors around their works. But readers should remember that this is merely a small list of possibilities. Transition class teachers will have much longer ones. Remember, if you can demonstrate a special interest, or belong to a club, you can make polite approaches to places that do not normally admit visitors. Use your head, and your neck to go places you want to go.

Chapter 9

Meath, the Boyne Valley and More

This is a book about Dublin, right? But sitting on County Dublin's head and shoulders, and with certain of its parts only twelve miles away from the city, is Meath, a county of ancient palaces, tombs older and more mysterious than the Pharaohs' Pyramids, castles, abbeys, beaches, battles

— and a Gaeltacht or Irish-speaking area. Thus, this book, *Out & About in Dublin*, has invaded the ancient kingdom of Meath and given it a chapter to itself.

Only that is not quite the full extent of the crime. There are bits of Louth in here too, just as there were when Meath was the home of the High King and one of Ireland's five provinces, along with Leinster, Munster, Connacht and Ulster. All that can be said as an excuse is that no other county has got a chapter to itself. You will just have to get to know royal Meath to see why it was worth the invasion. This chapter is merely an introduction. Dúchas sites are marked *. See page 15 for a note on value Heritage cards.

Tara Heritage Site*
County Meath
Tel: 046-25903
Entrance: signposted, just off the Dublin–Navan road.
Open: May–October: 10.00 a.m.–5.00 p.m.; mid-June–mid-September:
9.30 a.m.–6.30 p.m. Admission: free to site, fee for audio visual show
in adjoining church.

Cows are not supposed to wander around this ancient royal site but they do, and just like the Brown Bull of Cooley they seem to want a bit of the mythological action. They probably know all the secrets of Tara, which archaeologists are still trying to unearth. Some people believe that Tara lies on what they call the ley lines or natural meridians of the earth. A line that does exist — or did — was the Slí Chualann, which ran down the eastern counties of Ireland and was one of the four ancient roads that interchanged at Dublin. Try and see the film show first, or at least make sure to look at the site plan, otherwise Tara looks just like a very bumpy field. It takes aerial photography to reveal its splendour. The bumps are the earthworks of the palaces of the High King of Tara. St Patrick is supposed to have lit his Easter fire on the rival Hill of Slane across the plain in defiance of the King: he lived to tell the tale. Before that, Tara was one of the great ritual sites of Ireland and there is also a passage grave here. There is also a site at Tara that is supposed to be the grave of the beautiful Gráinne who eloped with the beautiful Diarmuid instead of marrying Fionn Mac Cumhail. More recently Tara had its Indiana Jones moment when it was claimed as the hiding place of the Biblical Ark of the Covenant — large doses of salt required. On a fine day it is a splendid place with a view across almost all of royal Meath. Check the churchyard for the stone carving that the plan calls 'rude' — it is called a *sheelagh-na-gig*. Also in the area is **Dunsany Castle**, which is open for approximately ninety days of the year: telephone 046-25176 for opening times, they vary; and the **Dalgan Park Mission Interpretative Centre** near Navan: Tel: 046-21525.

Brú na Boinne*
Newgrange and Knowth
Slane, County Meath
Tel: 041-24488
Entrance: via Visitor Centre. Signposted from Dublin–Slane road and from Drogheda.
Open: all year round. Different closing hours, ranging from 5.00 p.m. (November–February); 5.30 p.m. (March, April, October); 6.30 p.m. (May–end September); 7.00 p.m. (June–mid-September). Admission fee varies. It is possible to visit the Centre alone or combine it with either or both of the actual sites. NB: try to arrive in the morning to be sure to get on the tour you wish. In summer this is a very busy place.

This is a fabulous excursion. Very cleverly the Visitor Centre is located in a bend of the fast-flowing River Boyne complete with lush trees all around it. These were exactly the kind of attractions that drew the early Stone Age or Neolithic people to settle here and then to build their extraordinary passage tombs. That was over 5,000 years ago. The tombs are called **megalithic** — meaning made of huge stones — and the great boast is that they were built before the Pyramids of the Nile Valley. Their openings are astronomically aligned with the tracking of the sun during the year. The superb exhibition in the Centre will tell you all the background, and the guides and the bus drivers will add to that if you take the tours, which you should. Although Newgrange is the most popular tour (because you get to enter the passage tomb) Knowth is even more astonishing. Its great tomb is still being excavated although it will never be open to the public (the passageways are so low and so narrow that stomach-crawling is necessary, but the guides *must* do it at least once during their training). It has all its historical levels on display; satellite tombs like South Sea huts, a kiln, graffiti, secret passageways and just about most of the greatest megalithic art in Europe. Snakes and runes and moonstones, oh my! A brand-new theory is that some of the artwork on these stones represent sophisticated moon maps.

> Also in the Slane area: **Newgrange Farm** (see page 109), the **Francis Ledwidge Cottage Museum** for poetry lovers (041-24285), the **Hill of Slane** with the ruins of Slane Abbey, from which you can see the river and work out why the great tombs fit in so well.

Mellifont Abbey* and Monasterboice
County Louth
Tel: 041-26459
Entrance: Mellifont is signposted off the Slane–Collon road;
Monasterboice is four miles further and signposted from Mellifont.
Open: daily May–October.

In Latin Mellifont means the font of honey and it was the first Cistercian monastery in Ireland. Built by a river in rich farmland as most monasteries were, it was both splendid and huge, although now it is almost completely in ruins. St Malachy was the monkish developer and although the abbey was founded in 1142 there were several eras of further building before King Henry VIII closed it down.

You can still trace out the shape of the church and its great columns from the ruins which are plain to be seen. There is an unusual and beautiful octagonal building off the cloister green called a _lavabo_ where the monks did their ritual washing and a chapter house (if this is locked you can ask to go in) very like St Mary's Chapter house (see page 56). Trace the lines of the beautiful doors and windows, (one with low-hung gargoyles) and the delicate medieval tiles that still survive. Storerooms, crypt, infirmary, river, fields — the monks had everything. There is a centre with some stone carvings on display and a history of the monastery and the masons' work that was used to built it.

Monasterboice

This is a much older place than Mellifont. That is not hard to guess because of the round tower and the two (and a half) High Crosses, all standing in the modern graveyard that has grown around them. The crosses date from the tenth century and are, literally, sermons in stone. The carvings are scenes from the Bible plus some exotic extras that the masons added into the Celtic decorations and weavings. St Muiredach's Cross is the sturdier one and it has the better carving. Check for St Michael weighing souls and the devil grabbing them, and for the two evil-looking cats at the base. The more you stare, the more they grow on you....

Kells
County Meath

Kells is the town of the famous Book and it has High Crosses like other places have billboards. Which is not surprising because High Crosses were billboards in their day, and Kells was a Great Site of Irish Christianity. The monastery was founded here in 804 by monks fleeing from Vikings at Iona, in Scotland. So naturally they provided themselves with a Round Tower, whose windows face each of the roads leading into Kells. That form of burglar alarm didn't stop someone stealing the Book in the eleventh century. It was found in a bog shortly afterwards, its jewelled cover missing. If you haven't already seen the Book of Kells in Trinity College, you can have a peek at the expensive facsimile on display in the Town Hall.

You will find three Crosses in St Columba's churchyard and you can see what pictures you can make out of the carvings which now have a soft covering of lichens. Outside the churchyard lies a tenth-century monastic building called St Colmcille's House. Some people think it might have been a scriptorium. The tall Market Cross, which until recently stood in the town centre, has been removed for restoration while a medieval tower, complete with some interesting heads, now houses stores. The best way to see these, and the rest of the heritage of Kells is to take one of the guided tours which are conducted throughout the tourist season — enquiries can be at the Town Hall tourist office. About a mile outside the town is the People's Park and its Tower of Lloyd. This pretend lighthouse was built in 1791 as a tribute from a son to his father. It is 100 feet high and commands spectacular views of the area — it's open from March to September. The park contains a famine graveyard which had its own path to the nearby workhouse. More cheerfully there is a small adventure playground and picnic seats.

If you go west from Kells towards Oldcastle you will find signposts for **Loughcrew** passage graves and for **Sliabh na Callaighe**. This Irish name means 'the Witches' Hill' and it's the highest hill in the county — a not very difficult climb of 910 feet; bring good shoes — with a huge cairn on top called the Hag's Chair. Underneath is a passage tomb — and what a place for it. If you have been to Newgrange you will recognise some of the markings on the entrance stones but this tomb is older. There are thirty tombs in the area — with entrance possible into two of them, Cairn T and Cairn L. There are guided tours of both of these cairns from mid-June to mid-September, but you can climb the hill at any time. It is said that you can see fourteen counties from here. Maybe only witches could, but the view is superb. Telephone 049-854 2009 for information.

There are many prehistoric sites in this region. Ask for more information in Kells tourist office.

Rathcairn is the Gaeltacht set up in 1935. You can find it signposted on the road from Athboy to Navan and walk into any of the shops or pubs to try your Irish. There is a festival in the first week in July.

You can take scenic walks along the River Boyne from many of the towns in County Meath. Some walks meet up with the quiet, disused Boyne Canal (parts of which, if you have a canoe, is fine paddling territory). Try the walks from **Navan, Trim, Slane** or **Drogheda.** Near Drogheda you will find the site of Oldbridge, with a map and a vantage point on the north bank. There is an ENORMOUS green-and-orange signpost so that you won't miss it. This is where the **Battle of the Boyne** was fought on 1 July 1690, with much crossing of the river because the tide was low. Neither army had uniforms so the soldiers wore different colour badges to show who was who. About 2,000 died on the day. What you need to know is that William of Orange defeated King James, that William was riding a chestnut horse not a white one, and that this was really a European battle not an Irish one. Only nothing is ever that simple.

The north-bank drive from Slane to Drogheda is very beautiful on a sunny day. You could picnic by the river, or else in the woodland estate of Townley Hall, managed by Coillte and open to the public, with nature trails and streams to follow. In summer there is a family arts weekend held at Townley Hall — it's well worth the journey.

Trim

In Trim you are still in the Pale but about to leave it if you cross the river and go behind the Castle. The Pale was the area of Ireland controlled by English government before the big plantations of settlers came along in the sixteenth century. It was bounded by walls and stout castles of which Trim Castle was the largest and one of the stoutest (it's still here) and oldest, with a starting date of 1173. If you lived in the Pale, which of course included Dublin, you were supposed to shave off all nasty Irish facial hair and to adopt an English surname. This could be a colour, a trade, or an English name of a town (Green, Cooper, Sutton). The first owners of Trim Castle were the de Laceys, a Norman family.

The Castle is being renovated for visitors and it will soon be one of the great attractions of royal Meath. If you wish to get a preview, have a look at the film *Braveheart* which was filmed here in 1994.

Meanwhile you can visit **The Power and the Glory — Medieval Trim** in the town's Visitor Centre (open: April–September. Tel: 046-37227). It's a multimedia exhibition like Dublinia (see page 75) that tells the story of lofty and lowly life in medieval Trim. In the season there are regular walking tours of the many other medieval landmarks in the town. Check with the Visitor Centre.

You could also combine your trip to the town of Trim with a visit to **Butterstream Gardens** (open: April–September. Tel: 046-36017) just outside the town, though note that children are required to be kept 'on a short leash'. Small gardens lead like different rooms into one another alongside a stream. One is a Pompeiian villa garden.

Drogheda
County Louth

Any view of Drogheda shows spires, towers and the giant railway viaduct across the Boyne. But a good place to start is **Millmount**, on the Dublin road. You can drive right up, or else park in town and walk up the steep steps to the Martello tower. It sits like an egg over a Norman motte and bailey site. The tower, opened to visitors in summer 1999, both for its view, and for its exhibition of the site's history. The former army fort alongside houses craft shops, a restaurant and the **Millmount Museum** (041-983 3097) and **Governor's House** which tell the story of Drogheda, especially that of its trades. There are beautiful guild banners — the Carpenters' one shows St Patrick grinding the snakes down wearing a fine pair of walking shoes and the Boyne Fishermen's one is truly a work of art. Other items include a round coracle boat which looks Stone Age but was used in this century, a map which shows the size of medieval cities around Europe, Drogheda being bigger than Dublin, and there is also a geological collection.

The Tourist Office here can provide walking maps of the town with which you can tick off some of the soaring towers and spires. There are also guided walking tours throughout the season. Ghouls will find plenty in Drogheda. The handsome **St Peter's Church of Ireland** on Magdalene Street has a gruesome history — here, in 1649, Oliver Cromwell and his soldiers set fire to an earlier church and burned to death all the people inside. Cromwell claimed to have killed over 2,000 Drogheda inhabitants, including the poor garrison commander who was allegedly beaten to death with his own wooden leg.

Outside in St Peter's graveyard search for the creepy **'Black Death'** tombstones. In the Catholic **St Peter's Church** on West Street there is a shrine with the decapitated head of St Oliver Plunkett. It doesn't take much to figure why Old Abbey Lane got its name but all that is left on this oldest church site in Drogheda is the belfry.

St Laurence Gate is a typical medieval town gate. You can walk down to the dockside from there and get a flavour of Drogheda's once huge shipping trade. A nice place to eat is Monk's on the Quays just by the main bridge.

> O'Connell Street, Dublin was once called Drogheda Street. Henry Moore, Earl of Drogheda, had a healthy ego. He called the key streets of his estate Henry Street, Moore Street, Earl Street and Drogheda Street, and, just to be entirely proper, he named one of his smaller thoroughfares Of Lane.

Combine Drogheda with a Boyne walk, a seaside visit, a trip to Sonairte, or the summer Townley Hall Family Arts festival.

Meath Beaches

There are only seven miles of coast in Meath but they pack a lot in. **Laytown** is stony in parts, but has a great river with a footbridge and train bridge where you can fish. It's also got the ecology centre Sonairte (see below), an unexcavated prehistoric tumulus that looks like a Dennis the Menace head bump, and its unique summer strand races. Make sure to call in to Laytown's extraordinary Catholic church. It has kept its old front as a belfry, but behind, across a 'moat', is a round modern space with a window cut away so that at full tide the altar seems to float on the sea behind. **Bettystown** is crowded at weekends but at other times it is a wide and wonderful stretch of sand. It has qualified as a Blue Flag beach. There is also a resident funfair complete with vintage painted amusements. **Mornington** has a sixteenth-century tower that can be climbed, some very fine sand dunes and a wonderful view up to the Mourne Mountains. Watch the Boyne flow into the sea, spot its estuary birds or try fishing, but do not *attempt* to swim anywhere near the confluence. **Mosney** and **Gormanstown** have long wide beaches too although the sea is rather shallow here. Mosney also has **Fun Tropica**, a holiday camp with theme pools, a boating lake and funfair, that is open to day visitors from end of May to the end of August (Tel: 041-29200). All of these places are signposted from the Dublin–Drogheda road or you can take the train from Connolly Station to Mosney or Laytown.

Sonairte

Laytown, County Meath
Tel: 041-27572
Open: all year except for January.
Admission fee.

This lovingly restored Big House and its five acres on the banks of the slow and serpentine River Nanny might just be the greenest place in Ireland — it's the National Ecology Centre. All during the year there are guided school trips which are tremendous fun (Sonairte send a Secret Package to the school beforehand). You can see solar energy working, water power and windmills. School trips even get to eat the an organic meal grown in the different gardens and orchards. It appears to cook by satellite dish, but actually what you see is a solar cooker. Anyone can attend the weekend courses on different environmental themes from growing to cooking to recycling. There is a nature trail by the river, indoor and outdoor play areas, a coffee shop and the Sonairte shop which sells eco-products. The guides and staff will discuss any questions about ecology and energy-saving. The local birds are very fond of Sonairte.

Horses in Meath

Kildare may be the best horse-breeding county; Meath certainly races those horses. If you like a day at the races, you are spoiled for choice. Remember children under 14 are usually admitted free to meetings. You can obtain a racing calendar from the Irish Horseracing Authority, Leopardstown Racecourse, Dublin 18 (Tel: 289 2888). There are special race buses from Busáras to Bellewstown and Fairyhouse.

Laytown: real racing on the beach makes this a unique occasion. All the betting paraphernalia moves from turf onto sand. It's in early summer at a date determined by spring tides.

Fairyhouse: The big meeting here is the Irish Grand National each Easter Monday but there are races held almost all the year round.

Bellewstown: July. A family day out kind of race meeting.

Navan: There is a weekend race meeting here almost every month.

Plus: Near the beaches, you could take riding lessons at Castlehill Equestrian Centre, Julianstown (Tel: 041-982 9430). Meath Tourism has a brochure on equestrian sports — ask at any tourist office.

Tourist Offices: Navan 046-73426; Trim 046-37111; Kells 046-49336; Slane 041-988 4055; Oldcastle 049-854 2303; Drogheda 041-983 7070.

For information on bus tours of the Boyne Valley see page 216.

day-tripper/excursions/
getting out!

This is a list of suggested day trips out of Dublin which require car transport. The rough rule is that two to two-and-a-half hours-plus of a journey is the maximum comfortable time, so the selection below is mainly a Leinster one, with a very few forays beyond. Also, it is a selection only: if a place is not here it's no reflection on its merits or, indeed, its 'two-hour' measurements. To help those with the travelling bug I have included the names of guidebooks and regional tourist office addresses that will help you plan other excursions. You should check museums and houses for prices and last admission times before setting out. An ordinary road-touring map of Ireland should be sufficient, along with local signposting for most destinations. For farm destinations it's wise to telephone for precise directions.

The following list is compiled on a county-by-county basis. Wicklow and Kildare are shorter than they might have been because many of their sites are already covered elsewhere in the book (it's called colonialism) and 'jammy dodger' County Meath already has an entire chapter all to itself.

The attractions are marked ██ for museum or heritage site; 🏛 for houses and gardens; or a for activity.
✱ means a Dúchas site: see page 15 for a note on good value Dúchas Heritage cards.

Wicklow

Wicklow Gaol

Wicklow Town
Tel: 0404-61599
Open: March–October.

Rough-speaking gaolers lead their paid-up victims through the different holding quarters of this (originally) eighteenth-century gaol that got itself super-busy during the 1798 Rebellion, and again during the Famine. Shackles and a 'sea journey' are part of the experience.

Glendalough*

Tel: 0404-45325
Open: daily. Signposted from Kilmacanogue on Dublin–Wexford road.

St Kevin's ancient complex of tiny monastic buildings is in a spectacular position, hard by two spooky glacial lakes. There is a Visitor Centre with an audio-visual presentation. Glendalough also boasts several well-maintained climbing forest trails.

Arklow Maritime Museum

St Mary's Road, Arklow
Tel: 0402-32868

A presentation of the town's seafaring history — also includes a hands-on trawler wheelhouse.

Avoca Mines *(see page 235)*

Avondale House and Forest Park
Tel: 0404-46111
Signposted, just outside Rathdrum.

Spectacular and exotic trees planted by the ancestors of Charles Stewart Parnell, whose house this was. The National Forestry School is now here. The house offers a video presentation and is a shrine to the Home Rule hero. The park is free to explore.

Wicklow Mountains National Park*

Tel: 0404-45425
Entrance signposted from Upper Lake, Glendalough.
Education centre and information point. Guided tours at certain times.

Blessington Lakes Adventure Centre

Tel: 045-865092
Signposted just south of the town.

So much to do! Canoeing, sailing, windsurfing on the lake, lake cruises in summer by boat or Galway hooker, orienteering, archery, abseiling, pony trekking.

Wicklow Hills Quad Trekking

Cronelea, Tinahely/Shillelagh
Tel: 055-29260
Open: April–October.

A four-mile farm trail to ride the fun, all terrain vehicles (for ages 13 upwards). You must book and six is the maximum number per group. The livestock, even the pot-bellied pig, are now used to four-wheeled humans. Helmets and waterproofs are provided and there's a view of five counties at the summit.

Pottery Trail

Wicklow Tourism have a brochure/map of six potteries dotted along a scenic route. Pick one up in any Wicklow tourist office.

Wexford

The first five sites listed are on the east-coast side of Wexford; the remainder are on the western or southern side. Lucky Wexford — this long list could be much longer. For more ideas, drop into local tourist offices while you're in the area.

Irish National Heritage Park, Ferrycarrig

Tel: 053-41733
Open: March–October.

A fabulous riverside setting for a theme park that presents ways of life in Ireland from 9,000-year-old skin-clad houses to lake dwellings, Viking shipyards and working *fulacht fiadh* ovens. Actors help with the experience. Picnic and restaurant on site.

Yola Farmstead Folk Park

Tagoat, Rosslare
Tel: 053-31177
Open: March–November.

A village has been created, with forge, schoolhouse, miniature church, windmill and several homesteads including one that serves good meals. Nature trails, farm animals, craft shop and genealogy centre.

Wexford Wildfowl Reserve*

North Slob, Wexford
Tel: 053-23129
Open: all year. Admission free.

Come in winter to see the range of Arctic visitors. Information centre and audio-visual show.

Shrule Deer Farm

Ballygarret, Gorey
Tel: 055-27277
Open: daily: June–August; weekends: May and September.

Home to various types of deer including red deer. There is also a selection of farm animals as well as a good playground.

National 1798 Visitor Centre

Enniscorthy
Tel: 054-37596
Open: all year.

Offers guided or self-wandering tours around this interactive presentation of the Great Rebellion of 1798. The centre was completely revamped for the bicentenary in 1998.

Kilmore Quay Maritime Museum

Kilmore Quay Harbour
Tel: 053-29804
Open: June–September.

Welcome on board the former lightship *Guillemot II* now noted for its shipboard quarters, whalebone and history of Irish shipping. Come early to KQ and ask about boat visits to the bird sanctuary on the Saltee Islands with its wonderful gannets, its weird palm trees and its king. There are also non-landing sea tours of the area on the *Saltee Princess* in summer. Or a day's deep-sea fishing can be arranged (Tel: 053-29704).

Berkeley Costume and Toy Museum
Berkeley Forest House, New Ross
Tel: 051-421361
Open: by arrangement only, May–October. Groups of five and upwards preferred.

A remarkable private collection of dolls, toys and period clothes dating from the 1740s to the 1920s. There is also a small pretty garden open for inspection.

Barrow Cruise

New Ross Quay
Tel: 051-421723

This is a food idea. Galley lunch cruises from New Ross: May–October at 12.30 p.m. Children half-price. Afternoon tea: June–August 3.00 p.m.

JFK Arboretum*

New Ross
Tel: 051-388171
Open: all year round.

A sloping forest park with nearly 5,000 different species and lots of colour. Summer pony-trap rides and miniature railway.

Dunbrody Abbey Visitor Centre

Campil
Open: April–September.

The remains and the history of a large thirteenth-century Cistercian monastery. Its other considerable attractions include a delightful castle doll's house and outside, a yew-hedge maze in the shape of the castle; also pitch and putt.

Kilmokea

Great Island, Campile
Tel: 051-388109
Open: April–November.

Come for the animal statues, topiary and the secret garden through the wall. Children are free with adults.

Duncannon Fort

Tel: 051-389454
Open: June–mid-September: 10.00 a.m.–5.30 p.m.

The fort, which was built by the order of Elizabeth I during the Spanish Armada emergency, sits on its own promontory overlooking the fine Blue Flag beach situated below. It was rebuilt for use by the Irish army after being burnt in 1922 and now guided tours reflect all the periods of

Duncannon's history; battlement walk and cell visits also included.

Hook Lighthouse Visitor Centre

Tel: 051-389454 (information)
To open in 2000.

Said to be the oldest lighthouse in Europe, being either a Norman one built with bullocks' blood mortar, or a fifth-century one — whichever, you can expect a good story. Either way, monks ran the lighthouse for hundreds of years.

Carlow

Carlow Town Guided Tours

Tourist Office, Kennedy Avenue
Tel: 0503-30411/0503-30446
Open: mid-April–mid-October, Tuesdays, Thursdays, Saturdays:
2.30 p.m.

Evening mystery tours also available as well as day-long countryside walks. Alternatively pick up a Barrow Way map in the Tourist Office and DIY on foot or bike. Combine with **Browneshill Dolmen** which you can get to through the car park. Come to see the biggest dolmen in Ireland, perhaps in Europe, dating from before 2500 BC.

St Mullins: the site of an early Christian settlement by a beautiful part of the River Barrow. There is a penal altar here where an open-air Mass is said every year on the Sunday before 25 July. This is also the burial place of the feisty king, Art Mac Murrough.

Altamont Gardens

Tullow
Tel: 0503-59128
Open: Sunday and Bank Holiday afternoons, April–October.

Everybody's dream summer garden. The oak walk by the Slaney river offers a real chance to see wildlife and also a variety of flowers which brings butterflies to this spot in summer. Don't miss the clever little temple from where a panoramic view of south Leinster can be seen.

Adelaide Memorial Church

Myshall
Tel: 0503-57671
Open: by consulting neighbouring key-holder.

This is Ireland's tiny Taj Mahal. It was built in 1913 by a grieving father and is a replica of Gothic Salisbury Cathedral, complete with beautiful stained glass and tiles. Combine with **Ballykeenan Pet Farm**, Myshall, which is open all year (tel: 0503-57665).

Country Quads

Moloney's Farm, Borris
Tel: 0503-24624
Open: by appointment.

All-weather quad driving on safe farmland. Helmets and weather gear provided. From Borris you can also walk part of the **South Leinster** *Way* towards Graiguenamanagh, a glorious riverside trail, or turn east to climb Mount Leinster.

You may get hooked by the Barrow. There are several companies offering barges for hire (though not for day trips) in Carlow, Kilkenny and Laois. Ask for the Barrow Cruising brochure at the Tourist Office.

Laois/Offaly

Clonmacnoise Monastic Complex*
Shannonbridge, County Offaly
Tel: 0905-74195
Open: all year.

See the audio-visual show first for an understanding of this amazing sixth-century religious city which was founded on

the Shannon by St Ciaran. Clonmacnoise is both ancient
and wonderful.

Clonmacnoise and West Offaly Railway

Bord na Móna Works, Shannonbridge, County Offaly
Tel: 0905-74114
Open: April–October.

Five miles' journey in a little bog train across a typical
raised bog.

Cloghan Castle

Lusmagh, Banagher, County Offaly
Tel: 0509-51650
Open: July and August: 2.00 p.m.–6.00 p.m., or by appointment.
Guided tours.

The castle was originally built in 1336 and was expanded
in Cromwellian times. It is still occupied and contains
contemporary furniture. Nearby is a callows territory, rich
in bird life. Combine with a Silver Line trip on the
Shannon from Banagher (tel: 0509-51112).

Slieve Bloom Environment Park Trails

Tel: 0509-37299

Check with Birr Tourist Office (seasonal) for maps and
ideas, or drop into the Slieve Bloom Rural Development
Society in the Community Centre in Kinnitty where there
are experts, and sometimes guided tours. The froggy trail
to the Barrow headwaters is recommended; there are also
geological and waterfall trails.

Birr Castle and Historic Science Centre
Tel: 0509-20336
Demesne open all year round. Science Centre open all year round:
9.30 a.m.–6.00 p.m.

The grounds are splendid, but the unique draws are the
Great Telescope of 1845, for many years the biggest in the
world, and the new Halls of Science, celebrating the
amazing astronomical, photographic and engineering feats

of the resident Parsons family. Birr was once called Parsonstown.

Emo Court and Gardens*

Emo, County Laois
Tel: 0502-26573
Gardens open all year. House tours mid-June–mid-September.

The house which was designed by Gandon looks like a small parliament house. The gardens and lake-shore are full of surprises, including a giant (baby giant: only 150 years) sequoia walk. This walk was laid with a mile-long red carpet for the visit of King Edward VII.

Heywood Gardens*

Ballinakill (near Portlaoise), County Laois
Tel: 0502-33563
Open: all year; tours in July and August. Sundays: 3.00 p.m.

World-famous architect Sir Edwin Lutyens (of Dublin's Memorial Park) designed this series of linked gardens and pools.

Kildare

Lullymore Heritage Park

Rathangan
Tel: 045-870238
Open: all year.

An indoor and outdoor theme park of Irish rural life from Stone Age to hedge school and fairy bower. Crafts and teas.

Peatland World
Lullymore, Rathangan
Tel: 045-860133
Open: all year.

Everything you could possibly want to know about bogs and their inhabitants. Lullymore is built on a mineral island in the middle of the Bog of Allen.

Ballitore Quaker Museum

Ballitore
Tel: 0507-23344
Open: all year (it shares space with the library).

A tiny stone dwelling with all the elements of early Quaker life and schooling. Combine it with:

Crookstown Mill and Heritage Centre

Tel: 0507-23222
Open: April–October.

A corn mill dating from 1840 which explains the district's milling and baking history.

Robertstown Barge Tours

from Grand Canal Hotel, Robertstown
Tel: 045-860260
Sunday afternoon barge trips from April–September. Educational tours for groups by appointment.

Combine with the Robertstown Local Walk, marked in purple, along the Barrow Line.

Ballindoolin House & Garden

Carbury
Tel: 0405-31430
Open: May–September.

An interesting and pretty-well undiscovered heritage house and grounds. Includes original furniture, a working walled garden and nature and folklore trails through the woods.

Furness (near Naas)
Tel: 045-866815
Open: daily, September and October.

An elegant small house that was built in 1731 and which is of great architectural interest. In addition to the house itself, there is also an ancient Celtic church, a ráth and a large dolmen which all lie behind the main building. Expensive to visit.

Kilkenny

> A visit to the Tourist Centre will get you maps and other worthwhile information. Here are some of the attractions of Kilkenny City both medieval and modern.

Cityscope, Tourist Office
Rose Inn Street

A miniature model exhibition using SFX, to get you started on explorations. A studio sideline is an exhibition of doll's houses.

Open-top bus tours
April–October. Leaves from Castle.

Kilkenny Castle*
Tel: 056-21450
Open: daily, except Mondays, during October–March.

It has a glorious riverside setting, ancient twelfth-century bits and a lot of later improvements. Guided tour and art exhibitions.

Rothe House
Parliament Street
Tel: 056-22893
Open: all year.

An Elizabethan house with extensions which was built by a prosperous father for his twelve children. Contains a costume display.

St Canice's Cathedral
Irishtown
Open: daily except during Sunday services.

A thirteenth-century cathedral with an earlier round tower that can be climbed for a superb view.

Craft trail: Pick up a map of participating craft studios in the area.

Walking tours: Tynan walking tours (tel: 056-65929). Details from Tourist Office.

Dunmore Cave*

Ballyfoyle
Tel: 056-67726
Signposted from Castlecomer road.
Open: daily, March–October; winter: weekends only.

Not only did the geological combination of water and limestone do their 'fingery' business in these caverns but ancient historians recorded a Viking massacre here which occurred in the tenth century. Unfortunately, Dunmore Cave is not wheelchair accessible.

Jerpoint Abbey*

Thomastown
Tel: 056-24623
A twelfth-century Cistercian monastery with lots of atmosphere. Its carvings include dragons and a person with stomach trouble. This site can be combined with Kilfane Glen and Waterfall (see next entry) to make a full day out.

Kilfane Glen and Waterfall

Thomastown
Tel: 056-24558
Open: daily, July and August; May–September, Sundays only.

A wild natural garden complete with waterfalls, cliffs and a gingerbread cottage.

Woodstock Park

Inistioge
Woodstock is now owned by Coillte, since the Big House there was burned down. It's a great picnic spot; there is also a long monkey-puzzle avenue which is well worth checking out. Free.

Westmeath

Tullynally Castle and Gardens

Castlepollard
Tel: 044-61159
Gardens open: May–September each afternoon. Castle open: mid-June–end July; 1–15 September.

A huge rambling Gothic pile with lots of Victorian household items on show. The gardens are splendid, with lakes, a Chinese garden and spectacular trees.

Athlone Castle

Tel: 0902-72107
Open: Easter–October.

A sprawling riverside castle and former barracks, with audio-visual show and several exhibitions (river life; UN peacekeeping, singer John McCormack, to name a few). Don't miss the opportunity to hire a boat and crew your way on the mighty Shannon. Or travel on the *MV Ross* riverboat. Ask at quayside or Tourist Office.

Locke's Distillery

Kilbeggan
Tel: 0506-32134
Open: all year.

A museum of how whiskey was made in the country's oldest licensed distillery. Delicious food. The perfect stop on the road to Galway.

Lough Owell and Lough Lene

Near Mullingar, both of these lakes have swimming facilities if you fancy a lake dip. The tiny beach on Loch Lene has even qualified for Blue Flag status. Sailing and fishing are also possible from these shores. Close by is **Fore Abbey**, the ruins of a large Benedictine establishment, and nearby a more ancient hermit's chapel can be found. Even more famous are the alleged Seven Wonders of Fore, all science-defying! Ask at Mullingar Tourist Office for further information.

Belvedere House
Mullingar

A mansion dating from 1740, currently under restoration for public visiting. Its grounds are open and offer forest and lake walks plus a view of the barrier folly called the Jealous Wall.

Longford

Corlea Bog Centre and Trackway*
Keenagh, Ballymahon
Tel: 043-22386
Open: June-September.

Here lies a wooden road that was laid in 148 BC. No potholes! This is an interpretative centre about Iron Age life on the bog and how bogs were managed.

Carrigglas Manor
Longford Town
Tel: 043-45165
Open: May–September, Mondays, Fridays; June– August, Mondays, Tuesdays, Sundays.

There are guided tours of this Gothic house which was built by Jane Austen's sweetheart. A costume and lace museum is housed in the stable-yard. Woodland gardens. Combine with a trip, just a bit further on, to Cloondara to see the Royal Canal joining the Shannon.

Cavan/Leitrim

Cavan and Leitrim Railway
Dromod, County Leitrim
Tel: 078-38599
Open: May–October.

Both diesel and steam trains offer narrow-gauge railway trips on track taken from the famous West Clare railway.

There is also a museum, model railway, and engine sheds on display.

Lifeforce Watermill

Cavan Town
Tel: 049-436 2722
Open: May–September.

You mix a loaf of bread here which is then baked while you tour the water-powered mill and works.

Drumcoura City

Ballinamore, County Leitrim
Tel: 078-44676
Open: all year.

Western rodeo-style ranch open to day visitors or for residential weekends. Lashings of cowboy fun and ranch-style food on offer.

Ballinamore is on a restored canal line. Enquire at the marina about barge or boat hire.

Roscommon

Strokestown Park House

Gardens and Famine Museum, Strokestown
Tel: 078-33013
Open: Easter–October.

Strokestown House has been completely restored together with its own furnishings, a large walled garden, and a micro-history of the Great Famine as it happened locally. Please note there are separate charges for each aspect.

King House

Boyle
Tel: 079-63242
Open: Easter–October.

This early Georgian mansion became the home of the legendary Connaught Rangers and both its family and military history are on exhibition here. Also featured are interactive displays for children, including dressing up in costumes. Combine with **Boyle Abbey*** (tel: 079-62604) which dates from the twelfth century and was home to Cistercian monks. Architecturally, it is split down the middle between Gothic and Romanesque style.

Lough Key Forest Park (near Boyle)

Tel: 079-62363
Open: all year.

Forest trails, ringforts, cairns and tunnels together with boats for hire on the lake which has thirty-three islands.

Louth

Drogheda
(see Meath chapter: more colonialism!)

Carlingford

Holy Trinity Cultural and Visitor Centre
Old Quay Lane
Tel: 042-937 3454
Open: Easter–August, every day; rest of year weekends only.

Carlingford is a small port and is full of castles. The Visitor Centre shows a video history of the town and also provides information of what else there is to explore. There is a medieval town trail leaflet and Carlingford Medieval Week is in June. Combine with **Riverstown Mill**, Cooley; open all year from 12.30 p.m., (tel: 042-9376157). The famous Brown Bull, which Queen Maeve coveted so much, was a native of this area. You can walk some of the signposted Táin Trail from Carlingford — 19 miles of forests and hills.

Louth County Museum

Carroll Centre, Jocelyn Street, Dundalk
Tel: 042-932 7057
Open: all year; weekends: afternoons only.

The museum is housed in a handsome nineteenth-century bonded warehouse building and is an exhibit in itself.

Inside there is a lively and interactive presentation of local history.

Armagh

All of the following are in Armagh town, so if you set out early enough in the day, with enough money in your pocket, you can return the same evening penniless, but happy.

Armagh Planetarium

College Hill
Tel: 080-1861-523 689
Open: all year; weekends: afternoons only. Book star-shows to avoid disappointment.

Everything about astronomy and earth science, including star-shows and computer models. Great shop.

Navan Centre

81 Killylea Road
Tel: 080-1861-525 550
Open: all year.

This centre is at the site of a ringfort complex whose proper title is Eamhain Mhacha. Over these earthworks warrior Cú Chulainn strutted his stuff with the Red Branch Knights and the Kings of Ulster raised their royal palace. Video and interactive presentation of the history of this site, and the archaeological research in deciphering its story.

Palace Stables Heritage Centre
Palace Demesne
Tel: 080-1861-529 629
Open: all year.

An exploration of Big House life in the eighteenth century. Carriage rides in summer. Adventure play area.

St Patrick's Trian

40 English Street
Tel: 080-1861-521 801
Open: all year.

The interpretative centre of Armagh, the ecclesiastical capital of Ireland. On offer for younger visitors in particular is The Land of Lilliput, a fantasy experience based on *Gulliver's Travels*.

Down

> The first three of the following entries are all found on the Ards peninsula. A short cut can be made by taking the Portaferry car ferry at Strangford. It's quite expensive so you could return the inland way.

Exploris

Castle Street, Portaferry
Tel: 080-12477-28062
Open: all year.

This is the biggest aquarium on the island of Ireland. Special emphasis is placed on the unusual sea life of Strangford Lough, and there are open sea and shoaling tanks on view, touch-tank sessions and a well-equipped shop.

Mount Stewart House and Gardens

Newtownards
Tel: 080-12477-88387
Open: April–October: weekends; May–September: daily.

A comfortable classical house with plenty to see. The gardens are spectacular and no one will forget the Dodo Terrace with its charming animals. Also includes lake and wood walks and the famous 'Greek' Temple of the Winds — separate entrance fee for this.

The Somme Heritage Centre
Newtownards
Tel: 080-1247-823202
Open: all year.

The only dedicated First World War Museum in Ireland and, lest we forget, it's based on the bloodiest of all battles. There is a trench re-creation and an audio-visual presentation.

Ulster Folk and Transport Museum
Cultra
Tel: 080-1232-428428
Open: all year; October–March: weekends only.

This museum is situated just outside Belfast, but the city can be avoided — follow the signposts. It comprises acres of farm and village sets; a superb transport section with great locomotives — also featured is a *Titanic* exhibition. Allow several hours for this trip, it's well worth it. (You can also do this excursion as an Iarnrod Éireann Family Rail-break, see page 218.)

Brontë Homeland Interpretative Centre
Drumballyroney Church, Rathfriland
Open: March—October.

You can combine a visit to this site with any of those mentioned above, or with a trip to the Carlingford area. The Interpretative Centre offers a small exhibition about the famous Yorkshire literary geniuses whose father, Patrick, was originally from this part of the country. Return via Mourne Mountain drive.

More Information

A Visitor's Guide to Heritage Sites in Ireland, published by Archaeology Ireland, is an excellent collection of listings. It also includes the names of key-holders to many of the national monuments which do not have the usual open access.

Houses, Castles and Gardens of Ireland lists many places that are not in conventional guides. Available in tourist offices, or telephone 286 2777.

Heritage Sites is published by Dúchas, who also publish smaller regional listings.

Midlands-East Tourism have an excellent brochure called *Mountains and Waterways: Rural Walking Holidays*, which shows walking trails in all their designated counties. See below.

Bord Fáilte have several different publications available. Tel: 602 4000/1850-230 330 or visit their office at Baggot Street Bridge. (See also websites page 338.

Regional tourist offices will send information on the counties they administer or else direct you to local offices.

Concerning the counties covered above, you can contact the following:

> **Midlands-East** (Kildare, Laois, Longford, Louth, Meath, North Offaly, Westmeath, Wicklow), is located at Dublin Road, Mullingar, County Westmeath. Tel: 044-48650.

> **North West** (Cavan, Leitrim), is at Áras Reddan, Temple Street, Sligo. Tel: 071-61201.

> **South East** (Carlow, Kilkenny, Wexford), 41 The Quay, Waterford. Tel: 051-875823.

> **The Northern Ireland Tourist Office** is at 16 Nassau Street, Dublin 2. Tel: 679 1977.

> **The British Tourist Authority** is at 18 College Green. Tel: 670 8000.

Chapter 11

joining in

This chapter means just that. All of the societies and associations listed are glad to hear from young people — in fact, some of them are entirely youth-orientated. Many welcome families, others (and this is great if you are a bit shy) offer you facilities and information to get on with your own particular bug on your own terms. Whether you want to build your own telescope or tap-dance your way in the St Patrick's Day Parade, whether you're sporty or slinky, digitally adept or double-jointed, a completely indoors person or happy only when tumbling through white water, this chapter has tried to fit you in somewhere. Teachers may also find this chapter useful, because several of the organisations and facilities mentioned are tailored specifically for schools. It's a reference chapter, so at the end you will find lists — swimming pools, riding schools and libraries. But before you get that far, with any luck you will have started wondering why you thought all the good things happened to someone else, somewhere else....

> Where just a private address and number are given, this is a contact, usually an annually elected secretary, who will give you the information you need. So, if you write for information _please do_ enclose a stamped addressed envelope.

CREATION! From Art to Science

Arts Centres

Ark Cultural Centre for Children
Eustace Street, Dublin 2. Tel: 670 7788

Offers a full programme of music, drama, visual arts and dance throughout the year, with school attendance during the week and family attendance at weekends. Booking is essential for both. Its theatre offers both an intimate indoor space and a summertime outdoor space fronting onto Meeting House Square. Check the programme or become a Friend of The Ark.

City Arts Centre
Moss Street, Dublin 2. Tel: 677 0643

This Liffeyside centre is a focal point for visual arts, in the display of new work (including computer art) and in community involvement. Schools and groups are welcome to work on designated projects with the Education Officer. The Centre is also the venue for Very Special Arts Ireland (see below) who run an arts encounter programme for teenagers.

IMMA (Irish Museum of Modern Art)

Royal Hospital, Kilmainham, Dublin 8. Tel: 612 9900

IMMA acts as a resource for primary-school teachers. A programme of workshops, tours, talks and courses help teachers to develop classroom-based art projects. Contact the Education and Community Department for further information.

The Grainstore Youth Arts Centre

Cabinteely Park, Dublin 1. Tel: 285 0175

The Grainstore Youth Arts Centre is a superb new arts venue for young people in the Dún Laoghaire/Rathdown area. The restored outbuildings of Cabinteely House house a workshop, indoor and outdoor performance space, a music room, exhibition space and darkroom facilities. Community groups offering activities in dance, drama, film making, visual arts and so on, can apply for space/hours at the Centre.

Tallaght Community Arts Centre

Virginia House, Blessington Road, Dublin 24. Tel: 462 1501

The Tallaght Community Arts Centre offers regular workshops for young people of different age groups in drama and visual arts. Rehearsal space available for bands and concerts.

IntroArt

27 Great Strand Street, Dublin 1. Tel: 872 7930

IntroArt is a centre that supports and provides facilities for disabled people of all ages. It's affiliated to the National Youth Council and offers space, training, information, links and other resources, covering different areas of art and disability.

CAFE — Creative Activity for Everyone

143 Townsend Street, Dublin 2. Tel: 677 0330

A resource group for community arts groups and artists (visual and dramatic).

> **The Travellers Resource Warehouse** collects
> factory and industrial waste (examples: card, wool,
> paper, foam, newsprint and so on) as art materials
> and resources for schools, playgroups, youth clubs.
> Information from TRW, Pavee Point, 46 North
> Great Charles Street, Dublin 1 (tel: 874 3087).

Art Workshops and Classes

Dublin Corporation run art and craft classes in various
city and suburban centres, mainly the libraries. Contact
Youth Information Centre, Sackville Place for details
(tel: 878 6844); **The National Gallery** (tel: 661 5133)
(see page 19) have an annual programme for families and
for schools, as well as summer courses and Christmas
holiday painting sessions — you can check the current
programme in their free Gallery Guide; **The Hugh Lane
Gallery** (tel: 874 1903) has Saturday morning classes most
weekends of the year; **The National Museum** at Collins
Barracks (tel: 677 7444) have a full programme of themed
workshops for young people throughout the year; **Pine
Forest Art Centre** in Glencullen (tel: 294 1220) run
summer and year-round classes for different age groups in
various aspects of art and crafts, with portfolio work for
older students — a bus picks up students from various
southside pick-up points; **The National College of Art
and Design**, Thomas Street, Dublin 8 (tel: 636 4200)
offers summer courses in visual arts, including portfolio
preparation, for over 16s; **Tiggy's Art School**, Tarva, The
Green Road, Dalkey (tel: 285 1514) have afternoon and
weekend classes during the year, and summer courses, for
ages 4–14.

> The separate county council Vocational Education
> Committees will advise which of their schools and
> colleges offer full-time art, music, film/animation/
> media and drama courses.

The councils also run Youth Reach programmes and Dublin has a special Artsquad programme for people who have dropped out of schools. The different offices are Dublin city (tel: 668 0614), Dublin County (tel: 451 5666), Dún Laoghaire (tel: 285 0666).

Ballyfermot Senior College (tel: 626 9421) runs school-leavers' courses in art, animation, computers and photography during June, July and August.

See Science below for details on the annual RDS Youth Science and Arts Week — it's for arty types as well as boffins.

Computers

Futurekids
Dublin centres at: Tallaght (tel: 462 8808); Dún Laoghaire (tel: 269 6738); Stillorgan (tel: 278 1064); Rathfarnham (tel: 493 9622); Lucan (tel: 628 0301)

Futurekids is a nationwide company which specialises in offering children's programmes in computer skills.

Arthouse
Curved Street, Temple Bar. Tel: 6056800

Arthouse offers courses in multimedia skills, with a view to mixing art and technology. They also have regular family days in CD-ROM familiarising and computing skills.

The Irish Centre for Talented Youth
Tel: 704 5634

The Irish Centre for Talented Youth offers Saturday courses in computing throughout the year and also as a part of their multi-subject summer courses. A SAT assessment is required.

ClubMac
Tel: 260 5204

A Macintosh users' group that meets in Merrion Cricket Club, Donnybrook on the first Wednesday of every month. Telephone above number for details.

Dance

Classical Ballet

Pauline Magrath ARAD

39 Whitehall Road, Terenure, Dublin 12. Tel: 455 5946

There are many classical ballet teachers and schools throughout Dublin, and boys and girls from 6 years of age and upwards are welcome to join the classes. For a list of teachers and schools in local areas who conform to the standards of the Royal Academy of Dancing, contact Pauline Magrath, the Irish administrator, at the above address or consult Ballet Schools in the Golden Pages.

The Russian Dance Academy

Tel: 833 1406

This organisation teaches a Russian-based approach to classical ballet. Classes are held at different venues (at the time of this book going to press).

The Irish Junior Ballet

Tel: 475 5451

The Irish Junior Ballet is funded by the Arts Council. It's a performance-oriented company of dancers aged 10–21, who are chosen by audition, and work to a European training programme. Applicants must maintain a minimum dance study requirement of two hours per week in their own dance schools; company training takes place at weekends. Telephone above number for details.

De Valois House

5/6 Meeting House Lane (off Capel Street). Tel: 873 5536

This is the largest centre-city dance studio, and is called after the legendary Wicklow-born dancer and teacher, Ninette de Valois. Several dance schools and companies perform here. It's also a base for the Association of Professional Dancers of Ireland, offering classes, information and workshops to resident and visiting dancers. Telephone above number for details.

Ballroom

The Granby Dance Works
10 Granby Place, Dublin 1. Tel: 872 1812

City Dance Centre
150 Capel Street, Dublin 1. Tel: 872 9197

Contemporary/Jazz

Dance Theatre of Ireland
13 Clarinda Park North, Dún Laoghaire. Tel: 280 3455

Evening classes for over 15s.

Dublin School of Classical and Contemporary Dance
13 Stamer Street, Portobello, Dublin 8. Tel: 475 5451

Hip-Hop/Modern

Parnell School of Performing Arts
14 Sackville Place, Dublin 1. Tel: 878 6909

Irish Dancing

Coimisiún Rince
6 Harcourt Street, Dublin 2. Tel: 475 7401
An administration organisation which provides details of local teachers and schools.

Stage, Tap and Musical

Dublin Theatre Arts School (tel: 677 0040); this school is based at De Valois House; National Performing Arts School, The Factory, 35A Barrow Street, Dublin 4 (tel: 668 4035); Helen Jordan Stage School, with branches in the centre of the city and also at Crumlin, Tallaght, Clondalkin, Naas (tel: 451 1023); Billie Barry Stage School, Clontarf, Dublin 3 (tel: 833 9644).

Dance in Education

Daghdha Dance Company
Tel: 061-202804
The Daghdha Dance Company is based at the University of Limerick and travels to schools throughout the country to

which it presents its selection of dance and theatre in education programmes.

Coiscéim Dance Theatre
7 South Great George's Street, Dublin 2. Tel: 670 4906

Coiscéim offers occasional dance workshops in tandem with their in-theatre productions.

Dance Theatre of Ireland
13 Clarinda Park, Dún Laoghaire. Tel: 280 3455

This company also offers DancePOP (Performance Outreach Programme) for schools.

Very Special Arts

City Arts Centre
23 Moss Street, Dublin 2. Tel: 671 6518

Very Special Arts runs a dance programme called CounterBalance in which young people, with and without disabilities, work together.

Drama and Theatre

As a distinguishing feature only, I have divided this section so that **Drama** means acting, directing, mime, backstage work — all those getting-involved things, while **Theatre** means being in an audience.

Drama

Two large city-centre schools are:

Gaiety School of Acting
Meeting House Square West, Temple Bar. Tel: 679 9277

Caters for all ages, plus full-time student course, and summer Young Gaiety theatre workshops.

Betty Ann Norton Theatre School
Clonbrook House, 11 Harcourt Street, Dublin 2. Tel: 475 1913

All ages welcome, year-round and summer courses, with other centres in Dún Laoghaire and Rathmines.

Southside:

National Performing Arts School
The Factory, 35A Barrow Street, Dublin 4. Tel: 668 4035

Independent Theatre Workshop
Tel: 496 8808
Centres at Ranelagh, Rathgar, Tallaght

Irish Children's Theatre Group
19 Whitebarn Road, Churchtown, Dublin 14. Tel: 298 6636

Stagecoach Theatre Arts Schools
Blackrock. Tel: 280 3336

Dún Laoghaire Drama Workshop
Tel: 230 2691/284 4679

Northside:

Dublin Theatre Arts School
De Valois House. Tel: 677 0040

Summit Drama School
Tel: 832 0941
Also branches at Sutton, Clontarf, Glasnevin, Malahide, Castleknock and Swords.

If you are interested in film acting, or 'extra' work, check first with the drama schools listed above. Most of them work with casting agencies and pupils can be placed on their books.

Dublin Youth Theatre
23 Upper Gardiner Street, Dublin 1. Tel: 874 3687

Dublin Youth Theatre holds workshop auditions every year for its company of 14–22-year-olds. Entry requirements are balanced according to age, locality and gender — all that is required is a genuine interest in any or all aspects of theatre. Workshops are held on Saturdays and public productions are staged every year in a major theatre.

The National Association of Youth Drama (NAYD)
34 Upper Gardiner Street, Dublin 1. Tel: 878 1301

NAYD is a co-ordinating body for youth theatre in Ireland. The Association publishes a magazine, organises residential courses (scholarships available), runs the National Youth Theatre and the National Festival of Youth Theatres, and works with European Youth Theatre Encounter. A list of local youth theatre groups in Dublin city and surrounding counties is available on request. NAYD is also the contact for Reach Out, Youth Theatre for the Deaf.

Pan Pan Theatre
Tel: 280 0544; Fax: 230 0918

Pan Pan Theatre, in association with NAYD, runs a summer workshop, Deaf Youth Theatre.

> There are many other local youth drama groups, both community based and those attached to adult amateur drama groups. Your local library should be the first place to check out addresses; try also the National Youth Council.

Very Special Arts at City Arts Centre
23 Moss Street, Dublin 2. Tel: 671 6518

Very Special Arts Ireland runs a Young Playwrights Programme throughout the year. In the workshops it runs, 15–18-year-olds with and without disabilities, work together creating original plays which explore different attitudes to disability. Each year the overall winning play is publicly produced.

Theatre

Team Educational Theatre
4 Marlborough Place, Dublin 1. Tel: 878 6108

TEAM is a touring company. Based in Dublin it visits schools in other counties with original plays. They have workshops too and involve the audience with chosen themes.

Iomhá Ioldánach
The Crypt, Dublin Castle, Dublin 2. Tel: 671 3387

This group visits primary schools and performs original plays which are based on themes and stories from Irish mythology. Shows can be bilingual, or in all-Irish or all-English.

Down to Earth Theatre Company
The Boneyard, Schoolhouse Lane West, Dublin 8. Tel: 670 5734

Down to Earth produces original plays with environmental themes for primary schools and community youth groups. This company also offers workshops.

The National Theatre (Abbey and Peacock)
Abbey Street, Dublin 1. Tel: 874 8741

The National Theatre operates an Outreach/Education programme which offers experiences to community and youth groups. Details of the annual programme and events which are open to the general public are available from the Office and Projects Manager.

Calypso
7 South Great George's Street, Dublin 2. Tel: 670 4539

Calypso commissions theatre work that highlights human rights and anti-racism issues. They run workshops and offer information packs to schools.

The Lambert Puppet Theatre
Clifton Lane, Monkstown. Tel: 280 0974

The master puppeteer, Eugene Lambert, runs this theatre with his family. Shows are varied, touring in winter with shows in Dublin every Saturday and Sunday. The theatre has a collection of over 300 puppets and marionettes.

Second Age Theatre Company
Tel: 679 8542

Second Age bases its productions on each year's examination drama texts. The productions are well-publicised and patronised.

Storytellers Theatre Company
Tel: 671 1161

This company does similar exam-based work to that of the
Second Age Theatre Company but their texts tend to be
novels explored through dramatisation.

Dublin Yarnspinners
Tel: 280 8322

Dublin Yarnspinners offers regular entertainments, proving
that the ancient arts of storytelling are alive and well. They
meet in the Teachers' Club, Parnell Square, Dublin 1, on
the second Thursday of the month, except during summer
months. All welcome.

> Plays with juvenile interest are performed season-
> ally in almost all Dublin theatres. The Dublin
> Children's Theatre Festival in October is based at
> The Ark and features invited international acts.

Literature in Education

Poetry Ireland
Bermingham Tower, Dublin Castle, Dublin 2. Tel: 671 4632

Poetry Ireland has a register of several hundred writers (of
all kinds, not just poets) who will travel and read/perform
in primary and secondary schools.
(See also The Ark above.)

Film/Media

Irish Film Centre
Eustace Street, Dublin 2. Tel: 677 8788

The annual Junior Dublin Film Festival takes place each
autumn at the IFC and various local venues.

The Film Institute of Ireland
Tel: 677 8788

The Film Institute of Ireland runs an educational programme for schools and operates regular screenings and

seminars (contact the Education Officer for details at the above number). It also produces a guide to careers in film and television for school-leavers — viz., a directory of all the post-Leaving Certificate training opportunities. The VEC (see telephone directory for the different VECs) will also provide details of the schools and colleges in their areas that offer film, animation and multimedia training.

Terenure College
Terenure
Tel: 490 4621
Terenure College runs a summer-time course for young filmmakers aged 15–18 years.

Young Irish Film Makers
St Joseph's Studios, Waterford Street, Kilkenny. Tel: 056–64677
An Arts Council-funded organisation that offers courses and workshops in different aspects of film-making.

> *Ireland on Screen* offers useful addresses for anyone wishing to try the difficult task of landing Transition Year work in this hot area. It's available at the Irish Film Centre. The Film Institute of Ireland also have a library that can be accessed by students.

Film competitions for young people

Limerick-based Fresh Film Festival
3 Upper Hartstonge Street, Limerick. Tel 061–319 555

Mobil Green Site
Tel: 679 6600
A competition for Transition Year students who wish to enter 10-minute videos on environmental themes.

For film 'extra' work see Drama section above.

UCI Cinema Complexes
Blanchardstown, Tallaght, Coolock, Santry Omniplex
All of these cinemas hold cheap Saturday morning film screenings for children (accompanied adults no charge).

Information available in newspapers or from the cinemas themselves.

Music

Dublin has always been super-rich in music training and this section could be pages longer. I have had to choose a range of options but the list could be added to indefinitely. Where possible, an umbrella contact group is given which can supply details of local organisations.

Principal Music Schools

These schools teach all levels in all the classical orchestral instruments, in singing, music theory and appreciation. Performing groups are often formed within the schools. **DIT College of Music**, Chatham Row (tel: 402 3000); **Royal Irish Academy of Music**, 36 Westland Row (tel: 676 4412); **Leinster School of Music**, **Griffith College**, South Circular Road (tel: 475 1532); **Walton's College of Music**, 69 South Great George's Street (tel: 478 1884); **Kylemore College of Music**, Ballyfermot (tel: 626 5901).

Local Music Teachers

Local music teachers do not have an association, but since many are attached to one of the colleges on the list above, a query for a *local* piano, strings or brass teacher will usually be answered. The Golden Pages lists only a small number of people under Music Teachers. Your local library or community centre may also be able to help.

Music for Very Young Children

The Suzuki Violin Method

This approach, which teaches children of ages 2–5 how to love and handle a violin, has a few teachers in Dublin. For names, telephone 286 8297 or 282 9798.

The Kodály Method

This method is based on the pioneering work of Hungarian composer Zoltán Kodály, with music skills and theory acquired through folksong and choral work. For details of teachers and courses, telephone 668 7148, or send a SAE to KSI, P.O. Box 4569, Dublin 7.

Newpark Music Centre
Newtown Park Avenue, Blackrock. Tel: 288 3740
Newpark offers both Gateway to Music and Gateway to Instruments courses for children aged 4–7 years.

Leeson Park School of Music
Kensington Hall, Grove Park, Rathmines, Dublin 6. Tel: 496 7890
Includes a Music Kindergarten for the very tiny and children up to 6 years of age.

Parnell School of Music
14 Sackville Place, Dublin 1. Tel: 878 6909
Parnell School of Music has an introductory music programme for children aged 4 years and upwards.

Irish Traditional Music

Comhaltas Ceoltóirí Éireann
32 Belgrave Square, Monkstown. Tel: 280 0295
Comhaltas teaches tin whistle to children on Saturday mornings and there are evening classes in fiddle, flute, accordion for all ages from 7 years and upwards. Informal sessions and group playing happen on certain evenings.

Walton's (see Music Schools above) also run summer workshops in traditional playing.

Clontarf School of Music
11 Marino Mart, Fairview. Dublin 3. Tel: 833 0936
Clontarf School of Music specialises in traditional instrument teaching.

Wind and Brass

All the music schools listed offer individual tuition. The Irish Youth Wind Ensemble (minimum standard grade 6) give concerts and have a summer school for players.

Contact Pat Mullen (tel: 846 1216/855 7481). Another contact for brass and concert bands is the Irish Association of Marching Bands, c/o 57 Alderwood Avenue, Springfield, Tallaght, Dublin 24 (tel: 874 6911/452 1239). All youth bands provide instrumental training.

Jazz/Rock

Newpark Music Centre
Blackrock, County Dublin. Tel: 288 3740

Lessons in sax, guitar, drums and jazz improvisation.

Parnell School
Tel: 878 6909

Rock seminars and summer workshops.

Walton's School
Tel: 478 1884

Walton's School teaches rock and jazz styles of instrumental playing.

The Metropolitan School
59 Baggot Street Lower, Dublin 2. Tel: 454 0753

Lessons in rock and jazz styles of instrumental playing.

Ballyfermot Senior College
Tel: 626 9421

Ballyfermot College teaches rock music and rock management as a third-level course.

Orchestra

The National Youth Orchestra of Ireland
37 Molesworth Street, Dublin 2. Tel: 661 3642

The Orchestra has over 200 members between its two sections — NYO Under 18s (12–17 years) and NYO (18–24 years). Both orchestras perform in concert and for broadcast, and go on tour, nationwide and abroad. There are twice-yearly residential rehearsal sessions. Existing and new members must apply for auditions each autumn, in the various disciplines of strings, woodwind, brass and percussion.

Dublin Youth Orchestras
12 Wesley Heights, Sandyford, Dublin 16. Tel: 295 4206

Comprises four different orchestras in all: Junior Strings, Intermediate, Transitional and Symphony — they play all-year round, give concerts. This organisation also runs a summer school and arranges European exchanges. Contact Carmel Ryan at the above number for general orchestra details, and you can also telephone 235 2233 for summer course details.

Young European Strings
21 The Close, Cypress Downs, Templeogue, Dublin 6W.
Tel: 490 5263

Offers training in orchestral skills for string players in three age groups from 4–12 years. There are weekly sessions and occasional performances. Contact Maria Kelemen.

Other local youth orchestras are **Liffey Valley Orchestra,** c/o 22 Weston Drive, Lucan (tel: 628 2264); **West Dublin Youth Orchestra,** c/o Wesley College, Ballinteer, Dublin 16 (298 7066); **Young Dublin Symphonia**, c/o 190 Seapark, Malahide, County Dublin (tel: 845 1666); **Greystones Youth Orchestra** c/o 6 Silverpines, Bray, County Wicklow (tel: 282 9594). Certain schools and music schools maintain youth orchestras which perform in concerts and festivals.

The umbrella group for youth orchestras in Ireland is the **Irish Association of Youth Orchestras**, 6 Alexandra Place, Wellington Road, Cork (tel 021–507 412) and additional information and advice can be got from there.

Choral Music

There are choristers (boys only) in St Patrick's Cathedral (for pupils of the Cathedral school only), St Ann's on Dawson Street, St Bartholomew's on Clyde Road, and the Pro-Cathedral (the Palestrina Choir). On the other hand,

Christ Church Cathedral has girl choristers. You need an exceptional voice for these choirs. Other churches have less formal choir arrangements — ask locally.

Another choir is Piccolo Lasso, the Lassus Scholars' junior branch. It takes children from nine upwards. Contact Newman House, St Stephen's Green (tel: 453 9663).

There are many local young people's choirs. For a list of affiliated choirs in your area, contact **Cumann Náisiúnta na gCór**, Drinan Street, Cork (tel: 021–312 296) for information regarding youth choirs in local areas.

Three nationally known choirs are: **Cór na nÓg**, who perform with the National Symphony Orchestra (there are annual auditions — for information write to the Director, Cór na nÓg, RTÉ Music Department, RTÉ, Donnybrook, Dublin 4); **The National Children's Choir** (tel: 278 3283); **Irish Youth Choir** (17–29 years) (tel: 021–312 296).

All the large music schools teach singing and voice training. Newpark Music Centre (see above) have two choral classes, one for children of 7–10 years and Newpark Youth Choir for children of 10–14 years. The Kodály Method (see above) teaches musicology through song.

The Churchtown-based **Irish Children's Theatre Group** also offer performance-based singing (tel: 298 6636).

Sound Training

The Sound Training Centre
Temple Bar Music Centre, Curved Street, Dublin 2. Tel: 670 9033

This centre offers a range of courses, summer, part-time and full-time, in sound engineering for music and television production. You must be aged 17 years or over.

Music in Education

Two companies with a tradition of working in education are **Opera Theatre Company** (tel: 679 4962) which stages performances in schools along with prior workshop activities, and the DCU-based **National Chamber Choir** (tel: 704 5665) which works with a broad range of schools and produces a combined opera at the end of the training period.

The Irish Times operates, in conjunction with the RTÉ orchestras, a Music in the Classroom programme. Contact the Education Department of *The Irish Times* (tel: 679 2022) very early in the school year — it gets booked up almost immediately.

World Music for Youth

RDS, Ballsbridge, Dublin 4. Tel: 668 0866

This is a music education festival for schools run by the Royal Dublin Society during the school year. Concerts and workshops in different types of music are presented at several venues. For further information contact the Art and Development Officer, World Music for Youth, at the above address.

Jeunesses Musicales in Ireland

19 Ludford Park, Dublin 16. Tel: 298 7596

This is a branch of an international UNESCO-sponsored association dedicated to involving young people in all kinds of music, via clubs, festivals, competitions, and also summer courses.

Music Network

Ship Street Gate, Dublin Castle, Dublin 2. Tel: 671 9429

Music Network is a national music development association aiming to make classical, jazz and traditional music accessible to all. It also produces a Music Directory.

Music Association of Ireland

69 South Great George's Street, Dublin 2. Tel: 478 5368

This is a contact association for many music societies and organisations.

Slógadh

26 Merrion Square, Dublin 2. Tel: 676 7283

Contact Slógadh for details of the annual schools performance competition.

Feis Ceoil
37 Molesworth Street, Dublin 2. Tel: 676 7365
Contact Feis Ceoil for details of the annual competition.

And last but not least:
Bell-Ringing
So many churches have electronic or mechanical bell-ringing that it's delightful to know that Dubliners can still learn the ancient art of bell-ringing or **campanology.** You do *not* end up like Notre Dame's Quasimodo but rather get involved in a skill that adds to both social and civic life. Courses are held in Christ Church Cathedral. Either write to Leslie Taylor at Christ Church Cathedral, Dublin 8 (tel: 677 8099) or check the bell-ringers' page on the Cathedral's website (see page 339).

Photography
An Óige Photography Club
61 Mountjoy Square, Dublin 1. Tel: 830 4555

Membership is open to all age groups and An Óige Photography Club offers training and facilities in developing and printing.

The Gallery of Photography
Meeting House Square, Dublin 2. Tel: 671 4654

The Gallery of Photography runs workshops for young people throughout the year and also offers darkroom facilities.

Dublin Camera Club
10 Lower Camden Street, Dublin 2. Tel: 662 4464

The Photographic Society of Ireland
38 Parnell Square, Dublin 1. Tel: 873 0263

The Grainstore Junior Arts Centre
Cabinteely. Tel: 285 0175
The Grainstore offers darkroom facilities.

Many youth clubs have photography groups. There are classes in almost all community schools and the VEC run classes too.

Ten Photo Opportunities:

Head in the stocks outside Dublinia (see page 75)

Under Temple Bar's Palm Tree sculpture

Crossing the locks on the Grand Canal (see page 121)

In the Viking Boat on the quay outside the Viking Adventure Centre

Feeling the rays at the Bray Aquarium (see page 41)

On top of the Jameson Chimney

Standing beside a human statue busker on Grafton Street — same pose (unfair)

Patting a Stephen's Green horse

Sitting beside Oscar Wilde (see page 163)

Spray painting the U2 Wall

Politics

You can visit the Dáil by arrangement. But how about participating in a junior version of the United Nations or the European Parliament? The Model United Nations takes place in Dublin during the Easter holidays every year. This event offers a chance for about 800 secondary school pupils (fourth, fifth and sixth Years), from Ireland and abroad, to debate in Assembly conditions and to represent different UN member states; during the exercises the participants follow actual parliamentary procedures. Applications must be made at the start of the school year to The Model United Nations, St Andrew's College, Booterstown Avenue, Blackrock, County Dublin (tel: 288 2785). St Andrew's College also provides information on the organisation of the Model European Parliament, which follows a similar course, except that it takes place in different countries each year. So, unless it happens to be Ireland's turn, taking part in the Model Parliament will involve airfare and accommodation expenses.

Science

The RDS

Ballsbridge, Dublin 4. Tel: 668 0686

The RDS employs a Youth Science Officer and provides the venue for the annual Young Scientists Exhibition; it also runs a Youth Science and Arts week every summer. There are about 250 places for 14–17-year-olds so book early to avoid disappointment — it's usually held in July. The RDS also runs a Young Science Writers competition for 12–19-year-olds, with a closing date in early spring. Enquiries to the Youth Science Officer, RDS.

Archaeology

For a taste of how our ancient forefathers and mothers lived, ate, slept and celebrated, plus all the detective work involved in finding these matters out, you could join the Irish Young Archaeologists. The group is based at Dublinia, Christ Church, Dublin 8. Contact the Curator for details (tel: 679 4611).

Astronomy

Astronomy Ireland, PO Box 2888, Dublin 1. Tel: 459 8883

Astronomy Ireland welcomes youth and family members and also issues a newsletter. On fine weekends they have star-gazing sessions in Enniskerry, County Wicklow, as well as more public displays in the Phoenix Park (advertised in the papers). The organisation runs a telephone hotline (1550–111 442), has an astronomy shop, and holds public lectures monthly on the DCU campus. Send an SAE to the above address for more information.

See how to get into Dunsink Observatory in the Inside Jobs chapter (see page 230).

Academically Gifted Students

Irish Centre for Talented Youth

c/o DCU, Griffith Avenue, Dublin 9. Tel: 704 5634

The Irish Centre for Talented Youth offers an academic programme in various science and humanities subjects to students aged 8–16 years who are of exceptional academic ability. The Dublin programme is based at the Dublin City University campus. Fees are payable, but scholarships may be awarded. The Centre operates nationwide Talent Searches which require a SAT (Scholastic Aptitude Test). Courses are at weekends and during the summer. They do not supplant ordinary schooling but, based at first-year university level, offer extra stimulation to gifted students. All applicants can attend the Centre's Discovery Days in Science and Technology, from computers to archaeology.

Dublin Public Libraries

Dublin libraries are usually very busy places, with the larger libraries running regular activities for children, ranging from exhibitions to drama, from storytelling to fancy dress. Not all of the activities listed are available in all libraries and you will find space and staff numbers vary from library to library. If you are interested in any particular activity check with your local library for details. (See list and phone numbers at the end of this chapter.) Listed below are some of the activities that the Dublin Public Libraries have on offer.

Arts and Crafts: which means anything from drawing and collage to painting big beautiful wall murals or making junk sculpture. Some libraries give scrolls, others exhibit your work.

Book Clubs: these can be found in larger libraries, and often hold discussions and quizzes.

Drama Workshops: in libraries with enough space.

Exhibitions: include the display of children's art and writing, and books of special interest.

Music Listening Facilities: tapes can be borrowed for home use.

Project Files: Several libraries have built up a collection of Project Files to help with hobbies and schoolwork. Ask at the desk.

Quizzes: The Dublin Inter-library Quiz takes place each summer. Quiz heats take place in local libraries during the year.

Slide Shows and Film Strips: Available to teachers and youth club leaders.

Storytelling: in most libraries, for younger children — often takes place outside in the open air during fine weather.

Children's Book Festival: towards the end of October, offers two weeks of creative activity in libraries, with competitions, author interviews, fancy dress and more. Book Lists of recommended reading are published for each season.

Apart from the activities above, the following two libraries should be particularly noted.

The ILAC Centre library has a specialised programme of computer learning in many subjects, including computers! In addition, foreign language conversation exchanges take place on different days.

The Gilbert Library, based at Pearse Street Library, has a dedicated collection of national newspapers in its archive, together with books and other materials relating to Dublin city and county. You must sign in before you can consult this valuable reference collection whose premises are to be refurbished.

Summer Projects & Summer Camps

Summer Projects are excellent holiday activities/ workshops/excursions and are either free or very cheap. They are usually based in schools, but that's for convenience not for similarity. If you don't know about your local Summer Project through your school, contact the **Dublin Corporation Youth Information Centre**, Sackville Place (tel: 878 6844) or the **Catholic Youth Council**, 20–23 Arran Quay (tel: 872 5055), either of which will tell you all you need to know.

Summer Camps (the Dublin-based ones) vary greatly. Some are quite academic and are pointedly intended for catching up on school work while others are more like Summer Projects; some are conducted through Irish, and others again are quite like their American counterparts. All are fee-paying. Some regulars include: **Camp Blackrock**, based in Blackrock College — most sports as well as swimming, drama, arts subjects and computer workshops (tel: 288 8681); **Camp Portmarnock**, which is based at Portmarnock Sports and Leisure Club — most sports, swimming and soccer camps (tel 846 2122); **Camp Glenalbyn**, based at Glenalbyn House, Stillorgan — sports, swimming, and knockout activities (tel: 288 0857); **Kings Hospital Sports Camp**, Palmerstown — covers everything from swimming to karate and canoeing (tel: 626 5933).

For the 3–14 age group there are the following: **DCU Sports Camp**, Dublin City University, Glasnevin — sports include rock climbing, orienteering as well as soccer, tennis, dance. Drama and gymnastics are also on offer (tel: 704 5797); **Leixlip Activities Centre**, Leixlip, offers a multi-activity camp, including swimming (tel: 624 3050).

Special interest summer courses for young people include **Drama** — Gaiety School of Acting, Sycamore Street, Dublin 2 (tel: 679 9277); Betty Ann Norton Summer Drama, several centres (tel: 475 1913); Dún Laoghaire Drama Workshop, summer camp (tel: 230 2691); **Art** — Pine Forest Summer School, Rathfarnham (tel: 295 5598); Tiggy's Art School, Dalkey (tel: 285 1514). **Cooking** — Busy Bee Summer School of Cooking (for ages 11–16 years), Killiney (tel: 285 8674); **Basketball** — National Basketball Arena (coaching for boys and girls), Tallaght (tel: 459 0211); **Soccer** — FAI Soccer Clinics (for both boys and girls), at various venues. Information from FAI, 80 Merrion Square, Dublin 2 (tel: 676 6864); **Film and Media** — Terenure College (for teenagers aged 15+) Terenure (tel: 490 4621); **Modelling** — Geraldine Brand, one-week summer courses (for ages 14–18 years), (tel: 832 7332); **Music** — Walton's School of Music (offers summer courses in traditional Irish music), 69 South Great George's Street, Dublin 2 (tel: 478 1884); Parnell School of Music (offers rock seminars as well as workshops), 14 Sackville Place, (tel: 878 6909); Dún Laoghaire Music Centre (has a multi-arts summer school for ages 5–12 years), 130 George's Street (tel: 284 4178); **Sailing** — Irish National Sailing

School (varied summer courses for young people), West Pier, Dún Laoghaire (tel: 284 4195); Surfdock (offers various sailing, canoeing and windsurfing courses for ages 8–16 years), Grand Canal Dockyard (tel: 668 3945); **Snorkelling and Scuba** — Oceantec, 10/11 Marine Terrace, Dún Laoghaire (tel: 280 1083); **Windsurfing** (as well as rafting and canoeing and kites) — Wind and Wave Windsurfing, 16A The Crescent, Monkstown (tel: 284 4277); also Surfdock (see Sailing); **Athletics** — Morton Stadium (courses for groups in July and for individuals in August), Santry (tel: 862 0635); **Irish** — Gael-Linn (various Dublin-based courses for young people), 26 Merrion Square, Dublin 2 (tel: 676 7283) **European Languages** — CBC Monkstown, (offers a mixed languages/sports/computer camp for Irish and foreign students), Monkstown (tel: 280 4964).

There are many more courses available each year — consult your local newspapers, youth clubs and sports complexes for further details on what is available. See also the separate listings for sports below; you can be alerted to special summer courses in your chosen sport. Newspapers will also carry details of out-of-Dublin residential adventure camps of various kinds as well as Gaeltacht holidays.

The Big Youth Organisations

These organisations do not fall into any special category — they are broad-based, and could have their members doing all or any of the activities in these pages. You probably know about some of them, and you can look them up in a telephone book, but it's handy to have them all together.

Scouting Ireland CSI
36 Harrington Street, Dublin 8. Tel: 676 1598

Scouting Ireland SAI
Scout Den, Ballygall Road East, Dublin 11. Tel: 857 0132

The two Scouting organisations are set to amalgamate in the near future, but meanwhile aspiring Beavers, Cubs,

Scouts and Venturers (ages 6–20 years catered for) can join either association. Telephone for details of your nearest branch. Both organisations offer year-round outdoor activity, camping holidays and varied opportunities in sports, skills and self-development. Sea and Air Scouting are optional activities offered in certain areas. People with disabilities are integrated into general scout branches although deaf scouts have their own branch.

Irish Girl Guides
27 Pembroke Park, Dublin 4. Tel: 668 3898

Brownies, Guides and Rangers (ages 6-21 years).

Catholic Guides of Ireland
36 Harrington Street, Dublin 8. Tel: 475 1774

Brigidine and Guides (ages 6 years and over).

Girls Brigade
5 Upper Sherrard Street, Dublin 1. Tel: 836 5488

Explorers, Juniors, Seniors, Brigadiers (ages 5–15 and over).

Boys Brigade
Lower Abbey Street, Dublin 1. Tel: 874 5278

Anchor Boys, Juniors, Company (ages 5–17 years).

An Óige
Irish Youth Hostel Organisation
61 Mountjoy Square, Dublin 1. Tel: 830 4555

An Óige Hostels which are situated throughout the country provide cheap, clean accommodation. The organisation also offers a range of sports and hobby clubs. Members can stay in cheap-rated hostels world-wide.

USIT
Union of Students in Ireland, 9 Aston Quay, Dublin 2.
Tel: 677 8117

USIT issues student travel discount cards, and also offers cheap travel deals for secondary-school (scholars) and third-level students.

National Youth Council
3 Montague Street, Dublin 4. Tel: 478 4122

The NYC represents many voluntary youth organisations and clubs and runs a range of education and awareness projects.

National Youth Federation
20 Lower Dominick Street, Dublin 1. Tel: 872 9933

The National Youth Federation represents youth organisations and summer projects and also has a library of material on youth issues. (It also has beautiful Georgian plaster-work ceilings!)

Catholic Youth Council
20-23 Arran Quay, Dublin 7. Tel: 872 5055

The Catholic Youth Council organises Catholic youth clubs, youth information centres (Bray, Clondalkin, Dún Laoghaire) and non-denominational Summer Projects.

Church of Ireland Youth Council
30 Phibsboro Road, Dublin 7. Tel: 830 0299

The Church of Ireland Youth Council offers youth leader training and resources.

Foróige National Youth
Irish Farm Centre, Bluebell, Dublin 12. Tel: 450 1166

Foróige operates clubs and sports in the community.

Ógras
6 Harcourt Street, Dublin 2. Tel: 475 1487

Ógras offers sports and activities through the Irish language, at primary and secondary level.

Dublin Corporation Community and Youth Information Centre
Sackville Place, Dublin 1. Tel: 878 6844

Information on sports clubs, jobs, grants and so on. Youth literature and videos also available for consultation from this centre.

City of Dublin Youth Service Board (CDVEC)
70 Morehampton Road, Dublin 4. Tel: 668 3198

The Youth Service Board offers services and training to youth and summer project leaders.

Slógadh
26 Merrion Square, Dublin 2. Tel: 676 7283

Community Games
5 Lower Abbey Street, Dublin 1. Tel: 878 8095

Hobbies and Skills

Cookery

The Busy Bee Summer School
54 Ballinclea Heights, Killiney. Tel: 285 8674

You can learn to cook from a book or from the cook in your family. But learning the clever tricks to cordon bleu land can be fun. The Busy Bee School offers two-week courses for ages 11–16 years. DART pick-up service is also offered.

Design

Grafton Academy of Dress Design
6 Herbert Place, Dublin 2. Tel: 676 7940

Art classes are a help if you are interested in dress design and the Grafton Academy runs a summer course for older teenagers (and all ages) who would like to have a trial run in the rag trade.

Family History

The National Library
Kildare Street, Dublin 2. Tel: 603 0200

The Library has a special family-tracing service and will point you on the right track to starting serious genealogy. Dublin Libraries publish a short guide to the basics of genealogy, which is on sale in their branches.

Mormon Family History Centre

Finglas Road, Glasnevin (suitably opposite the cemetery).
Tel: 830 5803/830 6899
Open: Wednesday and Thursday nights but check by telephone first.

What not many people know is that from Dublin you can also check out the biggest family history database in the world, containing over ten billion names. It's managed by the Mormon Church, and their computers and hard copy are kept in a bomb-proof vault inside a mountain near Salt Lake City, Utah, USA. You can access it, as well as extensive Irish records, at the Mormon Centre at the above address.

First Aid

St John's Ambulance Brigade

29 Upper Leeson Street, Dublin 2. Tel: 668 8077

Order of Malta Ambulance Corps

32 Clyde Road, Dublin 4. Tel: 668 4891

Both of the above organisations offer basic first-aid classes at various locations, and you can decide to join either one of them at a later stage if you wish to do so. With further first-aid training, you can get to participate with your chosen first-aid organisation at concerts, matches and other big events.

Model Car Racing

If the weather is fine, come to Belfield car park (beside the Science block) on Sundays at noon to see the racing of radio-controlled cars. If you or any of the family are bitten by the bug any of the racers there will give you news of club events.

The Dublin Model Car Club

Taney Centre, Dundrum. Tel: 621 0014

The Taney Centre hosts indoor meetings of model car enthusiasts on Saturdays.

Science Fiction

Science Fiction Ireland
c/o 43 Eglinton Road, Dublin 4. Tel: 260 5204

This is the main organisation for other-worlders. Meetings are held on the first Tuesday of every month in The Squealing Pig, Amiens Street, Dublin 1. Notice-boards also in The Flying Pig Bookshop, Crow Street, Dublin 2, or The Forbidden Planet comic shop, Wellington Quay, Dublin 2. Octocon is the annual Sci-fi festival — further details available from the above number.

Stamps

An Post Philatelic Service
Room 2322 GPO, O'Connell Street, Dublin 1. Tel: 705 7400

An Post's Philatelic Service runs the Voyager Club for young stamp enthusiasts.

Steam Railways/Train Spotting

The Irish Railway Record Society
Heuston Station, Dublin 8

The Irish Railway Record Society actually hold its meetings at Heuston Station and can be contacted there by post.

The Railway Preservation Society of Ireland
PO Box 74, Blackrock. Tel: 288 0073

The RPSI organises several steam-train outings per year, which are open to everyone. For details of meetings and other information contact the Society at the above address.

War-games

Games Workshops
Lower Liffey Street, Dublin 1. Tel: 872 5791

Games Workshops supply actual games as well as kits and equipment and there is also a branch at Blanchardstown Shopping Centre (tel: 822 3868).

Serious gamesters could try the Dublin Games Guild meetings on Wednesdays at 6.30 p.m. at the Ierne ballroom, 12 Parnell Square East (tel: 874 5228).

Two regular events in the fantasy calendar are Gaelcon and Leprecon (usually October and January, respectively) and you can ask in the shops about these massive moots of fantasy gamers.

Money and Glory or Work and Work

The Law

By law you must be aged 14 years or over to get even a part-time job during school holidays. The Protection of Young Persons Act (1996) is quite specific — if you are under the age of 16 you are a 'Child' and if you are aged 16–18 years you are a 'Young Person'.

If you are over the age of 15 years and full-time at school you can be employed in **work experience or training** during holidays but are not allowed to work more than 8 hours a day, or 40 hours in a week. You can also do light work during term time but not more than 8 hours in a week.

Shops, bars, fast-food outlets and so on, are perfectly aware of the law in this regard. They are required to take full responsibility in certifying your age and seeing proof of parental permission to work. *You* are obliged to disclose your real age. The restrictions are protective. Remember that in far too many countries around the world young children are actually enslaved. It can be tempting to try and earn money during term time but if you exceed the hours allowed you can jeopardise both your health and your study prospects — not a good idea.

An area where work is available outside the restrictions outlined here are cultural, artistic, sports and advertising activities. But film and theatre people must fulfil strict chaperone responsibilities for young people (see under Drama above).

Whatever the area you want to work in, if you apply in person always do so togged out in your best, and where possible, always have references to hand. It is also very important to make sure that you clearly understand the work you are being hired for, the conditions of your employment as well as the amount and method of payment. You can always ask for the details in writing if they are complicated or if there are a lot of them to remember. Apply locally to find work where possible. It cuts down on travel expenses and time. Local shops often have small-ad notice-boards. If you have casual work hours, always let someone in your house know where you are going and when you expect to be back. And if you are hired for a job and come to hate it, *do* offer the employer notice that you intend to quit. First, it's a courtesy; second, they probably have some of your money in hand.

If you have particular interests like animals, fashion or motor bikes/cars, you should try to get a job you'd enjoy. When you're known at a garage, a hairdressing salon or stables/kennels, obviously it's all that much easier.

Ideas for Under 14s

Some people make a lot of commission selling lines: you need to be charming or be cheeky. Ask the next person you see doing it — they should be able to tell you how to get started.

Run your own Sales of Work — for profit or for charity, but always say which. Tables will do for stalls if you are going to hold the sale in the garden. Food can be made, while books, comics, records will sell quickly if they are cheap enough. You can have extra attractions — I used to charge one old penny to shake hands with our cat — a talented animal!

Deliver local newspapers — the free ones. These papers have to be distributed quickly by efficient delivery people. Write to or phone the distribution department of your local paper.

If you are photogenic you could be a model. The Morgan Agency, 13 Herbert Place, Dublin 2 (tel: 676 6625) will put suitable people of all ages on their books. You will have to send photographs and proof of parents' permission.

FÁS

FÁS is a statutory body which provides apprenticeship training in a wide variety of careers. FÁS offices also offer information and advice to job-seekers who satisfy the law concerning employment and young people. Its head office is at 27 Upper Baggot Street, Dublin 2 (tel: 607 0500) and there are seventy offices throughout the country.

Volunteer Work and Campaigning for Justice

Many of these organisations offer education programmes through schools. Some are also interested in hearing from individuals, although they may not be able to provide you with a work placement unless you are of a certain age (usually 16–18 years). There are many ways of helping people in the world and sometimes just making yourself aware of the facts can be the most important way to start.

Co-operation Ireland

37 Upper Fitzwilliam Street, Dublin 2. Tel: 661 0566

Co-operation Ireland organises cross-border exchanges between secondary schools from Northern Ireland and the Republic, and fosters cultural interchange.

The Society of St Vincent de Paul

8 New Cabra Road, Dublin 7. Tel: 838 9896

This charity has a programme for Transition Year students (and upwards). Activities include: working in Homework Clubs with disadvantaged primary school pupils, home visiting and fund-raising.

Trócaire

Booterstown Avenue, Blackrock, County Dublin. Tel: 288 5385

Trócaire is an international aid organisation. It has an active schools programme, produces a newsletter, and also works through youth groups and workshops; its annual fund-raising campaign is well-established. Trócaire also runs campaigns to highlight issues of injustice that exist throughout the world and young people are most welcome to become involved.

Afri
Grand Canal House, Lower Rathmines Road, Dublin 6.
Tel: 496 8610/496 8595

Afri is committed to issues of justice and peace world-wide. It is best known in Ireland for its Great Famine Project and its annual walks. Afri also campaigns against the international arms trade. Young people are welcome on all campaigns.

Concern Worldwide
Camden Street, Dublin 2. Tel: 475 4162/1850-410 510

Concern works throughout the developing world. It offers information on development issues, organises debates within schools and also works with Transition Year projects. Its annual fund-raising fast is supported by many young people.

Oxfam Ireland
19 Clanwilliam Terrace, Dublin 2. Tel: 661 8544

Oxfam is keen to inform students of all ages about the realities of the lives of their contemporaries in developing countries, and how global issues affect people in these areas. Write or telephone for details.

Amnesty International
48 Fleet Street, Dublin 2. Tel: 677 6361

Amnesty International has a youth branch of its organis-ation which assists in its worldwide campaign.

East Timor Campaign
Room 16, 24–26 Dame Street, Dublin 2. Tel: 677 0253

The East Timor Campaign actively involves schools, both primary and secondary, in raising awareness about the reconstruction needed, at all levels, in that small island-country that recently achieved independence after a particularly bloody invasion by Indonesia. Individuals are welcome to drop in to the above address and meet young East Timorese people.

Comhlámh
10 Upper Camden Street, Dublin 2. Tel: 478 3490

As a result of the support it provides for returned aid workers, Comhlámh can offer development education workshops and lectures which link home and overseas issues.

The Irish Red Cross
16 Merrion Square, Dublin 2. Tel: 676 5135

The Irish Red Cross has a youth section. Some of the activities it offers to young people include hospital entertainment troupes and storytelling; first aid, safety and baby-sitting courses through schools; learning therapeutic manicure care (for ages 16 years and over) and occasional international exchanges.

UNICEF
28 Lower Ormond Quay, Dublin 1. Tel: 677 0843

UNICEF is the UN body concerned with the rights of children throughout the world. Here you can find out about the Charter on Children's Rights, and also, unfortunately, information on human rights abuses that concern children. If you wish to fundraise for UNICEF as part of an aid campaign, the organisation will be delighted. The UNICEF shop is well-stocked with attractive paper goods.

African Cultural Project
4 Lower O'Connell Street, Dublin 1. Tel: 878 0613

The African Cultural Project operates cultural and educational programmes in partnership with festivals, schools, arts centres and so on. Activities include an African-Irish Youth Drama Group, Youth Choir and Junior Literature Week.

Celts and American Indians Together (CAIT)
c/o Aidlink, 46 Lower Rathmines Road, Dublin 6.
Tel: 496 6956/455 5453).

This group was set up to commemorate the historic donation from the Choctaw Nation to victims of the Great Irish Famine and is dedicated to addressing issues of famine and injustice throughout the world.

The following are two busy organisations that are not directly involved in education or campaigns but can provide information and also redirect enquiries:

Pavee Point Travellers Centre
46 North Great Charles Street, Dublin 1. Tel: 878 0255

Irish Refugee Council
40 Lower Dominick Street, Dublin 1. Tel: 872 4424

Local youth clubs can alert you to other volunteer work and some hospitals work with Transition classes on visitor programmes.

Peata
Tel: 296 4474

Peata is an organisation that brings friendly pets (customarily dogs) on visits to certain hospitals and homes. The animals must be vetted for size and temperamental suitability and their families must be committed to regular visits. This service brings a lot of joy to people who otherwise have no contact with pets.

DSPCA
(Dublin Society for Prevention of Cruelty to Animals)
Stocking Lane, Dublin 16. Tel: 493 5502

The DSPCA has a youth section and young members are welcome to help fund-raise for animal welfare.

Sports

You will not find one word about most common school sports below — if they are your passion, you already know how to follow them up. No — this is a connoisseur's list so don't just skip it because you ain't the sporty type. Some of these are exciting spectator sports that would make a great family outing — others are all action. I have divided sports into categories of my own that would probably put the Olympic Council into paroxysms of laughter, but to me they seem highly efficient.

> This book goes to press before either an Olympic 50-metre pool or the West Dublin soccer stadium are built. However, these facilities *are* on the way, we are assured.

Useful Addresses

Institute for Children's Sport in Ireland
House of Sport, Long Mile Road, Dublin 10. Tel: 450 2527

The Institute provides lots of information and ideas for teachers and group leaders.

Irish Sports Council
21 Fitzwilliam Square, Dublin 2. Tel: 676 3837

Cospóir — National Sports Council
Hawkins House, Dublin 2. Tel: 873 4700

Dublin International Sports Council
1 Merrion Square, Dublin 2. Tel: 662 2855

The Council is seeking to raise the national standard of sports facilities to international levels.

Olympic Council of Ireland
27 Mespil Road, Dublin 4. Tel: 668 0444

Department of Tourism
Sport and Recreation (Sports Activities Unit), Floor 3, Frederick Buildings, South Frederick Street, Dublin 2. Tel: 631 3800/1890-383000

Community Games Organisation
5 Lower Abbey Street, Dublin 1. Tel: 878 8095

Adventure Sports

You will need the following addresses for many of the sports listed in the following pages. They specialise in what is known as 'adventure sports' — which is, basically, any outdoor, non-competitive (except against the elements) exciting sport.

AFAS, the Association for Adventure Sports
House of Sport, Long Mile Road, Dublin 12. Tel: 450 9845

The National Outdoor Training Centre
Tiglin, Ashford, County Wicklow. Tel: 0404-40169.

Caters for groups and individuals, but booking is essential. Canoeing, river trekking, rock climbing, walking in all terrain, orienteering, caving, rescue skills, navigation, mountaineering at home and abroad.

An Óige
61 Mountjoy Square, Dublin 1. Tel: 830 4555

An Óige offers a wide range of adventure sports to its members.

Other centres offering adventure sports in the Dublin region are as follows:

Adventure Activities Limited
5 Tritonville Avenue, Dublin 4. Tel: 668 8047

This company organises canoeing, hillwalking, rock climbing, and abseiling.

Adventure Company
136 Seafield Court, Killiney. Tel: 276 2800

The Adventure Company organises hillwalking, orienteering, rock climbing and abseiling.

County Dublin Outdoor Education Centre
c/o Clondalkin Sports and Leisure Centre, Nangor Road, Clondalkin. Tel: 457 4858

The Centre organises archery, canoeing, orienteering, rock climbing and abseiling.

Blessington Land and Water Sports Centre
Blessington, County Wicklow. Tel: 045-865 092

The Blessington Land and Water Sports Centre is a multi-activity centre situated on the shores of a lake. It is open to families, schools and groups of all kinds. You can drop in, but at weekends it is advisable to book in advance, and while doing so you can also check out what clothing and/or equipment you will need. On offer are canoeing, windsurfing, sailing, pony trekking, tennis, orienteering and archery.

Paintball 'war' games are strictly speaking not sports. However, if it's your fancy to spend a day in the woods making very dirty realism from 'virtual reality', you will find a list of firms offering you the chance. Check the Golden Pages under Adventure Sports. Different age qualifications apply.

Air Sports

Flying

The minimum age at which a person can obtain a solo flying licence is 16 years. Weston Aerodrome, Celbridge, County Kildare (tel: 628 0435) offer pilot training. It's a very expensive sport, but introductory lessons are relatively cheap. Eirecopter (tel: 628 0059), also based at Weston, offer helicopter training. First Flight Aviation (tel: 890 0222) offer introductory helicopter pilot flights, and sight-seeing plane and helicopter trips out of Dublin Airport. Plane-spotting is free and the best place, apart from Weston, is anywhere along the back road to Dublin Airport (straight through Ballymun and keep going).

Gliding — Dublin Gliding Club
Tel: c/o 458 0340

Glider pilots meet at Gowrangrange, off the Punchestown Road (3 miles past Naas), on Saturdays and Sundays. A gliding licence is also only obtainable by people over the age of 16, but (at the discretion of the tutors), younger people can take lessons. There's no age limit for passengers, and it's possible to get a trial membership to try it out.

Para-gliding/Hang-gliding

Hang-gliding & Para-gliding Centre, Kilmacanogue, County Wicklow. Tel: 830 3884

The Centre organises summer courses for people over the age of 16, and also runs weekend courses from March to September. As well as practical gliding techniques, students learn meteorology, navigation and rules of the air.

Hot Air Ballooning

Balloons over Ireland

Tel: 260 0744

> All air sports are necessarily expensive because of the intensive level of training required to learn them, the high-tech equipment used and the relatively high cost of the appropriate insurance cover.

Water Sports

Angling

Dodder Anglers' Club

c/o R. O'Hanlon, 82 Braemor Road, Churchtown. Tel: 298 2112

The Dodder Anglers' Club has many young members, and runs courses in winter which cover the basic techniques of angling.

The Irish Federation of Sea Anglers

Tel: 280 6873

Some youth clubs have angling groups. Enquire at your local club.

Canoeing

The Irish Canoe Union

House of Sport, Long Mile Road, Dublin 12. Tel: 450 9838

The Irish Canoe Union has details of local clubs and the various kinds of courses available (see Adventure Sports above also).

Rowing

Dublin Municipal Rowing Centre

Islandbridge. Tel: 677 9746

The Rowing Centre is run by Dublin Corporation and caters for school groups and youth clubs. The facilities are excellent but booking is essential.

The Irish Amateur Rowing Union

House of Sport, Long Mile Road, Dublin 12. Tel: 450 9831

Sea Scouts teach rowing, and rowing boats can be hired in several places like Dalkey and Rush, if there's an experienced oarsperson with you.

Sailing

Fingall Sailing School

Malahide. Tel: 845 1979

Irish National Sailing School

West Pier, Dún Laoghaire. Tel: 284 4195

Both of the above schools teach sailing in small boats, according to Irish Yachting Association rules, to anyone over the age of 10 years. You can also contact the Irish Sailing Association, 3 Park Road (tel: 280 0239), for details of local clubs and the various courses on offer in the Dublin/Wicklow region.

Surf Dock offers safe training in Grand Canal Docks (tel: 668 3945). You can also take sailing as an option at the Blessington Adventure Centre (see above), and also with AFAS. Sea Scouts, not surprisingly, excel at sailing (see Youth Organisations) and Glenans Irish Sailing Club,

5 Lower Mount Street, Dublin 2 (tel: 661 1481) organise cheap residential sailing courses for families.

Coiste an Asgard
Infirmary Road, Dublin 8. Tel: 679 2169

Asgard II is Ireland's first sail training ship and it gives exciting sea-faring experiences to accepted applicants over the age of 16, both male and female. It sails on voyages through Irish and international waters. You can write or telephone for details of costs and sailing itineraries.

Scuba diving

The National Diving School
c/o 8 St James's Terrace, Malahide. Tel: 845 2000

The Diving School has a range of training options, beginning with Discover Scuba (which is open to competent swimmers aged 12 years and upwards), and progressing (for advanced and older students) to deep-sea and wreck diving.

Oceantec Adventures
10/11 Marine Terrace, Dún Laoghaire. Tel: 280 1083

Oceanic Adventures offers junior courses in snorkelling and Discover Scuba.

Irish Underwater Council
78a Patrick Street, Dún Laoghaire. Tel: 284 4601

Swimming

The most basic water sport of all, and suitable for anyone over three months of age. There is a list of the various kinds of swimming pools at the end of this chapter. Lessons in swimming and water safety are available in most pools at various times — ring your local pool for details.

Swim Ireland
House of Sport, Long Mile Road, Dublin 12. Tel: 450 1739

Contact Swim Ireland for details of clubs and intensive training.

Water Polo

Irish Water Polo Association
Tel: 402 5537/086–820 1567)

Contact the Irish Water Polo Association for details of clubs and training.

Windsurfing

Surf Dock (tel: 668 3945), Fingall Sailing and Windsurfing School (tel: 845 1979), Wind and Wave Windsurfing, 16A The Crescent, Monkstown (tel: 284 4177). All of these organisations offer junior-sized boards and specialised training. You can also take windsurfing as an option in some of the adventure sports centres mentioned in the above listings.

Details of windsurfing clubs are available from the following:

Irish Association for Sail Training
c/o 84-86 Lower Baggot Street, Dublin 2. Tel: 660 1011

Life-saving and Water-safety

Certificates awarded. For details of classes held in local pools contact:

National Safety Council
4 Northbrook Road, Dublin 6. Tel: 496 3422

General

You can do watery sporty things right in the very heart of Dublin city at Surf Dock, The Grand Canal Dock, South Dock Road, Ringsend, Dublin 4 (tel: 668 3945). There are one-day 'taster' events and various other packages of canoeing/windsurfing/sailing for schools, plus individual classes in these activities. There's even a dry-dock high wind simulator for advanced surfers! Junior windsurfing classes are also available during summer months for children aged 8–14 years. Junior-sized boards and wet suits available.

Motor and Machine Sports

Cycling

As a sport rather than a means of getting from here to there, cycling is divided into touring and racing. Many youth clubs take touring trips. A bike needs to be well maintained for both categories — get yours checked by an expert.

Touring:

An Óige Cycling Club
Tel: 830 4555

Touring, Racing and Mountain-biking:

Irish Cycling Federation
619 North Circular Road, Dublin 1. Tel: 855 1522

The Federation has details of clubs throughout the city and country that offer all kinds of cycling activities.

If you want to get involved in campaigning for better everyday facilities for cyclists you might want to join the Dublin Cycling Campaign, c/o Square Deal Cycleworks, Temple Lane, Dublin 2 (tel: 679 0838).

Motor Racing

Mondello Park
Naas, County Kildare. Tel: 045-860 200

Mondello will provide a calendar of their motor sports events which include motorcycles, karts, racing trucks, rallycross and superprix car racing. The Mondello Racing School is open to those who can drive and are over 18 years.

Karting

Kylemore Indoor Karting
Killeen Road, Naas Road, Dublin 10. Tel: 626 1444

This facility offers cadet karting for drivers aged 9–13 years, with Junior Race Meetings on Sundays, as well as regular Karting at other times.

Phibsboro Indoor Karting
Cross Guns Bridge, Dublin 7. Tel: 830 8777

Phibsboro Indoor Karting has a minimum age requirement of 12 years.

Kart City
Old Airport Road, Dublin 9. Tel: 842 6322

Kart City has outdoor and indoor circuits, and also junior karting for children aged 8–12 years.

Motorcycle Training

'Star Rider' is a course in motorcycle riding, aimed at three levels of experience. It's run by the County Councils, Fingal (tel: 872 7777), South Dublin (tel: 414 9000) and Dún Laoghaire/Rathdown (tel: 205 4700), at several locations.

Quad Trekking

Wicklow Hills Quad Trekking
Cronelea, Tinahely/ Shillelagh. Tel: 055-29260
Open: April–October.

Road Safety

There is a Traffic Education School in Clontarf, which is great fun for a day. There are film shows and then you're out on the miniature road system, double yellow lines and all, as pedestrians, cyclists (bikes available) and motorists (pedal cars available). It's run by Dublin Corporation mainly for schools, but it is also open to scouts and summer project groups. You can contact the School directly (tel: 833 85050) or you can telephone the Road Safety Unit of Dublin Corporation (tel: 679 6111) either of which will provide information.

Sport for the Disabled

The Irish Deaf Sports Association
c/o Carmichael House, North Brunswick Street, Dublin 7

Irish Blind Sports
25 Turvey Close, Donabate. Tel: 843 6501

This organisation offers athletics, judo, soccer, bowling, golf and, in summer, water-skiing.

The Irish Wheelchair Association
24 Blackheath Drive, Clontarf. Tel: 833 8241

The Wheelchair Association has a Sunday Junior Sports Club at their HQ; on offer are basketball, swimming, table tennis, athletics, archery, and a type of boules called boccia.

Cerebral Palsy Ireland
Sandymount Avenue, Dublin 4. Tel: 269 5355

Offers boccia, soccer, swimming, track and field, fitness and circuit training for anyone aged 14 years or over. Swimming is also on offer for those aged 12 years or over.

The National Specialised Equestrian Training College
Brí Chualann Riding School, Old Connaught Avenue, Bray, County Wicklow. Tel: 272 0704/6

The College offers a programme of riding for people with disabilities.

Spruce Lodge Riding Centre
Kilternan. Tel: 294 1219

Spruce Lodge also has a specialised horse-riding centre.

The National Outdoor Training Centre
Tiglin, Ashford, County Wicklow. Tel: 0404-40169

Tiglin offers a range of adventure sports for people with disabilities.

Special Olympics Ireland
Ormond House, Upper Ormond Quay, Dublin 7. Tel: 872 0300

Offers year-round training and competitions for people with learning disabilities. Sports available include athletics, basketball, bowling, table tennis, soccer, golf, equestrian, swimming and gymnastics.

Land Sports

Baseball

Baseball Ireland
Tel: 280 6307

Irish Baseball and Softball Association
Tel: 493 0151

There are dedicated baseball grounds at Corkagh Park, Clondalkin.

Boules
Tel: 677 2273

Make believe you are in France with this fiendish family-friendly bowling game. Not too many *terrains* in Ireland yet, but the sport is growing.

Caving

AFAS
(see Adventure Sports Section for contact details.)

The Irish Speleological Union
c/o House of Sport, Long Mile Road, Dublin 10. Tel: 450 9845

Do *not* go caving anywhere without skilled company.

Mountaineering

AFAS/An Óige
(see Adventure Sports Section for contact details.)

Orienteering

Irish Orienteering Association
Tel: 456 9099/021-870 338
Orienteering is open to groups, families and individuals. It's a type of crossword-cum-treasure hunt and is great fun.

Pitch and Putt

The Pitch & Putt Union of Ireland
c/o House of Sport, Long Mile Road, Dublin 12. Tel: 450 9299

Tennis

You can enquire at your local tennis court about classes, but the best scheme for young people is the Dublin Parks Tennis League, which operates three seasons of the year in fifty-four centres throughout the city. Registration is very cheap, and if you don't have the gear, racquets and balls are provided. Thousands of young people are interested and the scheme is very successfully. For those aged 16 years or over, FÁS run a tennis coaching scheme in conjunction with the Dublin Parks Tennis League. For more information contact Kay Lonergan (tel: 833 8711) or Dublin Corporation Parks Division (tel: 679 6111 ext. 3392).

Apart from this excellent public scheme there are literally dozens of private tennis clubs in Dublin — if you don't know of one, consult Sports Clubs in the Golden Pages! Tennis Ireland is the official organisation and its HQ is at Argyle Square, Dublin 4 (tel: 668 1841). A lot of sports centres offer special indoor coaching — you can enquire from them directly. Several summer camps also offer coaching.

Walking/Hiking

AFAS/An Óige

(see Adventure Sports Section for contact details.)

Dublin Walking Club

c/o 61 Ardcollum Avenue, Dublin 5. Tel: 847 4578

Families and young people welcome.

Indoor Sports

Archery

Irish Amateur Archery Federation

c/o Roadstone Group Sports Complex, Kingswood Cross, Naas Road, Dublin 22. Tel: 459 1212

The Federation can supply details on Dublin clubs. Children and families especially welcome.

Some adventure centres offer archery as an option.

Acrobatics

Irish Sports Acrobatics Federation

17 Carrick Lawns, Coolcotts, Wexford. Tel: 053-41329/021-331389

Acrobatics for all ages from 6–30 years.

Bowling (Tenpin)

There are several bowling centres in the Dublin area. See Entertainment chapter for details. Booking a bowling lane in advance is strongly advised.

Boxing

Nearly all big youth clubs teach boxing. For more specialised training contact:

Irish Amateur Boxing Association

c/o National Stadium, South Circular Road, Dublin 8. Tel: 453 3371

Fencing

Salle d'Armes

St John's Road, Sandymount. Dublin 4. Tel: 269 3720

This is a fencing school, and there are classes for children throughout the year. There are weekend courses for older age groups which operate as trial runs for people.

Gymnastics

Irish Amateur Gymnastics Association

House of Sport, Long Mile Road, Dublin 12. Tel: 450 1805

Most clubs take members aged 6 years and over and there are local clubs all over the city.

Ice-skating

Silver Skate Rink

327 North Circular Road, Dublin 7. Tel: 830 4405

Dublin needs more and bigger skating centres to make this sport thrive the way it deserves to — it's a mystery that it's so neglected. Meanwhile this rink survives and it offers morning, afternoon and evening sessions. It is realistically cold so bring gloves and warm clothes. Skates are available for hire, but if you have your own, admission is cheaper. Group and private classes are available and initiates can play ice hockey at special times.

Judo

Irish Judo Association
79 Upper Dorset Street, Dublin 1. Tel: 830 8233

The Association can provide information on local classes and clubs.

Karate and Martial Arts

Irish Martial Arts Commission
23E York Street, Dublin 2. Tel: 478 3831

There are martial arts classes available all over the country and most community and leisure sports centres offer classes in various martial arts. You can also contact The Martial Arts Commission (above) or any of the following: Newpark Sports Centre, Blackrock (tel: 289 2044), offers Kung Fu at all levels; Portmarnock Sports and Leisure Club (tel: 846 2122), offers kenpo; the Martial Arts Federation of Ireland (tel: 842 6637), has details on kenpo training and clubs; the Tae Kwon Do Centre is at 10 Exchequer Street, Dublin 2 (tel: 671 0705).

Snooker

Press your waistcoat and polish your shades — you could be on telly along with the best of them. Seriously though, if you are interested, you already know your local pool hall, or table, and the rules of the place. The minimum age for playing League games is 16 but the bigger centres often run Junior League for those aged 12 years and upwards. For further information contact:

Republic of Ireland Billiards and Snooker Association
c/o House of Sport, Long Mile Road, Dublin 12. Tel: 450 9850

Table Tennis

Table tennis facilities exist at all youth clubs, sports centres and community schools. For more information and details about tournaments contact:

Irish Table Tennis Association
c/o 46 Lorcan Villas, Santry, Dublin 9. Tel: 842 1679

> There are many local purpose-built sports centres that between them offer a huge menu of indoor sports to choose from, as well as facilities in community schools — check sports clubs in the Golden Pages. Dublin Corporation have two large sports complexes, one is situated on Aughrim Street (tel: 838 8085), and the other on Glin Road in Coolock (tel: 847 8177). The Dublin Corporation Parks Department (tel: 679 6111 ext. 3392) can give you information on outdoor sports facilities.

Animal Sports

Falconry

Raptorco
Randalstown, Stratford on Slaney, County Wicklow.
Tel: 045-404965

Make no mistake, Falconry is a blood sport. Hawks take small animals and birds in the wild, and that is also what falconers train their birds to do when they fly them in captivity. Bird-flying-only experiences (no hunt) are offered, but no guarantee can be given that your hawk will not stoop on something furry and small. So be warned.

If you want to practise this ancient sport, Raptorco is the place to contact — it offers a variety of falconry outings. Wear outdoor gear and be prepared for long treks.

Horse-riding

There is a list of riding schools on page 335. For other information contact:

The Equestrian Federation of Ireland
c/o Ashton House, Castleknock. Tel: 838 7611

Show Jumping Association of Ireland
Anglesea Lodge, Anglesea Road, Dublin 4. Tel: 660 1700

The Irish Pony Club is a youth organisation for people under the age of 17 years who are interested in horses and horse-riding. They hold rallies during school holidays and lectures, films and instruction all year round. They say 'possession of a pony is desirable but not essential'. For details of the various branches (nearly all of which are affiliated to local hunts), membership fees and other information, telephone: 056-26186.

Horse-racing

The Irish Horse-racing Authority
Leopardstown Racecourse, Dublin 18. Tel: 289 2888

This is the main racecourse near Dublin — it guarantees lots of buzz and a great day out for everyone during race meetings. There are special buses that leave from Busáras which go further afield to the courses at Punchestown, the Curragh and Fairyhouse. There are admission charges to enclosures but people under the age of 14 years either get in free or at much reduced rates. An annual racing calendar can be obtained from the Irish Horse-racing Authority.

(Legally, you cannot bet unless you are 18 years of age or over.)

Harness and Trot Racing

Portmarnock Raceway
Tel: 846 2834

This very Kentuckyish sport can be seen at Portmarnock every Sunday at 3.30 p.m. from April–October — it's another good day out. Admission rates for children are very reasonable and car parking is free for those who have paid the entrance fee.

Polo

All-Ireland Polo Club
Phoenix Park, Dublin 8. Tel: 677 6248

Polo is played in the Phoenix Park on weekend afternoons from May to September. It is free to watch. The polo ponies are small, skinny and swift — a breed apart. For more information contact the above.

Cats

The Cat Fancy Governing Council
23 Butterfield Avenue, Dublin 14. Tel: 494 3751

This organisation can advise you which shows have categories for ordinary moggies as well as for aristocats.

Dogs

Racing, Training and Showing are not necessarily for your family dog, but you never know.

Racing

Shelbourne Park
Ringsend, Dublin 4. Tel: 1850–646 566
Mondays, Wednesdays, Thursdays and Saturdays.

Harold's Cross
Tel: 497 1081
Tuesdays, Thursdays and Fridays. (Currently undergoing renovations.)

Not as glamorous as horse-racing, but still a good night out. Race meetings at both of the above venues are at 8.00 p.m.

Training

Mansize Dog Training School
Swords. Tel: 840 1982

Wendon Kennels
Mount Venus Road, Rathfarnham. Tel: 497 2723

There are several centres for obedience training, if you can't manage it alone. Contact either of the above for details.

Showing

Irish Kennel Club

Unit 36, Greenmount Office Park, Dublin 6. Tel: 453 3300

'Showing' usually means pedigree dogs only, but small local shows often have 'all comers' class. There are no age limits (for the humans) but children can also show their dogs in a special class at several of the larger shows. Contact the above for details.

Pigeons

Dublin Homing Pigeon Club

2 Shaun Terrace, Dublin 3. Tel: 855 6960

Pigeon-racing is very popular in Dublin and pigeons are kept in a lot of backyards around the city. If you have any yourself then you probably know all about the sport, but if you want to know more contact the above.

Dublin Zoo

Phoenix Park, Dublin 8. Tel: 677 1425

Finally, why not join the Zoo? Membership helps support animal maintenance; there is an education department and you will be first to learn about the Zoo's summer activities.

Winter Sports

Skiing

Kilternan Hotel

Tel: 295 5658

The Ski Club of Ireland has classes that begin in autumn on the artificial slope at the Kilternan Hotel. The Club also operates Junior racing. Unfortunately, there is nowhere in Ireland to try the real thing, though you *can* ski in Scotland.

Tobogganning

Probably no-one needs to be told, but there are some great tobogganning slopes in the Dublin mountains, especially near the Pine Forest. Any slope will do with the right snow coverage and sports shops stock cheap plastic toboggans as well as the fancy ones with runners.

Ice-skating

Available all year round — see indoor sports.

Wildlife and Environment

Some of the societies listed below are dedicated to nature-spotting while others are more involved with conservation work. Either way, they all provide you with excellent opportunities to get out and about.

Centres:

ENFO — Environmental Information Service
17 St Andrew Street, Dublin 2. Tel: 1890-200 191

An exhibition centre with great facilities (see Inside Jobs).

Sonairte — The National Ecology Centre
Laytown, County Meath. Tel: 041-27572

Sonairte has special workshops with schools, open to all (see also County Meath chapter).

National Conservation Education Centre
Knocksink Wood, Enniskerry, County Wicklow. Tel: 286 6609

This is a drop-in centre for individuals — it also offers field studies for primary and secondary students.

Bull Island Interpretive Centre
Clontarf, Dublin 3. Tel: 833 8341

Activities

BirdWatch Ireland

8 Longford Place, Monkstown. Tel: 280 4322

BirdWatch organises regular local outings, lectures and activities and has a newsletter. Families and young people are welcome and discounts are offered.

The Dublin Naturalists Field Club

c/o 35 Nutley Park, Dublin 4. Tel: 269 7469

This club takes members on regular fascinating trips connected with every imaginable aspect of wildlife. Night lectures also available.

The Irish Seal Sanctuary

Clochán, Tobergregan, Garristown. Tel: 835 4370

The Seal Sanctuary does Trojan work in rescuing injured and stranded seals from the waters and shores around Ireland (which are a designated marine sanctuary). The Sanctuary mainly relies on members of the public to alert it of seals in distress. The Sanctuary organises seal back-to-the-sea launches at venues nationwide and has plenty of literature for junior members. A larger centre is underway. Telephone for emergency information on seals only — for other details it is better to write.

Dublin Bat Group

Harristown Lane, St Margaret's, County Dublin. Tel: 834 7134

The Dublin Bat Group aims to raise public awareness of bats (which are a protected species) and it organises summer bat-spotting activities. Its magazine is called _The Natterer_ and family and individual members are welcome to join the club.

Irish Wildlife Trust

107 Lower Baggot Street, Dublin 2. Tel: 676 8588

The Trust provides information and a wildlife notice-board, publishes a magazine and also organises regular outings.

Dry Stone Walling

Cornerstone
Larchill, Kilcock, County Kildare. Tel: 628 4518
Yes you can learn the ancient craft of building dry stone walls at the above address.

School Wildlife Gardeners Association
c/o Scoil Treasa, Donore Avenue, South Circular Road, Dublin 8.
Shares ideas and plans on creative wildlife gardening for primary schools.

Conservation and Campaigning

ECO — Irish Environmental Conservation Organisation for Youth
26 Clare Street, Dublin 2. Tel: 662 5491
ECO organises workshops and practical education for individual and group members. They also run summer camps and sometimes work with schools.

Earthwatch
7 Upper Camden Street, Dublin 2. Tel: 497 3773
Earthwatch welcomes new members and offers information to people interested in monitoring the environment.

An Taisce
Tailors' Hall, Back Lane, Dublin 8. Tel: 454 1786
A nationwide conservation organisation with a mainly adult membership. However, family membership is also offered with a broad range of activities and interests which can be availed of. An Taisce also produces its own magazine.

Irish Peatland Conservation Council
119 Capel Street, Dublin 1. Tel: 872 2397
Among other bog preservation activism, the IPCC works with schools on various campaigns. **Mónóga Wildlife Club** (tel: 872 2384) is the junior branch of the Irish Peatland Conservation Council. Mónóga runs exploring bog days, competitions, surveys and provides news.

Environmental Education

ENFO/*Sonairte* (see Centres above)

Coillte
Leeson Lane, Dublin 2. Tel: 661 5666

Coillte is a semi-state department concerned with forestry and it provides literature and forestry careers information.

Crann
Main Street, Banagher, County Offaly. Tel: 0509-51718

An organisation that promotes afforestation and gives advice to all kinds of tree-lovers and growers. Crann will provide information for school projects, has family membership and also produces a regular newsletter.

Dúchas — The Heritage Service
51 St Stephen's Green, Dublin 2. Tel: 647 3000

Dúchas has two environmental departments: the Wildlife Service at 7 Ely Place, Dublin 2 (tel: 647 2300), and the Canals and Waterways office at St Stephen's Green House, Earlsfort Terrace, Dublin 2 (tel: 678 7475/6).

Circus

Belfast Community Circus School
23–25 Gordon Street, Belfast BT1 2LG. Tel: 080 1232-236 007

Obviously, Belfast is not Dublin. Equally obviously, it's just over two hours away and its Circus School offers unique opportunities to learn aerial skills (trapeze and tightrope), juggling, clowning and more. The BCCS offers outreach programmes to disadvantaged schools, workshops for teachers and masterclasses for street theatre artists. It's funded by the Northern Ireland Arts Council but has plenty of cross-border contact. Plus, on Saturday afternoons, their Central Circus classes are open to anyone who pays a modest fee. So, if your heart is set on learning the trapeze or being a clown, this is the place to come.

Chapter 12

entertainment

Bowling

Leisureplex:
Blanchardstown, tel: 822 3030; Malahide Road, Coolock,
tel: 848 5722; Tallaght Village Green Centre, tel: 459 9411;
Stillorgan, tel: 288 1656

Metro Bowl
149 North Strand Road, Dublin 3. Tel: 855 7274

Bray Bowl
Quinsboro Road, Bray. Tel: 286 4455

XL Bowl
Kennelsfort Road, Palmerstown, Dublin 20. Tel: 626 0700

Cinema

UCI Cinemas:
Blanchardstown, tel: 1850 525 354; Coolock, tel: 848 5133;

Santry Omniplex, tel: 842 8844; Tallaght, tel: 459 8170; Coolock, tel: 8485133

These cinemas run Saturday-morning junior clubs which offer special rates.

IMAX
Virgin Cinema Complex. Tel: 817 4200

IMAX is a giant-format cinema. The Complex also offers virtual reality entertainment shows.

Circus

Advertised shows from Irish and visiting circuses in fairgrounds in Booterstown, Whitehall and Goatstown.

See also the Belfast Community Circus School (page 328).

Farms *(see page 107)*

Funfairs

> There are surely many spaces in the shopping mall-rich suburbs that could house a funfair. Sponsors — where are you?

Funderland
RDS Grounds, Ballsbridge, Dublin 4
Buses: 6, 7A, 8, 45.

Funderland is a huge fair that runs at Christmas, for one month only. It's got easy rides, thriller rides, side-shows and junk food.

Skerries (Bus 33) has a resident funfair with surely the cutest little Big Wheel in the world. **Bray** (Bus 45) also has resident funfair entertainment. Unfortunately, there are no permanent funfair facilities in Dublin City.

Games

Dr Quirke's Emporium
O'Connell Street, Dublin 1

Dr Quirke's has a range of games and simulated rides.

Atari Expo
The Square, Tallaght. Tel: 452 2828

Horse-racing

ICON

Leopardstown Racecourse, Dublin 18. Tel: 289 1000

Leopardstown racecourse, just south of Stillorgan, is the
principal racing ground for the Dublin area. Regular
fixtures are held here throughout the year. It's a huge
complex, with a crêche, and an amazing Romantic-Ireland
themed pub/restaurant tower called ICON, which is built on
so many levels, with towers, streets, mills and so on, that you
will get lost, dizzy, or have a great time. The Baileys Centre
here also offers a fifteen-minute audio-visual show that has
stolen a lot of stories from Newgrange. Just remember,
horses are fine, food is fine, but real Dublin and real
Ireland are out there waiting for you. A special ICON bus
leaves from Parnell Square — telephone for details.

Ice-skating

Silver Skate Rink

327 North Circular Road, Dublin 7. Tel: 830 4405

Three sessions daily. Skates available for hire.

Indoor adventure and play centres

Assault courses, slides, ball ponds, bouncing castles, are
some of the features of the following fun centres. Some of
these places have facilities for children aged 13–14 years.
All of them have toddler areas which are completely
supervised. Parties are also catered for and are rather a
speciality (See page 134).

Clonsilla has Giraffes and is located at Coolmine
Industrial Park (tel: 820 5526); **Leisureplex** has Zoo play
centres at Blanchardstown (tel: 822 3030), Coolock
(tel: 848 5722), Tallaght Village Green (tel: 459 9411) and
Stillorgan (tel: 288 1656); Santry has **Adventure World**
and **Omni Centre** (tel: 842 8856), Swords has **Kidzone**,
Feltrim Industrial Estate (tel: 840 8749). Bray is home to
Dawson's Amusements on Strand Road (tel: 286 0974).

Karting

Kylemore Indoor Karting
Killeen Road. Tel: 626 1444

Phibsboro Indoor Karting
Cross Guns Bridge. Tel: 830 8777

Kart City
Santry and Bray. Tel: 842 6322

Spawell Karting
Tel: 490 4401

Outdoor Play Centres

There are large free adventure playgrounds in **Marlay Park**, **Malahide Gardens** and the **Phoenix Park**. **Fort**

Lucan in Westmanstown, **Lucan** (tel: 628 0166) and **Clara-Lara** in Laragh, County Wicklow (tel: 0404-46161), all have summertime outdoor assault courses and water courses. **Blessington Lakes Land and Water Sports Centre** (tel: 045-86092) offer canoeing, sailing, abseiling and assault courses. The annual **Maze in the Maize** happens just outside Maynooth (signposted) each July. It's a real maze made out of tall corn.

Puppets

The Lambert Puppet Theatre
Mews, Clifton Lane, Monkstown. Tel: 280 0974
Buses: 7A, 8.
Offers a full range of puppet technology and magical tales. Shows every weekend.

Theatre

The Ark
Eustace Street, Dublin 2. Tel: 670 7788

The Ark is a dedicated venue for children's theatre. Family shows at advertised weekends.

There is a Children's Theatre Festival in October and special shows for young people during Christmas. And, of course, don't forget the Christmas pantomime. For other theatre ideas see the Joining In chapter.

Wildlife

See Joining In chapter. The Pearse Museum (see page 40) has a Nature Awareness Centre with free activities on Saturday mornings (tel: 493 4208).

Free Entertainment

Free entertainment is reasonably plentiful, but not such a regular thing that it can be faithfully listed. However, the following is a list of some ideas which you can play around with:

Navy Ships and Sailing Ships

Foreign navies often pay courtesy calls to Dublin port, and their ships and submarines are usually made open to the public, generally on weekend afternoons. They are usually moored at (a) Alexandra Basin, North Wall (Bus: 53A from Beresford Place or (b) Dún Laoghaire (Buses: 7, 7A, 8, 46A). Watch for sailors around town, or read the 'What's On' columns.

Street Entertainment

Meeting House Square in Temple Bar offers a full programme of weekend summer entertainment, that includes children's circus and theatre, free film nights and, during several music festivals, free concerts. Contact the Temple Bar Information Centre, 18 Eustace Street, Dublin 2 (tel: 671 5717).

Mimes and clowns of varied quality perform on Grafton Street. The St Patrick's Day Festival also offers high-class street theatre.

Park Concerts

Dublin Corporation has a full programme of summer band music in parks that have bandstands. St Anne's Park, Blackrock Park, the Phoenix Park have hosted free rock concerts in the past — such events are always well publicised. Bands also play in St Stephen's Green, and very occasionally, plays are also performed there.

> See also separate listings for art galleries which run free painting sessions.

Libraries

Dublin City: Ballyfermot, tel: 626 9324; Ballymun, tel: 842 1890; Central Library, tel: 873 4333; Charleville Mall, North Strand, tel: 874 9619; Coolock, tel: 847 7781; Dolphin's Barn, tel: 454 0681; Donaghmede, tel: 848 2833;

Drumcondra, tel: 837 7206; Finglas, tel: 834 4906; Inchicore, tel: 453 3793; Kevin Street, tel: 475 3794; Marino, tel: 833 6297; Pearse Street, tel: 677 2764; Pembroke, Ballsbridge, tel: 668 9575; Phibsboro, tel: 830 4341; Raheny, tel: 831 5521; Rathmines, tel: 497 3539; Ringsend, tel: 668 0063; Terenure, tel: 490 7035; Walkinstown, tel: 455 8159.

Fingal: Balbriggan, tel: 841 1128; Baldoyle, tel: 832 2549; Blanchardstown, tel: 821 2701; Howth, tel: 832 2130; Malahide, tel: 845 2026; Rathbeale, tel: 840 4179; Skerries, tel: 872 7777.

Dún Laoghaire/Rathdown: Blackrock, tel: 288 8117; Cabinteely, tel: 285 5363; Dalkey, tel: 285 5277; Deansgrange, tel: 285 0860; Dundrum, tel: 298 5000; Dún Laoghaire, tel: 280 1254; Shankill, tel: 282 3081; Stillorgan, tel: 288 9655.

South Dublin: Ballyroan, tel: 494 1900; Castletymon, tel: 452 4888; Clondalkin, tel: 459 3315; Tallaght, tel: 462 0073; Whitechurch, tel: 493 0199.

Riding Schools

(please note, this is a selection only)

Ashton Equestrian Centre, Castleknock, tel: 838 7611; Brennanstown R.S., Kilmacanogue, County Wicklow, tel: 286 3778; Brittas Lodge Stables, Brittas, tel: 458 2726; Broadmeadow Equestrian Centre, Bullstown, Ashbourne, County Meath, tel: 835 2823; Calliaghstown R.C., Rathcoole, tel: 458 9236; Carrickmines Equestrian Centre, Foxrock, tel: 295 5990; Donacomper R.S., Celbridge, County Kildare, tel: 628 8221; Killegar Stables, Enniskerry, tel: 840 3499; Kilmacredock R.C., Obelisk Lane, Maynooth, tel: 624 3747; Kilronan R.C., Swords, tel: 840 3499; Kinsealy R.C., Malahide, tel: 846 0010; Oldtown R.S., Oldtown, tel: 835 4755; Phoenix R.S., Castleknock, tel: 868 7000.

Most riding stables are quite far from the city centre so be sure to ask for specific directions when you are making your booking.

Swimming Pools

Dublin Corporation Pools

Open: Monday-Friday: 11.30 a.m.–3.00 p.m.; 4.00 p.m.–8.00 p.m.;
Saturday: 10.00 a.m.–1.00 p.m., 2.00 p.m.–6.00 p.m.; Sunday:
10.00 a.m.–2.00 p.m.

Corporation Pools are at the following locations: Ballymun
Shopping Centre, tel: 842 1368; Ballyfermot, Le Fanu Park,
tel: 626 6504; Coolock Shopping Centre, tel: 847 7743;
Finglas, Mellowes Road, tel: 834 8005; Markievicz,
Townsend Street, tel: 677 0503; Rathmines, opposite Town
Hall, tel: 496 1275; Sean McDermott Street, tel: 872 0752;
Willie Pearse Park, Crumlin, tel: 445 55792.

School and other pools

(open to public or club members)

ALSAA pool, Dublin Airport, tel: 705 2686; Blackrock
College, tel: 288 8681; Central Remedial Clinic, Vernon
Avenue, Clontarf, tel: 833 9458; Cerebral Palsy Ireland,
Sandymount, tel: 269 5608; Cheeverstown House, Temple-
ogue Road, tel: 490 5988; Clondalkin Sports and Leisure,
Nangor Road, tel: 457 4858; Coolmine, tel: 821 4344;
Dundrum Family Recreation Centre, tel: 298 4654;
Glenalbyn, Stillorgan, tel: 285 3107; Kilternan Hotel,
tel: 295 5542; King's Hospital, Palmerstown, tel: 626 4550;
Marian College, Lansdowne Road, tel: 668 9539;
Monkstown/Newpark Sports Centre, tel: 288 3720;
Portmarnock Sports Centre, tel: 846 2086; Presentation
College, Putland Road, Bray, tel: 286 7517; St John of God,
Islandbridge, tel: 677 4022; St Paul's College, Raheny,
tel: 831 6283; St Vincent's CBS, Finglas Road, Dublin 9,
tel: 830 6716; St Vincent's Pool, Navan Road, tel: 838 4906;
Stewarts Sports Centre, Palmerstown, tel: 626 9879;
Templeogue College, Templeville Road, tel: 490 1711;
Terenure College, Templeogue Road, tel: 490 707; Westwood
Club, Leopardstown, tel: 289 3208. Telephone individual
pools for available opening hours.

> **Ten Best Dublin Freebies:**
>
> Dublin Libraries
>
> Summer night open-air films in Meeting House Square
>
> St Patrick's Day Parade
>
> The National Gallery and its activities
>
> All three National Museums
>
> Summer steam train rides in Marlay Park, plus its adventure playground
>
> Phoenix Park Motor Races
>
> Temple Bar Blues Festival
>
> National Cinema Day (June), free admissions to all cinemas
>
> Glasnevin Cemetery Tour (honestly!)

Chapter 13

Surfing dublin ───────────

This is a small selection of websites. To state the obvious, there are many more out there. The first section is purely Irish; the end section is a trawl from all over the web of what might be useful or, even better, fun to use. Short website addresses only are given — exploration is up to you.

Three main Ireland servers to consult are:
www.iol.ie (contains a school's out section)
www.indigo.ie (or add /~discover)
www.niceone.com/

Those three will lead you to many Irish and Dublin-based sites from which details of events, facts, tours, sports, hobbies, weather and more can be obtained.

General information
www.visit.ie/dublin
The Dublin Tourism site.
www.ireland.travel.ie
The Bord Fáilte site.
www.dublincorp.ie
The Dublin Corporation site — information on all of the Corporation's activities.
www.entertainmentireland.ie
As its name suggests.
www.ireland.com
A huge information site from *The Irish Times*.

Museums and other venues
www.cbl.ie
This is a super starter address because it's so easy to remember. It is the Chester Beatty Library's site which is

worthwhile in itself, but also leads to most of Dublin's cultural sites such as museums and galleries — just click on 'Links'. The National Library site shows you genealogical know-how; the Archives link will take you all over the world and the Christ Church Cathedral site is excellent.

www.archeire.com/archdublin
An excellent site for learning more about the city and its buildings.

www.heritageireland.ie
This is the Dúchas site.

www.dublinzoo.ie

Media

www.foinse.ie
Includes lots of Irish language links.

www.rte.ie

www.irish-times.com
This is the best newspaper site and has its own archive. Available also on ***www.ireland.com***

www.fm104.ie

Political Parties

www.fiannafail.ie
www.finegael.ie
www.greenparty.ie
www.labour.ie

Environment/Science

www.enfo.ie
The ENFO library section is full of information.

www. wildireland.ie

www.astronomy.ie
This is Astronomy Ireland's site.

Web Goodies

www.britannica.com
This is the Encyclopedia Britannica site. It also carries website reviews.

www.artchive.com
An enormous gallery full of all the artists you can think of.
www.askjeeves.com
Type in any question and Jeeves gets to work.
www.cnn.com
24-hour news from CNN.
www.astronomynow.com
To the moon and back.
www.nasa.gov
To the moon and back — by NASA.
www.benjerry.com
Ice-cream on the net.
www.greenpeace.org
www.imdb.com
A movie database, more encyclopedia than movie site.

Children's Net

www.yahooligans.com
The junior Yahoo server — it leads everywhere.
www.researchpaper.com
This is an American homework helper. It is good as it offers
a choice between its own information and internet links.
www.ajkids.com
This is the junior 'Ask Jeeves'.
www.thekids.com
A very good junior site, especially its 'Best of the Net' links
page.
www.letsfindout.com
A busy encyclopedia.
www.realkids.com/adventure.htm
Just what it says — real life adventures.
www.petcat.com
All that cat owners could ever want to know.
www.disney.com
The Mouse and friends.
www.yucky.com
It's known as the yuckiest site on the internet.

Chapter 14

reading dublin

Now that you've read this book, you may wish to get more detailed knowledge of Dublin. The following list outlines a small selection of books on different aspects of the city which should be available in any library.

Walks

Walking Dublin by Pat Liddy (New Holland)
An illustrated guide to twenty-four original walks.

The Building Stones of Dublin by Patrick Wyse Jackson (Country House)
A fascinating guide to walks which follow the city's architectural materials.

Heritage Trails, (Dublin Tourism)
A guide to the city's signed trails.

Exploring Dublin — Wildlife, Parks, Waterways by Christopher Moriarty (Wolfhound Press)
Packed with interesting and unexpected facts.

On Foot in Dublin and Wicklow by Christopher Moriarty (Wolfhound Press)
Getting out of the city with an expert.

Sculpture in Dublin: A Walker's Guide is published by the Sculptors' Society of Ireland.

History

The Annals of Dublin by E.E. O'Donnell (Wolfhound Press)
Year by year events from 8000 BC.

Dublin the Fair City by Peter Somerville Large (Sinclair-Stevenson)
A biography of the city.

Guide to Historical Dublin by Adrian MacLoughlin
(Gill & Macmillan)
Sadly out of print, but excellent if you can find it.

The Neighbourhood of Dublin by Weston St John Joyce
(Gill & Macmillan)
First published in 1912, full of gossip and stories, but most
of the Dublin of Weston St John Joyce's time is now
covered with our houses.

Encyclopaedia of Dublin by Douglas Bennett
(Gill & Macmillan)
An A to Z.

Dublin — One Thousand Years of Wood Quay by
Jonathan Bardon and Stephen Conlin (Blackstaff Press)
This is a clever 'Anno's Dublin'-style picture-book.

Viking and Medieval Dublin, Curriculum Development
Unit (O'Brien Press)
A fine collection of essays and pictures.

Historic Dublin Maps (published by the National Library).
Do your own research with this excellent thirteen-map kit.

The Liffey in Dublin by John De Courcy Ireland
(Gill & Macmillan)
The story of every inch of riverbank.

Dublin Voices — an Oral History by Kevin C. Kearns
(Gill & Macmillan)
Wonderful stories of Dublin early this century.

The Vikings CD-ROM (National Museum)

Architecture

Dublin — A Grand Tour by Jacqueline O'Brien and
Desmond Guinness (Weidenfeld and Nicolson)
Wonderful pictures and histories of places, some of which
you can get into, and some of which you can't.

Dublin — an Urban History by Niall McCullough
(Anne Street Press)
Uncovers the layers of building and street-planning.

Dublin 1660-1860 by Maurice Craig (Allen Figgis)
The architecture of Dublin.

Miscellaneous

Dublin Tourism Handbook
Irish Youth Directory (National Youth Council)
Guide to Evening Classes in Dublin (Wolfhound Press)
Dúchas Heritage Handbook
Dublin in Books
A bibliography of several hundred books relating to Dublin
(up to 1991). Available to read or to buy at the Gilbert
Library, Pearse Street.

index